ORDER IN PARADOX

ORDER IN PARADOX

Myth, Ritual, and Exchange among Nepal's Tamang

DAVID H. HOLMBERG

MOTILAL BANARSIDASS PUBLISHERS
PRIVATE LIMITED • DELHI

Reprint : Delhi, 2005
First Indian Edition: Delhi, 1996
First published 1989 by Cornell University Press

ISBN: 81-208-1369-3

MOTILAL BANARSIDASS
41 U.A. Bungalow Road, Jawahar Nagar, Delhi 110 007
8 Mahalaxmi Chamber, 22 Bhulabhai Desai Road, Mumbai 400 026
236, 9th Main III Block, Jayanagar, Bangalore 560 011
203 Royapettah High Road, Mylapore, Chennai 600 004
Sanas Plaza, 1302 Baji Rao Road, Pune 411 002
8 Camac Street, Kolkata 700 017
Ashok Rajpath, Patna 800 004
Chowk, Varanasi 221 001

Printed in India
BY JAINENDRA PRAKASH JAIN AT SHRI JAINENDRA PRESS,
A-45 NARAINA, PHASE-I, NEW DELHI 110 028
AND PUBLISHED BY NARENDRA PRAKASH JAIN FOR
MOTILAL BANARSIDASS PUBLISHERS PRIVATE LIMITED,
BUNGALOW ROAD, DELHI 110 007

For Laura Hines Holmberg and
in memory of Allan Richard Holmberg

Contents

Introduction to South Asian Edition

The South Asian edition of *Order in Paradox: Myth, Ritual, and Exchange among Nepal's Tamang* is appearing almost twenty years after my initial long term residence among western Tamang from 1975-1977.[1] Several of the core ideas developed here took shape in the late 1970s in my original ordering of the artifacts of this ethnographic engagement into an overview of the structure of Tamang ritual and social formations (Holmberg 1980). The first American edition of the book appeared six years ago. The focus of the book—beyond the ethnographic—is on the structure of a complex ritual field composed of Buddhist, shamanic, and sacrificial practitioners and on the relation of this structure to the logics and contradictions of Tamang social exchanges, especially those associated with cross-cousin marriage. In the book, I sought to elucidate particular anthropological problems ranging from the specific theoretical problem of the analysis of complex ritual systems through the relation of ritual practice and exegetic "myth" to the more general problem of the conceptualization of "culture" as a coherent, unproblematic object of anthropological reflection. As importantly, I tried to offer a sympathetic translation of the genius of Tamang sociocultural productions with all the incumbent problems associated with such translations. The analysis works directly from and in an anthropological dialogue with the indigenous exegeses of Tamang myth.

My continuing involvements with Tamang, transformations in the discursive field of South Asian studies, recent political changes in Nepal—especially the place of identity in national and academic discourse—and a rich array of new scholarly contributions—indigenous and anthropological—all cast the book in a new light. My purpose here is not a rigorous update of the original text; too much

[1] See David Holmberg, Kathryn March, Bhim Tamang and Suryaman Tamang (1994), *Mutual Regards: America and Nepal Seen through Each Other's Eyes* (*nepālī ra ameirkiko dohorī namaste*). Kathmandu: Jivan Support Press.

has happened over the last decade to do justice to the complex transformations. I attempt, rather, to contextualize the original and propose additional vantages that can be brought to bear on the history of Tamang relations with the state of Nepal and the ritual forms that constitute the primary subject matter of the text that follows.

I situated my analysis historically but for the specific purposes of reframing received constructions of ethnicity/caste in Nepal and of framing the localized cultural productions which are the object of my study in the book. I invoked the history of state formation to counter the prevailing views of ethnicity/caste in Nepal as variations either on anthropological essentialisms or indigenous essentialisms. Anthropological models at the time—whose origins can be found in the earliest western constructions of social order in Nepal—reified groups like Tamang, implicitly or explicitly, as separate and primordial entities. Indigenous constructions likewise tend to stress the continuity of originary ethnic formations in Nepal from time immemorial, constructions now at the basis of claims of the *janajāti* (non-Hindu or Tibeto-Burman speaking "ethnic groups" who claim a status of "indigenous") movements of contemporary Nepal. My argument was simply that groups in Nepal could not be considered in isolation; they gained their "essences" in relation to other groups and that critical forces for understanding these relational processes were to be found in the formation of the state of Nepal which placed groups into categories of superordinate and subordinate tempered in the cultural constructions of the high caste Hindu rulers.

A second and related invocation of history relates directly to the particular place Tamang fell in the orders of the formative state of Nepal in the eighteenth century and its later elaboration during the Rana period in the nineteenth century and up until about 1950 (v.s. 2007). Tamang of the western region who constitute the ethnographic focus of the book were viewed by the dominant, national elite as a conquered population brought into the state on the pain of servitude to the economic infrastructure. From the early part of the nineteenth century up until the late 1950s, western Tamang held their subsistence lands only in return for corvèe-like labor in paper production, fruit plantations, butter production, the postal system, munitions factories (converted to tax in late nineteenth century), and the like. Active challenges to state authority would be met by confiscation of land, prison, or death. Within this overarching frame, I argued that the relations were not just ones of economic exploitation but were, in fact, produced by a culturally inflected discourse where Hindu elite figured and thereby produced "Tamang" in particular ways and vice versa. Tamang, however, were allowed considerable local and sometimes regional autonomy and state legitimated headman wielded considerable power. Rather than becoming acculturated to prevailing ideologies of the Hindu state, a rich and complementary Tamang culture evolved in containment and the object of the book was to unravel and make sense of those involutionary forms and their regular ritual recreation.

Where this history opens the book, its central arguments relate to processes of internal structuring—how the ritual strands formed a system of complementarities and oppositions which in turn related to dynamics of social order and its contradictions. The ritual forms in their most critical aspects were explained endogenously; history accounted for the presence of particular ritual strands (e.g. the Buddhist) but could not account for the continuity of elementary structural relations of the ritual system or its reproduction. The book argues that the exogenous forces of state formation set spatial, social, and political-economic limits on western Tamang, that they set in play the processes of involutionary containment.

The importance of external relations, however, did not stop there. This historical situation produced active defiance, resistance—as many now refer to the covert but never the less oppositional activity of groups like the Tamang—and complicity of some sections of local Tamang societies. The particular structures of domination produced within the nascent state of Nepal were the context for the elaboration of the social and ritual formations which in turn generated social solidarity and oppositional power.

The Tamang practices described below thus were not just complementary to those of the dominant populations of Nepal, they were *actively* complementary. It was not simply that Tamang claimed to be Buddhist in a Hindu state, that they exchanged food in balanced symmetrical reciprocities in opposition to the asymmetrical transactions so characteristic of Hindu systems, that they honored and were indebted to the brothers of their wives when their Hindu neighbors deprecated theirs, that Tamang women enjoyed measures of freedom and power unknown to their high-caste equivalents, or that death rites took precedence over marriage in the reproduction of social relations in an inversion of their Hindu neighbors. We must view the perpetuation of these differences not simply as the residue of an historical juxtaposition and a separation perpetuated in the state of Nepal by the enclosure of the Tamang, but as generated in an oppositional dynamic.

This elementary dynamic of interthnic relations has become visible in new manifestation in the now democratic Nepal where some political leaders of Tamang (mostly based in urban contexts) speak out and organize ethnic associations with overt political goals of advancing the lot of Tamang whom they view as economically exploited and discriminated against. At the time of my initial research in the 1970s, public organization in defiance of the prevailing order was against the law and was very dangerous. Many prominent Tamang leaders in the region where I worked had been jailed at various points in their lives for resisting the old Rana regime or its successor the Panchayat system. Others had been killed by government authorities or had to flee the country. At the time of my initial research, for instance, several Tamang men in nearby villages had been placed in preventive detention by the government out of fears that they had been enlisted to organize the regional population in support the Khampa guerilla activity taking place to the west on the frontiers with Tibet during the mid-seventies. The climate was repressive making Tamang reticent to discuss openly their opposition toward the government and its representatives. When I wrote *Order in Paradox*, I avoided direct or prolonged discussion of contemporary Tamang resistance in the text because of the potential harm it could cause my local friends and supporters. I had in fact been removed from the village by the government at the very conclusion of my research—"for my own safety"—because of accusations lodged against a local populist leader by his political rivals, accusations which implicated "foreigners" resident in his village. The accusations involved false but inflammatory charges calculated to create a climate of ethnic hostility.

The movement for democracy which reached its climax in late 1989 and early 1990 produced a new constitution and substantially transformed the political climate. Open political speech abounds—as my friends laugh everyone is a politician now!—and groups are free to organize on the basis of ethnic association. Urban leaders of these ethnic associations—including several Tamang groups—are laying claim to an "indigenous" status and calling for better representation in the new democratic power structure. Here is not the place to discuss fully these groups or the penetration of their convictions into village consciousness or ethnic movements in general as Nepal struggles to form a new construction of nationhood not dependent on the ideological order of the legal-cultural codes of the nineteenth century. I will only note that these developments represent the latest surge of what has been an undercurrent in the very structuring of the Nepalese nation since its inception.

Our recent research on the regional history of sectors of the western Tamang, suggest a long and sometimes tense accommodation between Tamang and the forces and representatives of the state. A few brief notes on some dimensions of Tamang challenges to state exploitation will provide a further contextualization of the book. Such contextualization is necessary in part because historical studies in Nepal are generally silent in reference to the effects of state formation on local communities like the western Tamang. Historical studies in reference to the state concentrate almost exclusively on the political history of the central elite and the intrigues of the great men and women of Nepal or the apparatus of central administration, military, and economic bureaucracy. In many ways, historical reconstructions of state formation in Nepal have been active in the legitimization of the status quo and rarely speak of forms of exploitation, expropriation, violence, or for that matter, the cultural politics which accompanied state formation, consolidation, and perpetuation.[2]

The earliest recorded Tamang encounters with the kings of Gorkha who were later to consolidate Nepal was one of active opposition. As I note in the text,

[2] For an alternate perspective see Pashuram Tamang, "Tamang under the Shadow" in *Himal*, May/June 1992.

Vajracharya and Shrestha (1976 [v.s. 2032]) report an attack in 1739 by a "Ghale-Bhote" force on the troops of Narabhupal Shah—the father of Prithvi Narayan Shah who consolidated the state of Nepal into the form we more or less know it today. Tamang lore includes conflicts and battles between local Tamang "kings" and the forces of Gorkha coming out of the west. Typical of such accounts is the following from the village of Bumtang:

> Before Prithvi Narayan Shah, the Gorkha kings sent soldiers to this area and the Tamang kings killed them. The Tamang were called to Salyān and they hid their weapons in the sand. When the Gorkha soldiers came they killed them. They [forces from Gorkha] came back and killed the Tamang king. They came here and killed them.

Likewise the local legends of Ghale kings throughout the region record wars with the Gorkha kings prior to consolidation.

Although hard historical information on Tamang defiance—especially in the earliest periods of state formation—is limited, there is no question that as the state formed, an oppositional relation framed encounters in the areas where I worked. Active confrontations become more visible in the last 40 or 50 years when challenges to Rana appropriation of local resources became bold, especially in the period immediately before and after the fall of the Ranas in 1950 (2007 v.s.). Moreover, in v.s. 2017 around the time King Mahendra dissolved the first democratic government of Nepal, poor Tamang debtors looted houses of Brahman immigrants in the area and drove them out of their villages—a movement which led to the killing of numerous Tamang villagers when troops were sent and fired into a crowd. Shortly thereafter, one group of Tamang actually briefly siezed a police station before fleeing to Calcutta. At the actual time of my research, the characterizations of Tamang made by the authorities of state and vice versa reveal conflict and mutual distrust. In the mid-seventies, for instance, a policeman was sent to the village to arrest villagers on outstanding warrants, an annual pilgrimage. While frustrated by the apparent absence of all the individuals he was pursuing (they had all fled to the forests when the call went through the village that the police were on the way!), he showed up on my steps for a cup of tea and told me how this was "enemy territory." Tamang villagers, for their part, would revel in stories of groups of women beating policeman and sending them on their way. Tamang regularly challenged state exploitation and mocked the representative authorities of the state in annual carnival-like inversions. This sort of commentary at the interface of representatives of the authority of the state and local Tamang echo through my notes to this day with state administrators, military officers, police and development workers complaining that Tamang villagers do not speak their language and that they are not of same country.

The situation is, of course, more complex and simple models of domination and subordination tempered in a cultural politics do not do justice to the patterns of interrelationship that took form. Accommodation—especially by sectors of local headmen who took advantage of opportunities for accumulating land and money—made the system work and an entrenched elite emerged in all local areas. Thus, tension as well as solidarity characterized the relations between local elite and more impoverished villagers. Full discussion of these historical developments must await forthcoming publications and I will confine myself here to reminding the reader to engage what follows in light of these observations on the oppositional frame of Tamang relations with the representatives of the Hindu state.

What changes have occurred in recent decades can likewise only be understood in light of Tamang articulations in more external socio-political orders. The most obvious transformations in Tamang village life in the last two decades can be attributed to a general process of the dissipation of local insularity which had been enforced during the Rana era on village communities, an insularity which had been perpetuated up through the 1970s. In this order, village headmen who derived their positions largely through hereditary mechanisms legitimated by the state prevailed over a local society whose orders were regularly confirmed and recreated in rituals supervised by sacrificers and Buddhist lamas. Most villagers remained based in their home territory extracting an existence—for many a marginal existence—from subsistence farming. Labor outside the village was occasional and the stage for social and economic experience was local. As I argue in the book, Tamang symbology was characterized by a mythic closure which related directly to a highly localized geography, society, polity, and economy. The world of Tamdungsa—the Tamang village where I resided—has now opened up. The horizons of villagers and their concommitant experiences are radically shifting in ways which make the communal closure of the village and region much less contained.

The connections to the greater region and to urban areas are accelerating rapidly. Many of the sons and daughters of the village have taken up residence in the district center or the city of Kathmandu in order to pursue wage labor in enterprises like carpet factories or road construction or to secure salaried sinecures mostly in the lower echelons of the police, military, or administration or externally in the military or police forces of Singapore, Great Britain, Brunei, and India. More successful entrepreneurs especially in the construction business have accumulated enough capital to purchase land and construct houses in the Kathmandu valley. Accomplished students move on to the district center or Kathmandu to receive education beyond the School Leaving Certificate. Yet others have stayed in the region working out of the village but not too distant in the forestry department, in lead mines high above the village, or in the postal system. Those with few skills have taken up porterage employment with trekking companies who lead foreign tourists through the mountains. This employment is relatively new to the western region. In the past, eastern Tamang had dominated the porterage business but trekking companies find western Tamang will work harder for lower wages, are unorganized, and are, as the managers of treks, say, "unspoiled." Finally, some travel to India or the Middle East in search of employment of various sorts.[3] Thus, a village that could be described in the mid-seventies as subsistence based, supplemented by occasional and seasonal wage labor, is now fully entwined in a monied economy where more villagers, especially the young, want to procure wage employment.

A new road across the river from the village where I resided makes Kathmandu a long half day away. People move back and forth with great regularity and are as likely to go to Kathmandu in search of medical treatment as to the nearby district hospital or the bazaar compounder. Everyone has relatives in Kathmandu and places to stay while visiting the city. The Sora Kutta neighborhood of Kathmandu—on what was the northwest outskirts of the city in the Rana period—is now the center of an expanding urban Tamang community. Tamang from all over the western region congregate here. The traffic of villagers back and forth from the hills on all types of conveyance from Chinese jeeps through jam packed minibuses to government buses is thick. When a new road is built linking the region with Kathmandu, the travel will be cut to one or two hours or a long daily commute.

This opening up of village society, polity, and economy and the extension of linkages—kin and otherwise—out into greater Nepal has had concomitant effects on the ritual life of Tamdungsa: rituals marking the village as a socio-political entity are in clear decline; the meaning of and attitudes toward ritual practices of sacrificers, shamans, and Buddhist lamas are also transforming; and, in some Tamang areas, conversion to Christianity has become common place. All these developments are linked in a way to the diminishment of the locality as the focus of order and experience.

The demise of one important community ritual and the apparent transformation of another point to the decline of the village as a key socio-political unit. *Chhe chu* or *tshe-chu*, a nine day dance festival, was historically focal in the legitimation of the principal headman of the village and in the definition of the village as a bounded socio-cultural entity.[4] Although performed both years I resided in the village and in the year immediately after my departure, it has not been staged since. In the past, *Dasaī* marked the village as part of the greater polity of the Hindu state and legitimated the headman's local primacy under the sanction of national authority appears to be celebrated in a new manner where kin affiliations as opposed to political affiliations receive the greatest elaboration.

These two rituals can best be understood as having performed complementary roles in the process of sanctioning the local headman and instantiating the village

[3] Tamang of the immediate vicinity of my research have yet to be implicated in any numbers in the prostitution trade which has had a significant impact on some districts of Tamang residence.

[4] See David Holmberg, "The Dance Drama of Chhechu among Western Tamang." *Syo mhendo*, 2.16:14-18.

as a bounded social and administrative entity. Chhe-chu ritually constituted the headman by village acclamation. He would receive the first blessing of power (*wang*) from the Buddhist lamas, a turban, and a special tormo or a dough image of Buddha all marking his position as the headman. The ritual emphasized the boundedness of the village as a social and political entity and likewise the identity of local villagers over and against the authority of the greater Nepalese state. The elder or great dance of the festival (which included some fifteen dances) mocked and derided representative outsiders who intruded into local life and the village sealed itself from exchanges with the outside for three days. The inversions of this festival challenged—as such carnivals are want to do—the very legitimacy of the state at the same time as they reinforced one of the key links in its order, the village headman.

The celebration of Dasain, the "national" festival of Nepal represented the authority of the headman as externally constituted. Early on in the establishment of political dominion of the state over the Tamdungsa region, headmen had to travel to the encampment of military commanders during the time of Dasain to receive turbans marking their office. They likewise received a mark on the forehead (*Tīkā*), a type of blessing, from those military officers, an act which signifies the ascendency *cum* patronage of the conveyer and the subordination of the recipient. In the village, some seven or eight buffalo were usually sacrificed in ritual recognition Durga, the heads of which were aligned in front of the headman's house and the headman dispensed blessings to a parade of villagers. For the nine nights preceding the climax of the tenth day, villagers would sing in front of the headman's house to assure well being and strength for the local community. Although several of these practices died out in the late Rana period, other practices remained in full force at the time of my residence in the mid-seventies. Village Dasain was a localized version of the rituals of state performed at the center and ritually confirmed relations of political hierarchy and patronage.

By 1993, Dasain had been reduced to a prolonged round of feasting among extended consanguineal and affinal kin with almost no ritual elaboration which marked previous performances. Recognition of Durga the focal goddess of this national rite was a cursory nod and there was no singing or dancing occurred at the houses of the headmen. No blessings were conveyed at all in 1993 celebrations ostensibly because of a death in lineage of headmen, however, villagers reported that this had been the pattern for the last decade. The political symbology which gave the local ritual substance had been translated in large measure into an idiom of kinship where kinship and polity are no longer coextensive as they have been in the past. Finally, villagers—provoked no doubt by the pronouncements of urban leaders of the ethnic and indigenous peoples' movements—were questioning whether Dasain was in fact a festival of theirs or one of the Hindus.

The cessation of feudal-like corèe labor, a new politics, and the breaching of village insularity have set the stage for the nonperformance of Chhe-chu and the devolution of Dasain. Not only have villagers turned their energies in new directions, they appear less dependent on allegiance to one or another local headman (but not entirely independent). Party politics tie villagers to outsiders on the one hand and bitterly divide them internally on the other. If the old politico-religious edifice is now in demise and in some quarters actively challenged, the tradition of indulgence in meat and millet liquor remained strong in 1993. Dasain celebrations remain an important interlude for villagers if for no other reason than those who work and live outside the village get leave and vacation at this time of year and return to visit family and friends—it is a time of state sanctioned leisure.

Other aspects of ritual life have also changed in the new landscape of village society, economy, and polity. The surface features of ritual life suggest continuity in practice yet the meaning of and the attitudes toward these practices have transformed as experience of villagers has been decentered from local space and society. The ritual system of the western Tamang—revolving around the practices of Buddhist lamas, sacrificers, and shamans—responds to the conditions of a people tied to a locality. Much of ritual symbology, especially in shamanic and sacrificial rites, relates to a finite geography and society. These rituals, on one level, fix persons into of a specific territory and social domain. Ritual performances always center on the place of ritual performance and in turn link that place into an order of known space the margins of which until the recent past was for most villagers up to Kyirong in Tibet and down to Kathmandu in the south. Each village on the trails to these end points of spatial consciousness, each temple, each unique spot in the trail, each divinity, each treacherous cliff would be enumerated in ritual chant or verse of song. These spatial recitations were directly relevant to the experiences of villagers who worked fields in specific locales, herded in the surrounding forests and hills, and who traveled annually to Tibet to trade grain for salt. These are not the trails of today's villagers who as I noted send their children to the local school where they learn to speak, read, and write proper Nepali and jump on buses to the big city. A more national, even universal construction of space is displacing and superseding the local. Social space has also reoriented from the more strictly face to face interactions with kin that not so long ago defined sociality.

As people move out spatially, they do so discursively as well. The shamanic and the sacrificial although still active local practices are now looked upon in a way similar to that Stacy Pigg has insightfully analyzed in her work on "Disenchanting Shamans" in eastern Nepal.[5] Shamans and sacrificers are more and more often constructed by those with external experience and education as "village" practices in direct contrast to that which is "developed." Many now position themselves at a remove from practices that were matter of fact for most

[5] See Stacy Pigg, "Disenchanting Shamans: Representations of Modernity and the Transformation of Healing in Nepal." Ph.D. Dissertation, Cornell University, 1990.

people a generation ago. This distancing reflects the infusion of "development" into local discourse. The rhetoric of the educated and administrative elite, primary and secondary school teachers, sophisticated urbanites, the now pervasive voice of Radio Nepal, returned soldiers, and indigenous or foreign development workers has created a self-consciousness in most villagers who now reconstruct practices dialogically. In its curative self justification, the shamanic comes directly up against the constructions of more universalizing "medical" knowledges. An array centrifugal forces challenge the viability of shamanic constructions. Shamanic practice though remains vibrant if for no other reason than the direct attention shamans accord to individual bodies and consciousnesses—an attention which has always marked their practice—has a compelling relevance in local life precisely because of those forces. Ties to a specific locale and kin continue to work in the identity constructions of even those villagers who have taken up monied employment elsewhere; they still eat village rice and know that if all else fails in their migratory pursuits, subsistence can be always found in their home villages.

Buddhism retains a prestigious if transformed position within the field of ritual practice and connections between village lamas and urban centers are increasing. Several boys in the region have been sent to reside for brief periods of time in the Tibetan Buddhist monastic communities of greater Kathmandu. To this point, however, none have returned to practice in their home villages. Ideals of celibate monasticism and more rationalized forms of Buddhism have yet to inspire active transformations of local Buddhism. Villagers have, though, constructed a fine new Gombo or temple and rebuilt the main village or stupa in a grander, more urban style. Memorial death feasts remain the most extensive of local social rites and now in the relative demise of village coherence play as important a ritual role as ever in the definition of local society.

Identity politics in greater Nepal and an active movement toward conversion to Christianity have, moreover, contributed to a more pronounced avowal of adherence to Buddhism among some sectors of Tamang. The historic propensity of Tamang to define themselves as Buddhist—to be called "Lama"—has received new emphasis the ideologies of Tamang ethnic associations which see Buddhism as a rallying point in opposition to the prevailing dominance of high caste Hindus in all the parties of the newly democratized polity and the recent florescence of fundamentalist Hindu organizations in Nepal—inspired no doubt by movement in India—who unabashedly denigrate non-Hindu populations. As I argue in the book, Hindu ideology stigmatizes groups like Tamang as inferior thus blocking them from positions of prominence and rationalizing the exploitation of their labor. For Tamang to accept these valuations would be not only to acknowledge an inferiority but would constitute adherence to an ethos at direct odds with the values of symmetrical reciprocity which frame Tamang interactions among themselves. Many of the leaders of the Tamang ethnic associations have substantial experience outside Nepal in places like Darjeeling and have transposed the terms of identity politics in India—especially its religious dimensions—into their representations of the plight of Tamang. The "Tibetan" Buddhist monasteries in the Kathmandu valley are populated largely by monks from ethnic groups like the Tamang[6] and Buddhism appears to be increasingly invoked in the identity politics of Nepal.

Buddhism, however, is now challenged by Christianity in several western Tamang communities and the intrusion of Christianity informs Tamang constructions of their Buddhism. An hour or so away from Tamdungsa there is a cluster of eleven nominally Christian households—one of several in the region. They have separated from their main village and constructed a simple roofed building where they meet on Sundays. Three men from these houses explained to me that they had converted because of the expenses incurred when they followed the instructions of shamans or other curers when sick. Shamans, they said, tell them to sacrifice chickens then goats and sheep and that in the process shamans impoverish them without really curing, echoing conversion tales repeated throughout the region and up into the Ankhu Khola where estimates are that some 80% of the population are now nominally Christian.

This very recent trend to Christian conversion is not a simple or well established phenomenon. It is not only—as some would argue—the economic advantages of conversion gained by poor Tamang (access to loans, markets for cash crops, free medical care and the like) although these inducements are part of a more complex convergence of social forces. To begin with the meaning of the bible in Tamang Christian mentality is in direct continuity with a tradition of respect for the sacred power of written words among Tamang, a tradition discussed at length below. Most Tamang Christians are non-literate and their confidence in the bible—which exists in a western Tamang translation—has a direct correlate in the metaphoric powers they historically have attributed to the books of Buddhist lamas. When I asked several Christians about how they cured themselves, they said they now place the bible on their foreheads and pray and avoid the expenses of sacrifice.

Conversion is not an act taken lightly. The state did not recognize the right of Tamang to convert until after the Peoples' Movement of 1990. One could be jailed for converting to Christianity and more certainly for proselytizing. Under the new constitution, freedom of religion is allowed but proselytizing remains technically against the law. Likewise, conversion is often accompanied by tension with close kin and leads to spatial separation of Christians. Many Christian households in the region have sold their land and moved to urban areas or bought land in Gorkha district and established a Christian community. Christians in the immediate area of my research live in separate hamlets and claim that they will only marry Christians. The act of separation is accompanied

[6] Personal communication from Abraham Zablocki.

in some instances by violent confrontations. The eleven houses of Christians in the immediate vicinity of Tamdungsa were, according to the Christians with whom I spoke, visited by a large, angry crowd from a neighboring village who, reputedly provoked by their village lamas, burned the only copy of the Tamang bible that they owned. Other villages have seen assaults by Christians on Buddhists. In one community where missionaries from the Summer Institute of Linguistics resided in the 1970s, Christian Tamang cut down the prayer flags of Buddhist lamas. Furthermore, conflicts are now beginning to arise over the performance of death rites, rituals at the heart of Tamang social reproduction. Nominally Christian households still resident in the hill villages have until this time performed no burials and villagers report that when deaths have occurred in a Christian household, lamas are still called to perform cremations and other rites surrounding death.

The social messages of Christian conversion are several. The non-recognition of lama, shaman, and lambu and the spatial separation of Christians from their communities of kin suggest a social transformation of some consequence. Christians not only disavow their practitioners they renounce the consumption of alcohol and the meat of sacrifice both intimately tied up with Tamang sociality and reciprocity. The motivation for such marked non-participation needs to be more carefully studied, however, we can identify in a preliminary way some important variables in the process of conversion. Conversion in the areas I am familiar with suggests it is most likely located among the poorer or more marginalized Tamang. Conversion to Christianity may well encode a challenge to the local elite and power structure. The association of headmen, lamas, and, in a secondary way, sacrificers and shamans constitute a mutually supporting power structure in local communities. Allegiance to Christianity provides an avenue for local Tamang to break from the bonds of alliance and patronage which tie them into this local structure and link them into external networks not mediated by local patrons.

Finally, Christian conversion would not have found such fertile ground if it was not for the relative lack of dynamism prevailing in the traditional ritual practice which has yet to respond significantly to the new social and experiential reality of villagers. Christianity may well provide a competitive religious perspective which speaks more directly toTamang as they move outward from their village and regional communities. Although the conversions in the vicinity of Tamdungsa are all inspired by indigenous preachers who hail from Gorkha District to the west. An identity as Christian also associates one with the dharma of rich and prestigious foreigners, modernity, and a new, more developed "truth" and may carry millenial overtones for converts. The shamans "lie" say the Christians and their doctors. Finally, allegiance to Christianity takes on meaning in the identity politics of Nepal. On the one hand, a Christian identity carries a certain stature and confronts Hindu hegemony in a rhetoric with international overtones but, on the other hand, poses contradictions for the declarations of the indigenous movements which make Buddhism one of their signs of distinction.

The ritual and social formations described below, thus, not only emerged in a set of historical relations with the outside, it is transforming in those relations. It would be an aberration, though, to see these external forces as the final determinants of structure in local Tamang communities. The forms described below and the new ones emerging today are the result as importantly of local and regional Tamang agents formed into a society which has not been without determinative power in the constitution of the greater Nepalese society. What formed Nepal in sociocultural terms in the past and what continues to form Nepal in the present emerges from a dialectic between local and central forces. If the resilience of Tamang in the past to the impositions of the encompassing state are any guide, we should expect the emergance of a transformed but distinctively Tamang society and culture within a state which can no longer—in its official ideology and in emerging political practice—relegate Tamang to the subordinate margins.

Maps, Figures, Table

Maps

Figures

Table

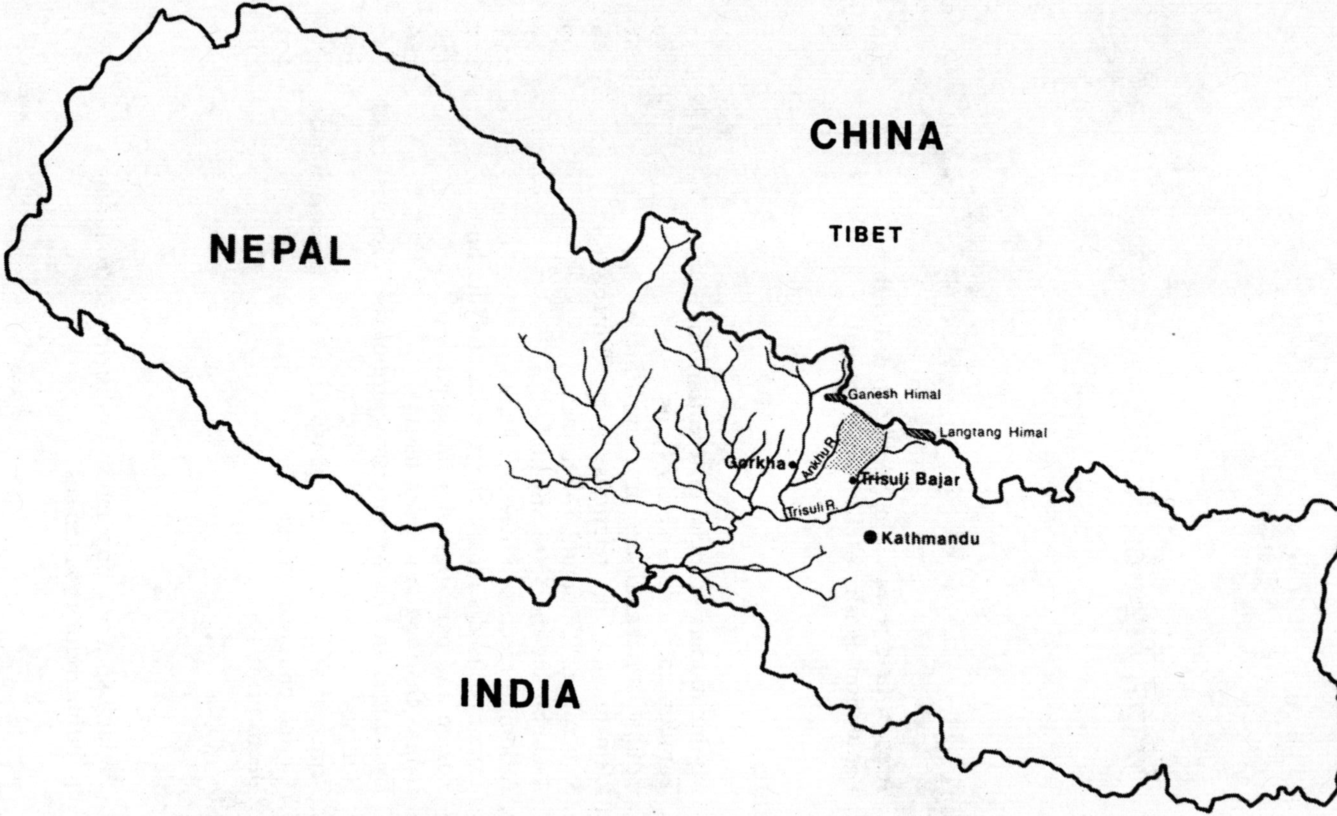

Map 1. Area of field research in Nepal (shaded region)

Preface

Throughout Himalayan Nepal one finds an abundant array of ritual expressions reflecting multiple Hindu, Buddhist, and indigenous forms. Lamas, Brahmans, shamans, sacrificers, monks, nuns, tantrics, ascetic mendicants, and other ritualists practice in innumerable temples, houses, fields, and forests, at crude and elaborate altars, at all social gatherings, at remote peaks and high lakes, in river valleys, along trails, and in bazaars. This book examines the ritual life of a community of western Tamang in sociological and historical perspective and compares Tamang culture with other cultures in the Hindu-Buddhist world.

It is directed to those who have an interest in the ethnology of Nepal, greater South Asia, Southeast Asia, and Tibet as well as to those interested in the study of religion and society and in theories of culture.

The project began in 1975 when I returned to Nepal, after two previous visits, to pursue intensive ethnographic study of a Tamang community. After months of visiting Tamang villages in several regions and beginning the study of Tamang language, I settled in a community of seventy-two households, which I call Tamdungsa in this book. This is not the real Tamang name of the village but of the mythic site of the events that yielded the two primary clans of the village. Tamdungsa is situated to the northwest of Kathmandu, to the north of the Salankhu River, and between the Trisuli and Ankhu rivers (see Map 1).

I arrived in the village in December 1975 and lived in a small mud and stone storage loft through July 1977 with brief returns to Kathmandu to renew visas and see colleagues and friends. Almost immediately upon my arrival in Tamdungsa, I was included in what I was later to learn was one of the most important rituals among Tamang, a memorial death feast. My halting ability in the Tamang language at that time and my mostly superficial understanding of Tamang social life made the complexity of this event overwhelming: I witnessed Buddhist ritual chanting, clans exchanging, weeping, dancing, singing, drinking, and feasting. All this took place around a colorful altar erected on freshly cut saplings. My immediate impression was of an event that although Buddhist in orientation was far from the orthodox renditions of Buddhisms described in most scholarly works. I attended several more of these feasts during my stay and talked on many occasions to villagers about them. By the time I left Tamdungsa, I had made reasonable sense of the basic form and ideology of the memorial death feasts even though participation in them required the consumption of numerous glasses of the local whiskey distilled from millet. It eventually turned out that most ethnographic roads in my study of the Tamang circled back to these ritual feasts. They contain and recreate essential orders in Tamang social life and cosmology, and they are considered in detail in this book.

The ethnographic effort that followed this fortuitous introduction to local culture and society, though, was directed toward understanding most aspects of village life. In particular, I delved into two other ritual domains that stand in complement to the Buddhist memorial death feasts—sacrificial rituals and shamanic rituals. My doctoral dissertation was a preliminary ethnographic reconstruction of these ritual practices and their relations to each other and was framed in brief descriptions of Tamang social order and local history. Although this book reconsiders and refines some of the arguments I developed there, it is a different text. After my initial reconstruction of Tamang ritual life, I saw more clearly the links between social order, Tamang history in Nepal, and the structure of the ritual field. Moreover, my first impressions of the death feasts as heterodox, an almost "tribal" (and I use this term cautiously) Buddhism, stood out even more as I compared the ritual forms of the Tamang with those of other Buddhist peoples. This book deals more directly and systematically with the interpretation of ritual, myth, and social structure and with comparative issues.

I have been in Nepal twice since 1977. I took a survey trip to the region north of Tamdungsa in the winter of 1982–83 and stayed in Nepal from mid-August 1987 until mid-January 1988. On the latter trip, made after this manuscript was substantially complete, I was struck by the changes in village economy and polity. I will not pursue discussion of these changes here except to note that the bounded nature of the Tamang communities I came to know is fracturing. Villagers, particularly the younger generation, are much more in communication with the greater Nepalese economy and society. This process was in an incipient stage at the time of my original research but is having a more profound effect now. Many more people are employed and searching for employment outside the village or are salaried in the village. The local polity is more bitterly divided and buffeted by the factionalism of district politics. Nevertheless, it is also striking how much remains the same. The Tamang emphasis on reciprocity and a distinctive ritual life are still strong, and a subsistence agriculture continues to provide the basis of local economic life. This book presents an image of the culture and society of Tamdungsa and the immediate area at the time I lived there, but its major themes are still applicable. The continuities in local culture—even with the changed experience of the younger generation—are profound, and the closure necessary in this ethnographic reconstruction is not entirely arbitrary.

My trips to Nepal have been possible only with the support of colleagues at Tribhuvan University and of others in Nepal. During my initial ethnographic research, I was affiliated with the Institute of Nepal and Asian Studies, and Dean Prayag Raj Sharma was always of graceful assistance. During my most recent trip I was associated with the Department of Sociology and Anthropology through the Research Division. I especially thank Professor Dor Bahadur Bista, whose perspectives on Nepal and the anthropology of Nepal have been of value to me for many years, Professor Om Gurung of the Department of Sociology and Anthropology, and Dr. Ratna Man Pradhan of the Research Division. I am also grateful to officials of the ministries of home and panchayat, foreign affairs, and education of His Majesty's Government of Nepal for kindly granting me permissions and assistance of many sorts over the years. Ann vB Lewis and the staff at the United States Education Foundation, Kathmandu, were a delight to work with on my last stay.

In the Tamdungsa area, I especially acknowledge the help of Suryaman Himdung Tamang, who introduced me to Tamang culture, taught me Tamang language, improved my Nepali, transcribed endless tapes of ritual chants, worked through difficult interviews with me, accompanied me on forays all over the region, and helped in the most important and the most mundane aspects of research. His immediate family, lineage, and circle of kin treated me for better and for worse as one of them and gave me a place in local society. Most people of Tamdungsa and neighboring villages—especially the *mukhiyā* or headmen, lamas, sacrificers, and shamans—not only tolerated my intrusions but showed me a hospitality and friendship I will never forget. I can only hope that my respect, affection, and gratitude are in some way evident in this book and that their genius, generosity, and irreverent sense of humor occasionally glimmer through the pages.

Many colleagues, teachers, students, friends, and institutions have supported, encouraged, and inspired me. The ethnographic research over the years was supported by the National Institute of Mental Health and the Fulbright Faculty Research program. Cornell University supported me with some helpful small grants and, most important, with a semester's leave in the fall of 1986 to devote to writing. Harihar Acharya, James Boon, Joan Brumberg, Bernard Faure, Thomas Fricke, David Gellner, Davydd Greenwood, Sharon Hepburn, David Hess, A. Thomas Kirsch, Daniel Maltz, James G. March, Sally McConnell-Ginet, Sarah Miller, Stacy Pigg, P. Steven Sangren, James Siegel, and Robert J. Smith have provided comments on portions of the manuscript at various stages or have engaged me in stimulating discussions relevant to this book. Many others, whether they know it or not, have played a significant role in my thinking. Co-panelists and commentators at various meetings and other colleagues have influenced my approach in large and small ways, and I have learned much from them: Michael Allen, Jane Atkinson, Ruth Borker, Merritt (Terry) Cooke, Michelle Dominy, James F. Fisher, András Höfer, Mary Katzenstein, Nancy Levine, Edward Martin, Ernestine McHugh, Stanley Mumford, Barbara Parker, Navin Rai, Robert Schroeder, Carmela Schwartz, Joy Shepherd, Linda Stone, Robert Yoder. My debts to others should be obvious in the references of this book. I also thank Charles F. Keyes, James Gair, J. Bruce Long, and Leighton Hazlehurst, who all helped me in the formative stages of this work. Members of the Nepalese community in Ithaca, especially Shambhu Oja and Banu Oja, kept my spirits up all along the way. Peter Agree encouraged me early on in the development of the manuscript and through its completion. The production of the manuscript owes much to Jill Warner, Kathryn White, Ann Peters, Thomas Volman, and Stacia Zabusky. All photographs are mine. Kathryn March was with me in Tamdungsa for the second year of my original stay and every trip since. Her insights and observations on all aspects of Tamang life have woven their way inextricably into my own thinking. Her support is beyond thanks. Mohan and Maya Holmberg have distracted me at all the right times.

DAVID H. HOLMBERG

Ithaca, N.Y.

Note on Transcription and Pronunciation

I used both Nepali and the local dialect of Tamang in my research. I am relatively adept in both but have studied Nepali for many more years. Nepali was my medium for learning Tamang, and I often asked for explanations in Nepali when I did not fully understand what had been said in Tamang. Many Tamang are bilingual, and I moved in and out of Tamang and Nepali while conversing. Tamang ritual orations and certain songs also employ an archaic form of Tamang, which most villagers, including ritual specialists, cannot translate completely word for word; they almost always know, though, the general sense and implications of their words. Nepali words, written in *devanāgarī* script, are transcribed here for the most part according to Turner's *Comparative and Etymological Dictionary of the Nepali Language* ([1931] 1965). I have made several exceptions to Turner's system to facilitate reading for nonspecialists. Turner's "c," "ch," "ṅ," and "ś" are rendered, respectively, as "ch," "chh," "ng," and "sh." The names of well-known ethnic and caste groups of Nepal and other well-known Nepali terms appear as they are commonly written without diacritical marks.

Tamang is an unwritten Tibeto-Burman language and has several significant tones. It varies from village to village and there is no standard. When I first began to live in Tamdungsa, I developed a rough-and-ready system for transcribing the local dialect into Devanagari. Thus, I have transcribed Tamang words, with a few exceptions, as I have transcribed Nepali words. What sounds approximately like "shy" to English speakers is rendered by Tamang in Devanagari as "sy." I have opted here to write "shy" for the Devanagari "sy" as in "shyingo." The Tamang phonemes "ts," "tsh," and "ds" are not recognized in

Devanagari, and I have transcribed them as in the beginning of this sentence. The only Tamang pitch or tone that is marked in this book is the breathy, which is indicated by an "h" after a consonant that does not have an aspirated form or after a vowel that succeeds a consonant that does have an aspirated form. The transcriptions are somewhat different from and more accurate than what I have used before (Holmberg 1980, 1983, 1984). I make no claims to linguistic precision, and many significant phonetic distinctions are lost in this system of transcription. For those who require more accurate transcriptions of western Tamang, many if not all the terms used here appear with greater precision in Höfer (1981).

As transcribed here, both singular and plural forms of Tamang words are rendered in singular form. The only exceptions to this practice are the recurring terms for ritual practitioners—*lama, bombo,* and *lambu*—which are made plural by adding an "s." Tibetan terms are transcribed according to the sources from which they were drawn. If no source is apparent, I have tried to be consistent with the Wylie system (Wylie 1959) as used in Tucci (1980). Sanskrit terms are written without diacritical marks and in approximation of English pronunciation. Non-English terms appear in italics and with diacritical marks only in the first instance of their use or when they are reintroduced after many pages. A glossary of the commonly used non-English terms appears at the end of the text. All translations are mine unless otherwise indicated.

Many readers, especially those who read this text from perspectives steeped in Tibetology, greater Nepal studies, Indology, or Asian studies, will be vexed by my use of Tamang terms instead of more standardized Tibetan, Nepali, or Sanskrit terms. For example, I use the local form *guru rhimborochhe* for a Buddhist hero instead of the Tibetan *Gu ru Rin po che* or Sanskrit *padmasaṃbhava.* This Tamang-centric practice conforms with the overall orientation of this text, which attempts to reconstruct cultural forms in Nepal from Tamang and Nepalese perspectives, and to understand Nepalese culture not simply as a derivation of greater Indic or Tibetan formations.

ORDER IN PARADOX

1 Introduction: Elementary Structures in Ritual Life

> The study of the concrete, which is the study of the whole, is made more readily, is more interesting, and furnishes more explanations in the sphere of sociology than the study of the abstract.
>
> Marcel Mauss, *The Gift*

> In the lama's house there is a conch (*dung*);
> In the bombo's house there is the beak of a hornbill (*khyung*);
> In the lambu's house there is a mouth (*sung*).
>
> Tamang Saying

What follows is a cultural study of the rituals and society of a western Tamang community in Himalayan Nepal. This investigation unfolds within, and speaks to, comparative problems in the anthropology of religion in general and of Buddhist societies in particular. It is also a study in culture theory and demonstrates that order, harmony, and resolution should not be privileged in conceptualizations of culture at the expense of contradiction, tension, and irresolution. The study examines the ritual field of the western Tamang, which includes the rituals of several specialists—rituals which on the surface appear contradictory—and relates this ritual field to an ideology of reciprocity and its inherent paradoxes. The Tamang ritual field points us to a new approach to elementary structures in ritual life, one based less on the generation of superordinate meaning through order than on the impossibility of final meaning. But let us begin with the ethnographic.

Tamang villagers to the northwest of the Kathmandu Valley engage some eight ritual specialists.[1] Three are prominent and are recognized as focal persons in the ritual system: *lama*, *lambu*, and *bombo*. Five

[1] Höfer (1981:26) isolates five practitioners in a neighboring area. In addition to the eight practitioners discussed here, many other laypersons in the local area provide specialized ritual services. Tamang villagers regularly consult those in the village who are conversant with the Nepalese calendar for astrological service and other individuals who have special curative knowledge.

fulfill subsidiary roles: *gurpa, shyepompo, pujāri,* Hindu priests, and *sangtung*. The rituals revolving around the practice of the prominent specialists mark out three spheres: the Buddhist, associated with lama; the sacrificial, associated with lambu; and the shamanic, associated with bombo. Each sphere proceeds from a distinct authority and is marked by a division of labor. A brief ethnographic synopsis of these practitioners and their practice provides an entrée into the problems this book discusses.

Lamas and lamaic rituals. Lamas are the most respected practitioners among Tamang, and villagers address and treat them honorifically, particularly during rituals. Lamas preside over memorial death feasts (*gral*) that rescue the shadow-souls of the dead into rebirth and regenerate order in the local society of intermarrying clans. These socially encompassing rituals are the most important lamaic performances and are integral to the meaning of lamas and Buddhism in Tamang imagination. Lamas also preside at a ten-day dance drama (*chhechu*) at the conclusion of which they distribute blessings of long life and general well-being.[2] In addition to overseeing these large-scale celebrations, lamas provide an array of protective, propitiatory, and exorcistic ritual services, many of which are important subrites of the encompassing memorial death feasts and dance dramas.

Lamaic authority stems from the activation of sacred texts conceived as oaths of ancient Buddhas. Lamas rebind the world into orderly form through their textual incantations. Gurpa are also invocational specialists and supplement lamaic efforts in the festival of dances. Shyepompo or learned singers lead choruses of villagers in songs glorifying the Buddhas and dance around the raised altars of the lamas. Although lamas are associated with the cosmology, texts, and ritual paraphernalia of greater Tibetan Buddhism, no monasteries exist in the western Tamang region in which this study was based. The lamas are not celibate renouncers; they marry and are linked to a clan-based social regime.

Lambus and sacrificial practices. Lambus sacrifice to propitiate divinities and to exorcise an array of harmful agents who constitute a society separate from, but in direct engagement with, human society. Much of everyday concern and ritual activity focuses on these beings. Lambus honorifically entreat divinities to stabilize the cosmos and society, to bring rain, to stave off earthquakes, landslides, and violent storms, and to resist evil onslaughts. Lambus also appease and deflect

[2]Some Tamang pronounce *chhechu* as *tshechhu*.

afflictive shades and evil spirits who insinuate themselves in human life. Lambus, like other practitioners, act to assure well-being. They have a special ritual relation to a divinity named *shyihbda*, the master/mistress of the earth and to an evil known as *nakhle mhang* or the winnowing-tray-evil. Along with lamas, lambus play a key role in rites of passage. Replicating the sacrificial services of lambus are the pujari, who propitiate divinities of greater Hindu Nepal. On rare occasions, Hindu priests from neighboring Brahman villages provide specialized propitiatory services for some Tamang households.

Bombos and shamanic rituals. Bombos recall lost shadow-souls, raise up life-force, and divine. They have special powers of mediation between human and divine or malevolent beings. During their rituals, they shoulder and toss about divinities and spirits and go into divine and demonic domains, unveiling the enigmas of experience. Where the rituals of lamas proceed from the authority of the text and those of lambus from the sacrificial act, bombos are inspired to practice by severe seizures brought on by ancestral spirits of deceased bombos and a relationship with spirit beings of midspace. Where lamaic and sacrificial rituals reaffirm a regime of measured exchange among local clans and among humans, divinities, and harmful agents, bombos in their rituals—referred to here as "soundings"—fathom the paradoxes and arbitrariness of these orders. Although bombos cure the living and counter morbidity, malaise, and misfortune, their cures are of a special sort. Lambus and lamas effect most everyday cures, and shamanic soundings deal ultimately with the preconditions of malaise. From our perspective bombos often assume a deconstructive stance that defies and sidesteps reductive glosses. *Sangtung*, like bombos, are also shamanic curers but are said to "shake harder" than bombos, and bombos look down on them. Sangtung provide many of the same services that bombos do but are not fully masters of controlled possession. They beat on bronze plates instead of drums and do not erect raised altars, don special costumes, or deploy elaborate paraphernalia essential to the soundings of bombos. Many bombos practice as sangtung before completing an initiation under the supervision of preceptors or *guru*.

Our concern here is with ritual logics and communications as much as with practitioners. Lama, lambu, and bombo mark out a tripartite field. The other five specialists are subsumed under the ritual domains of these three and are not discussed at great length here, even though each figures uniquely in the system and, in some instances, can provide specialized services. In general, they supplement or replicate the services provided by the other practitioners. For instance, pujari who supervise propitiation of greater Nepalese divinities and Brahman priests in their rare practice for Tamang do not introduce a Hindu component to ritual life but provide sacrificial services usually part of the lambu's repertoire. Likewise sangtung fall well within the shamanic fold and the shyepompo and gurpa within the lamaic. Tamang villagers are obliged—even though some may disparage one or another practitioner (if not all)—to engage most of these practitioners on a regular and continuing basis. Moreover, although rivalry often frames their relations, each practitioner will engage the others and they often combine their efforts toward specific ritual ends. It is central to my analysis that these three ritual domains be conceived not as exclusive but rather as complementary dimensions of a unified field.

Ritual Polarities in Anthropological Thought

This pattern of ritual differentiation is by no means confined to the Tamang. It is an essential feature not only of all the religious systems of the Himalayas but of those of South and Southeast Asia and many if not most ethnographic areas of the world.[3] Thus ritual differentiation is an integral problem for theories of religion. Anthropologists and historians of religion have traditionally approached multifaceted ritual systems from two primary vantages, which Kirsch has succinctly reviewed for the study of religious complexity in the Buddhist societies of

[3]Accounts of Indian religions stress the simultaneous practice of multiple specialists (Harper 1957, 1963; Dumont and Pocock 1959b; Rahmann 1959; Dumont 1970a:33–60; Wadley 1976; Babb 1975; Claus 1979; Kakar 1982). In the Hindu Himalayas, Brahman priests are opposed to shamans (Berreman 1964). The interpretation of multifaceted ritual systems has been focal in discourse on the Theravada Buddhist societies of Southeast Asia (Spiro 1967; Tambiah 1970; Kirsch 1977) and Sri Lanka (Ames 1964; Gombrich 1971a; Obeyesekere 1966, 1969; Kapferer 1983). Hindu Chetri-Bahun in Nepal employ specialists in possession along with Brahmans and other practitioners (Höfer and Shrestha 1973; Stone 1976; Winkler 1976). Multiple specialists are an integral part of all the religious systems of Tibeto-Burman-speaking groups in the Himalayas and are reported for Magar (Hitchcock 1966; Watters 1975; Jest 1976; Oppitz 1982), Chantel (Michl 1976), Thakali (Fürer-Haimendorf 1966; Greve 1981–82; Manzardo 1985), Gurung (Pignède 1966; Messerschmidt 1976a, 1976b), Sunuwar (Fournier 1976, 1978), Helambu Sherpa-Tamang and Langthang Tamang (Hall 1978), eastern Tamang (Fürer-Haimendorf 1956; Lama 1959; Miller 1979; Peters 1981), Sherpa of Solu-Khumbu (Fürer-Haimendorf 1955, 1964; Ortner 1978a; Paul 1976, 1982; March 1979), Thulung Rai (Allen 1976) and Athpahariva Rai (Dahal 1985), Limbu (R. L. Jones 1976b; Sagant 1973), Newar and other urban groups (Okada 1976; Toffin 1984; Van Krooij 1978; Slusser 1982), peoples of Kalimpong and Darjeeling (Macdonald 1975:113–28), Lepcha (1967), and Tibetan groups across the nothern regions of the Himalayas (Stein 1972; Berglie 1976; Samuel 1978a, 1978b; Paul 1982; Mumford n.d.).

South and Southeast Asia. He has identified a "stratigraphic" or "thin veneer" theory in historical studies and a "structural-functional" theory in anthropological studies (1977:242). The stratigraphic theory organizes components according to historical period and concentrates on accounting for the origins of various strands rather than their continuity. Structural-functional approaches are concerned "with the relationships of various components" and how these components reflect constraint from "nonreligious" spheres (1977:242). Spiro (1967, 1970), for instance, sees the strands of Burmese religion as "discrete" and "alternate" and explains them according to psychological underpinnings of ritual symbology and action; Ames (1964) approaches Sinhalese religion as a "single syncretized religious system" and invokes sociological correlates of ritual practice in explanation (Kirsch 1977: 242–43). Psychological interpretations usually proceed from clinical orientations and organize the symbolic processes of rituals in therapeutic idioms. Sociological approaches unfold in mechanical models and see rituals as serving particular social purposes. The two vantages often conflate into an approach toward ritual symbology as ciphers of psychosocial processes.

Closely related to these approaches in the history of the study of Asian religions are the articulatory concepts of "great tradition" and "little tradition." In South Asia "great" usually signified textually based Hindu or Buddhist practices and "little" a residual set of practices associated with divinities and spirits not found in the great tradition. This model, which in large measure reflects the influence of philological approaches in Western studies of Asia, presumes discontinuities between levels. Calling attention to structural, historical, and communicative continuities between these opposed poles, Dumont and Pocock (1959a), Obeyesekere (1963), and Tambiah (1970) interpret the social and cultural systems of India, Sri Lanka, and Thailand as unified systems and have criticized approaches that consider great and little as isolates. More recently, Kapferer, although accepting these critiques, links the practices of exorcism and demon celebration to class distinctions in Sri Lanka. He argues that working classes and peasants have special, although by no means exclusive, association with demon ceremonies in a religious system that also includes renunciatory Buddhism and the worship of divinities: "Demons are the terrors which prowl at the base of hierarchy" (1983:35).

Studies of religion in Nepal have conformed in large measure to these basic explanatory patterns; the tendency has been to approach the domains of ritual specialists in isolation, concentrating on "Hindu" practices, "Buddhist" practices, or "spirit possession." For instance, most studies of shamanism or spirit possession in Nepal have considered it a discrete system in complement to Buddhist and Hindu practices (see Hitchcock and Jones 1976:xii) and invoke historical or psychosocial forces to account for these distinctions. Nepalese shamanisms are regularly associated with a protoshamanism of Central Asia (Hitchcock 1967; Jones 1968; Watters 1975); Watters makes the following observation: "Many of the themes of classical shamanism can be found with varying degrees of modification in other ethnic groups of Nepal as well, at least in kernel form. . . . Does this suggest, perhaps, that there was a proto-tradition of the non-Indic peoples of Nepal which may have very closely resembled the classic Inner Asian tradition? The incidence of Kham-Magar shamanism shows that such a tradition can and does, in fact, exist in Nepal" (1975:155).

What these studies neglect—as do many studies of shamanism—is that shamanism even in its classical locales is usually associated ethnographically with other forms of ritual practice.[4] Peters (1981), R. L. Jones (1976b), and S. K. Jones (1976) stress the psychotherapeutic and sociotherapeutic aspects of shamanic practices in Nepal. In this study of Tamang religious complexity, I do not mean to dismiss historical, experiential, or sociological dimensions of ritual life, but rather to approach them as mediated at their formation in culture.

Several studies of religion in Nepal (Sagant 1973; Fournier 1978; Samuel 1978a, 1978b; Paul 1979), however, diverge from this pattern by considering various ritual strands as parts of systems in a dynamic interplay in which each part reflects a logic of the whole and in which the total religious field is more than the accretion of discrete strands. These representations share with this study a concern with the symbology that relates what are elsewhere considered isolates, whether Hindu, Buddhist, shamanic, sacrificial, or "folk." The initial comparative problem is thus less one of contrasting separable strands like "shamanism" or "Buddhism" than of contrasting total ritual systems, whether those of the Magar, Gurung, Chantel, Thakali, Newar, Tamang, Sunuwar, Sherpa, Rai, Limbu, Tibetan groups, or Indo-Nepalese Chetri, Bahun, Kami, Sarki, and Damai (to mention some more commonly cited groups in hill Nepal) or, more extensively, of the Hindu-Buddhist systems of greater Asia.

In large measure, then, this book follows the orientation developed

[4]For instance the Tungus, from whom the term *shaman* enters our language, have other ritual practitioners in addition to shamans, including lamas (Shirokogoroff 1935).

by Tambiah (1970) in his study of Thai Buddhism and its relation to spirit cults. There he attempts "to present the religion as a synchronic, ordered scheme of collective representations; then on the one side to demonstrate how the system of religious categories is woven into the institutional context and social structure of the contemporary villagers; and on the other to relate the same system to grand Buddhist literary and historical tradition." Tambiah conceives Thai religion as a "single total field" encompassing four "cults or complexes" that exist in relations of "opposition, complementarity, linkage, and hierarchy" (1970:2). Here, Tamang religion is also approached as a field composed of sacrificial, shamanic, and lamaic practices, but, as we shall see, the absence of state Buddhism in Nepal has allowed a system of balanced complementarities to emerge in Tamang religion, in contrast to the Thai case where a routinized Buddhism has—from Tamang perspective—come to reform and dominate the field in a totalizing way.

Furthermore, this book draws on and succeeds two semiological orientations within contemporary anthropology: structuralist vantages associated with Lévi-Strauss, which have concentrated on the study of myth, and interpretive ones associated with Geertz, Turner, and others, which have taken ritual as their primary object. The influence of structuralist approaches is obvious in the abstraction of a ritual field: attention to the total field over and above specific elements is a primary premise of structuralist analysis. The delineation of the Tamang field as composed of three ritual domains, though, should not be construed as rigid or final. Such a delineation is necessary and serves a heuristic purpose, but the closure imposed is temporary; the analysis it invites ultimately undermines itself. Not only does history impinge on structure, but the interpretation presented here suggests not an overdetermined structure of balance and harmony but a dynamic tension.

To gain access to this tension we approach ritual as world construction drawing on and reorienting an oft-cited conceptualization of religion as "models of" and "models for 'reality'" (Geertz 1973:93) which shape experience and orient action. Ritual systems like that of the Tamang, though, do not present us with a totalizing "general order of existence" (Geertz 1973:98). There are several orders of existence which often appear—as should be evident from the ethnographic synopsis above—to be mutually exclusive. For instance, lamaic ritual unfolds from a premise that the Buddhas bound the cosmos and society, including humans, divinities, and harmful agents, into orderly form through oaths, which lamas reactivate. Lambus sacrifice as though those oaths were basically sound, but insufficient. And bombos, in turn, sound on the premise that both lamaic and sacrificial rituals are intrinsically incomplete. The total field thus resists a final gloss and can only be apprehended in the apperception of its contrary versions.

Complementary vantages are, from the perspective of ritual as world construction, written into the system so that any ordination remains arbitrary and incomplete in its selectivity; each necessarily enables contradictions and antitheses. As Ortner has observed in her study of Sherpa ritual, "Religion, by virtue of being a metasystem that is separate from and yet addressed to the social order, itself engenders paradox, contradiction, and conflict" (1978a:152). In this book, I demonstrate that the logical origins of ritual multiplicity among Tamang reside in this dynamic, tempered in historical processes. The paradoxes and contradictions generated in one ritual construction are taken over in another ritual complex only to regenerate the other ritual forms. As Kirsch observed in his review of Thai ritual, "If the animistic component [of Thai religion] provides a kind of symbolic opposition to Buddhist world view, its perpetuation is linked closely to the perpetuation of Buddhism" (1977:266). And, we could add, vice versa. From the vantage, then, of each ritual construction revolving around one or another practitioner, the Tamang field never becomes fully represented. Each ritual makes its representations from the pretext that the others are not present, even though from an abstracted anthropological overview each is dependent on the others. On the level of rituals there is a perpetual oscillation through alternate vantages, each subsuming the other but without the formation of a totalizing ritual.

The complementarities that structure the Tamang field are ritually expressed only on the rare occasions when practitioners combine. The contradictions in these ritual constructions as they form a field, though, become the subject of exegetic reflection in what Tamang refer to as *ṭhungrap-kerap* or origination accounts, which we can gloss as myths.[5] The Tamang ritual field, then, takes us into a consideration of the relation of ritual and myth. I approach these accounts as, among other things, metalogues in which the Tamang themselves reflect on dimensions of their ritual and social life, including ritual divergences. They constitute an indigenous discourse on the very problems that have inspired anthropological studies. More often than not, when asked, Tamang invoke variants of these accounts to make sense of, and

[5]Detienne (1986) has shown that the history of mythology as a field calls into question our preconceptions of myth as a genre. When *myth* is used here it is in reference to these origination accounts.

to frame, their apparently contrary practices. These accounts, which are told both colloquially and chanted formally, provide in this study a means to shift back from abstractions of an anthropology of ritual and myth to a more concrete approach.

If this book has a conscious ethnographic strategy, it is to sustain an interplay between the metalogues of myth and the representations of ritual (including social representations).[6] The structure of the central argument about ritual complexity is reflected in the structure of chapters 5, 6 and 7, which delve into ritual spheres, discussing the authority, recruitment, and practices of lambus, bombos, and lamas, respectively. These chapters also examine focal rituals for each practitioner and delineate an overall ritual message for each domain. Chapter 8 addresses the field as a totality through an origination account of the ritual divergences of lamas, bombos, and, secondarily, lambus.

This book, though, does not confine itself exclusively to the symbology of a western Tamang community in synchronic suspension and isolation; it is both a more extensive ethnographic work and a theoretical work. It examines the ritual field in view of Tamang history, social life, and the relation of Tamang rituals to other ritual systems with a Buddhist component. Chapter 2 introduces the Tamang sociologically in greater Nepal through a historical consideration of their emergence as an ethnic group—a Buddhist caste/tribe—within an encompassing Hindu sociopolity. The chapter also describes the village of Tamdungsa. State formation not only created the group called "Tamang" but contributed to a process of cultural introversion in a local area, bounding and constraining ritual and social formations. Tamang communities became contained as clan-based local societies, and a nonmonastic—or what I label here "amonastic"—Buddhism took form tied to a regime of restricted exchange. This regime of restricted ex-

[6]Ethnography is an artifact of cultural differences, and this book was written in recognition of these differences. This may seem to be an obvious point, but it is often neglected in certain genres of ethnography as well as in some contemporary critiques of ethnographic practice. The former reduce humanity to variants on unitary themes (economic, political, psychological, biological), and the latter often myopically reconstruct ethnography as an unreflective effort to confine humanity to an authoritative idiom. I have included the words and texts of the Tamang as much as possible, but I make no pretense of speaking for the Tamang. This text makes no attempt to resolve what is a necessary contradiction of ethnographic writing: if ethnography is born with cultural differences, it cannot escape them. Even recent ethnographic techniques that attempt to weave the voices of the ethnographer's interlocutors into a textual dialogue shade more often than not into the exaggerated announcement of an ethnographic "I." This book focuses, moreover, on rituals with which one cannot have, in the strict sense, a discussion.

change among clans and a general ethos of reciprocity are the focus of chapter 3. An cthos of reciprocity orders social transactions and experience in encompassing ways and at the same time induces irresolvable contradictions. The breaches inherent in social differentiation are tied to gender, and reciprocity and gender are linked to ritual divergences, a subject that is taken up in chapter 8 again through mythic materials.

The convergence of Buddhism with a clan-based—from some perspectives "tribal"—society appears to be a violation of terms, for, more often than not, Buddhism is associated with state societies and a universalizing and rationalizing ideology. Tamang in their amonasticism suggest a new pole in the comparative study of Buddhist societies of greater Tibet, South Asia, and Southeast Asia. This comparative theme is addressed descriptively in chapter 7 in the discussion of lamaic institutions and practices and by comparison with other Buddhist systems in chapter 8. Moreover, chapter 5, on sacrifice, and chapter 6, on shamanic soundings, situate Tamang practices in more extensive comparative concerns with sacrifice and with shamanism and spirit possession as general ritual phenomena. The model of presentation, however, is that each domain of Tamang ritual life derives its meaning only in relation to other aspects of the system, and comparison should properly be framed with an appreciation of the total system and not discrete elements. In this study, the historical, sociological, and experiential facets of ritual life that have been the objects of anthropologists' reflections are presented as structures mediated in an encompassing cultural logic, including a dialectic between the production of meaning through order and a recognition of the arbitrariness of all orders.

2 Tamang Comparatively Reconstructed

> From now on, throughout our Gorkha Kingdom of Nepal, all Tamang [of the twelve clans] when referring to their own caste shall write and have written "Tamang"; [by the same token,] in all documents of the military and civilian administration, of government offices and regiments, in public and daily life, do not write or have written "*bhoṭe*" or "*lāmā*," but write or have written "Tamang" for the twelve [clans of] Tamang of the *bhoṭe* caste and only for that group of the *bhoṭe* caste.
>
> A Proclamation (1932) by King Tribhuvan and Prime Minister Bhim Shamsher Rana

Nepal bridges the Inner Asian plateau of Tibet and the Gangetic plain of India and circumscribes within its borders many climatic zones from steaming, humid jungles in its southern Terai plains to arid, arctic wastes in its high intermontane valleys. Between the extremes of the Tibetan plateau and the Gangetic plain, ranging in altitude from six hundred feet to over twenty-eight thousand feet and rising in a series from the plains are the rugged and precipitous ranges of the Himalayas: the Siwalekh, the Mahabharat Lekh, and the Himalayas proper. These ranges are carved perpendicularly and transversely by a number of river gorges and valleys that divide the country into distinct regions.[1]

Ethnographers generally invoke three main divisions in what is a stunning array of ethnic groups in this ecologically diverse country.[2] Tibetan-like peoples, including the famous Sherpa, inhabit the high reaches of the Himalayas along the borders with Tibet. To the south in what are called the midhills, ranging in altitude from low interior gorges to eight thousand feet or so, reside many Tibeto-Burman-

[1]See Karan (1960) and Hagen (1971) for general accounts of Himalayan geography.

[2]For more elaborate descriptions of this diversity see Bista's classic *People of Nepal* (1972). Höfer's (1979) study of the state and caste hierarchy in Nepal has the best and most comprehensive overview of diversity in Nepal. Several factors are making these ethnic group models obsolete. Migration, particularly within the midhills, to the southern plains, and to urban areas, confounds this neat picture. In some areas that have seen migration from many areas, ethnicity as usually conceived in the ethnography of Nepal is dissolving as a significant category.

speaking ethnic groups. The main groups that have attracted anthropological attention are (from roughly west to east): Magar, Chantel, Gurung, Thakali, Tamang, Sunuwar, Jiril, Rai, and Limbu. Included in this category but distinct from the majority of the hill groups are the Newar—the farmers, traders, crafts people, and city-builders of the Kathmandu Valley. Intermingled with these groups are the pervasive Indo-Nepalese hill groups. They speak Nepali—an Indo-Aryan language—which is the national language of Nepal. The significant sectors of these hill groups are the high-caste Bahun (Brahman), Thakuri and Chetri (*chhetri*)—both Kshatriya or "warrior" groups—and the low-caste Kami (Blacksmiths), Damai (Tailors), and Sarki (Leatherworkers). Sectors of the high castes came to political domination in Nepal in the late eighteenth century. Other distinct subgroupings of the Indo-Nepalese inhabit the low hills and plains of the southern borders of Nepal.

A Confusion of Cultures with Peoples

Contemporary Tamang are usually thought to be a group of people who descended from Tibet in time immemorial or to be an indigenous population of the central Himalayas (see Macdonald 1975:133). The use of the term *Tamang* has a complicated history. The Tamang as a named category of people—like many other groups found throughout highland Nepal—emerged not out of time immemorial from hidden Himalayan valleys but with the formation of the state of Nepal. There has been a tendency in the ethnography of Nepal to look at groups like the Tamang in isolation and to envision their cultures as presences in unchanging continuity with those of ancient residents of the Himalayas or neighboring regions but transforming and sometimes disintegrating in historical contacts with ascendant Hindu and Tibetan Buddhist peoples. Tamang culture, though, was as much created as undermined in the genesis of contemporary Nepal. Tamang cannot be considered outside this reality. In particular, what we can tentatively characterize as an insular or "tribal" character of Tamang culture emerged in response to the evolvement of sociopolities in the greater Himalayas where local sectors of Tamang turned in upon themselves in a process of involution.

Although there has been a recent florescence of research on Indo-Nepalese, Newar, and other societies, Nepal emerged, in Western imagination, as the home of autonomous "tribal" groups.[3] These groups, although subject historically to the acculturative forces of Indic and Tibetan civilizations, were often romanticized for their elevation and remoteness. During the 1950s, when the ethnology of India was turning attention to Indian civilizations and away from an almost exclusive focus on "tribal" populations or groups outside the Hindu mainstream, Nepal opened to the anthropological imagination; it was remote from Indic civilization to the south and close to Tibetan civilization to the north.[4] The first comprehensive monographs focused on the Sherpa (Fürer-Haimendorf [1964] 1972), the Gurung (Pignède 1966), and the Magar (Hitchcock 1966), while the urban Newar and the pervasive Chetri-Bahun and other Indo-Nepalese groups as well as other prominent Tibeto-Burman-speaking groups remained relatively unstudied. The focus on distinct and separate groups, although justified in a nascent ethnography, resulted in an image of Nepalese society as fragmented as its geography; as Nicholas Allen aptly notes, "The traditional and stereotypic ethnographic map of a tribal area [in South Asia] shows a patchwork or mosaic of subareas, each with its own language, customs and ethnonym, and the typical tribal study takes one such group as its unit of description" (1981:168). Early descriptions of groups, with notable exceptions (see Rosser 1966; Caplan 1970), minimized relations with greater Nepalese society in the pursuit of an ethnographic presence independent of more encompassing relations.[5]

Ethnographers often take contemporary named groups and teleologically reconstruct cultures backwards in time to presumed original (unsullied) forms, even though many Nepalese *jāt*—"sort, kind; tribe, nation; caste [or clan]" (Turner [1931] 1965:213)—are relatively new categories, unknown until recent centuries. Commonly named caste and ethnic groups such as Tamang, Gurung, Newar, Chetri, Bahun, Kami, Sarki, Damai, Thakali, Bhote, Sherpa, Magar, Chantel, Sunuwar, Tharu, Rai, and Limbu are not isolates with great historical

[3]Nepal is beginning to find a place in the study of South Asia and in Indological discourse, especially in French and British ethnology, where Nepal is not relegated to the peripheries of South Asian studies as it is in America.

[4]As Dumont remarked, "Up to about 1950, . . . most professional ethnologists at work in India concerned themselves with tribes, i.e. with groups which they believed had escaped, as the result of their isolation, the influence of Indian civilisation, just as if they were situated in Africa or Melanesia" (1970a:3). See also Cohn (1968:23).

[5]These relations, of course, can also be exaggerated as they have been in a study of Nepalese political-economy (Seddon, Blaikie, and Cameron 1979).

depth and continuity of form, but have acquired specific identities as Nepal consolidated.[6] For instance, even though ethnologists have speculated on a primordial Newarness, marked by language, culture, physiognomy, and common geographic origin (see Doherty 1978), Gellner argues that "Newar social structure is thoroughly South Asian in derivation" and that "their language has undergone at least 1600 years of influence from Indo-European languages" (1986:114).[7] Similar conjectures of origin have been made for many groups in Nepal.[8] Whether or not these conjectures are accurate, they prestructure ethnic groups as discrete entities and yield an image of Nepal as the agglomeration of groups who migrated at different times. In these formulations, each group becomes an artifact of its origins, and cultures are assumed to be inextricably linked to demographically closed and continuous populations: cultures have become confused with peoples. The Tamang are a case in point because they include groups that had little or no connection prior to the consolidation of Nepal. As is evident today, Tamang can incorporate non-Tamang into their fold over a period of time—a practice that is true of the Sherpa as well (Oppitz 1974).

This ethnographic cum historical tendency is related to an elementary opposition in the ethnology of South Asia between non-Hindu tribes and Hindu castes, an opposition that reflects one in greater ethnology. In South Asia, tribal societies in contrast to caste societies are characterized as geographically localized usually in isolated hilly or forested margins, egalitarian and stateless, occupationally undifferentiated, commensally and maritally open, nonliterate and out of the sway of Hindu civilization, and, despite their marginality, possessing some degree of socioritual autonomy and integrity.[9] Several groups in the Nepal Himalayas, though, do not readily conform to this problematic construction. Sherpa with their developed monastic institutions and Newar with their extensive urban civilization hardly qualify as tribes (see Gellner 1986); moreover, groups such as the Tamang have been conceived as both castelike and tribelike. From the perspective of the Hindu state, which took form in the late eighteenth century, Tamang are an endogamous jat or a caste separate from other groups and part of a hierarchy generated in the Brahmanical differentiation of groups

[6]For more comprehensive listings see Bista (1972), Frank (1973, 1974), Höfer (1979).

[7]Slusser remarks that the term *Newar* "appears to be of very recent origin" and "may have been bestowed by the Gorkhalis [in the eighteenth century]" (1982:9).

[8]Oppitz (1974) has located the origins of the Sherpa in eastern Tibet, and Höfer (1981) has suggested that the origins of the Tamang are in the region of Kyirong, Tibet.

[9]Tribe in Indian discourse as well can have the derogatory undertones of primitive and licentious.

according to relative purity; from the vantage of Tamdungsa villagers, the boundaries of the local group are, for most purposes, coextensive with the boundaries of society. They appear to themselves as an autonomous population composed of exogamous clans; in South Asian ethnology, they emerge as an egalitarian tribe. One of the anomalies of the sociology of Nepal is how to make sense of these two alternate perspectives, both of which have a medicum of descriptive power but remain incomplete.

The prevailing solution has been to view Nepal as involved in a process of Sanskritization, whereby historically isolated tribal societies—as well as some northern Buddhist groups and the urban Newar—have become increasingly acculturated to Brahmanical caste ideology.[10] Most attempts at ethnographic synthesis in Nepal situate the peoples of Nepal between Indic and Tibetan cultural influence, with Indic predominating because of the ascendancy of Hindu political authority. The Tibeto-Burman-speaking groups of the midhills of Nepal, in particular, are regularly approached as though they have been under pressure to assimilate from greater Hindu society, a process whereby their unique cultural systems become degraded by an infusion of caste principles into their egalitarian worlds. Whether or not this Indocentric reconstruction of Nepal is accurate, it neglects the intriguing dynamics of the convergence of Brahmanical caste ideology with the social reality of hill Nepal and unique configurations of caste generated in Nepal (Hitchcock 1978; Greenwold 1978). Furthermore, it downplays the observation that caste societies, including the historically continuous ones of India, allow for significant social and ritual variation across caste boundaries and regions.[11] There is no doubt that an assertion of orthodox Brahmanical ideology accompanied the formation of the state and that orthopraxic Hindus have been and remain the dominant political elite of Nepal; however, a social order has emerged that is irreducible to separate Indic, Tibetan, or tribal perspectives.

Any attempt to reconstruct the Tamang defies these reductions. Tamang, like all groups in Nepal, have a social reality only in contrast to, and in relations with, other groups, relations that took form in the rise of the Hindu state of Nepal; they were created and continue to transform in this history. Although the level and form of state intrusion

[10]The most extensive developments of this point of view are to be found in discussions of the Thakali (see in particular Fürer-Haimendorf 1966 and Messerschmidt 1982) and the Newar (see in particular Rosser 1966).

[11]For discussion of the similarities among castes in the Indian Himalayas see Berreman (1960).

varied from region to region, autonomous sociopolities do not exist in Nepal. As Levine suggests in her conclusion to a study of ethnicity in the Humla region, "Ethnicity in Nepal cannot be understood apart from the external political factors that have impinged on villagers' lives" (1987:86). Even in those areas of Nepal where enclaves maintain a measure of independence, this reality is and has been a function of relations with the ruling elite of Nepal. A more appropriate characterization of the configuration of groups in Nepal is one of a constant reordering subject to formation, reformation, and oscillation. State ideology and policy in conjunction with local conditions shaped ethnicity in Nepal. Fission reported among contemporary populations like the Thakali (Fürer-Haimendorf 1966; Iijima 1982; Bista 1971) and the fluidity of group boundaries in some regions of Nepal suggest that the contemporary array of named groups in Nepal—no matter whose reconstruction one takes—is, as in the past, dynamic rather than ossified (cf. Leach 1970). For example, Fisher has recently shown how Himalayan traders in the Dolpa region employ ambiguity in identity in their trading strategies (1986:94–95).

Although the state of Nepal played an articulatory role in the genesis of contemporary group distinctions (Sharma 1978; Höfer 1979), the history of Nepal is not simply one of Hinduization or Sanskritization (Srinivas 1966), that is, a movement toward standardized Hindu models; on the contrary, the encounter of Indo-Nepalese, Tibetan, and other Tibeto-Burman-speaking groups has resulted in a mutual accommodation of contrary cultures into structures uniquely Nepalese (Bista 1982).[12] To understand Tamang, we must unravel the genesis of this encounter and the dynamics of what was a discourse among different cultures and the combination and recombination of elements according to different cultural systems. Bateson's compelling organization of cultural contact around schismogenesis, a process that can result in a systemic complementary differentiation, is particularly appropriate to the Tamang case (1972:68).

Ethnographic Anomalies: Who Are the Tamang?

The referent "Tamang" exposes the problems of approaches to ethnicity that work from empirical criteria to define group affiliation. The

[12]The formation of the early Nepal or Gorkhali state was not an isolated event and relates directly to the presence of the British in northern India (see English 1985).

word *Tamang* apparently did not come into general usage in Nepal until well into the twentieth century. Older men in the village of Tamdungsa recount that about fifty years ago a touring government official required all the adult men of the village to affix their thumbprints to a document affirming that they would no longer refer to themselves or be referred to as "Lama" or "Bhote" but as "Tamang." This event corresponds roughly to a proclamation the central government issued in 1932 that made "Tamang" an official legal category superseding "Bhote" and "Lama" (Höfer 1979:147–48). The extent of the application of the term *Tamang* prior to this time is unknown. Höfer notes that *Tamang* appears in texts in Tibetan language as early as the thirteenth century and variants (*tapang* and *tamu*) are still used by the Thakali and Gurung to refer to themselves, suggesting a protogroup from which the contemporary Tamang/Gurung/Thakali historically diverged (1981:6–7).

The earliest Western uses of *Tamang* appear in mid-nineteenth-century documents in which the term is listed along with "Murmi, Lama, Bhotia, Ishang, and Sain" as a referent for a hill population in Nepal (Risely 1891:110). Groups now designated "Tamang" along with other populations were known primarily as "Bhote" and "Murmi" from the middle part of the eighteenth century through the nineteenth century.[13] *Sain* is probably derived from the general Newari term for Tibetans (see Manandhar 1986:253). *Ishang* or variants is a Sherpa referent.[14] Tamang in the Tamdungsa region referred to themselves most often as "Lama," although "Tamang" is gaining currency. Outsiders, particularly those at some social distance, referred to Tamang as "Lama" or as "Bhote"—the former term indicating respect, the latter term connoting "impure" and "unclean" (see Turner [1931] 1965:484).

Those now labeled "Tamang" constitute the largest Tibeto-Burman-speaking ethnic group in Nepal, numbering 555,056 and 522,416 speakers at the times of the 1971 and 1981 censuses (HMG 1975, 1984), respectively. These figures probably underestimate their population considerably. Peoples generally recognized as Tamang are grouped around the Kathmandu Valley: south along the hills of the frontal

[13]*Murmi* may well derive from the Tibetan *mur* for frontier and *mi* for people, making the Murmi "people of the frontier" (Macdonald 1975:129). The shift from the nineteenth-century Murmi to the twentieth-century Tamang reflects a transformation of the populations referred to by this term from the margins of Tibetan civilization to the margins of Nepalese civilization, a movement we shall examine in greater detail.

[14]*Ishang* may derive from the term *ashyang* or mother's brother, which is often used as an honorific within Tamang society.

Table 1. Tamang-speaking population in districts surrounding Kathmandu, 1971 census (HMG 1975)

District	Total population	Percentage, of total population speaking Tamang
Rasuwa	14,544	83
Makwanpur	72,332	44
Nuwakot	58,464	34
Sindhu Palanchok	61,905	30
Kabre Palanchok	72,605	30
Sindhuli	34,580	23
Ramechhap	30,039	19
Dhading	36,889	15
Dolakha	19,601	15
Total	400,959	27

range of the Himalayas, the Mahabharat Lekh; north on the southern slopes of the high range of the Himalayas sometimes to the borders of Tibet; west as far as the Buri-Gandaki River; east through the watershed of the Dudh River and continuing into the far east of Nepal. There are also established urban sectors of the Tamang, and just outside Kathmandu at Bauddhanath, now also associated with Tibetan immigrants, are important sectors of Tamang who have resided there alongside Newar for generations. According to the 1971 census, Tamang make up 35 percent of the total population in districts bordering the Kathmandu Valley plus Rasuwa district.[15] If districts immediately to the west and east are added, Tamang comprise 27 percent of the population of nine districts; 72 percent of the total Tamang-speaking population live in these nine districts (see Table 1 and Map 2). Tamang (along with other hill populations) have also migrated in significant numbers to the Terai plains, to Indian regions of Sikkim, Darjeeling, Assam, and elsewhere, to Bhutan, and as far as Southeast Asia. Moreover, the designation "Tamang" is not confined to these populations.

[15]Although all census data on language and ethnicity are notoriously slippery, I have used the 1971 data for extrapolations because they may well underestimate numbers of Tamang speakers much less than the 1981 census and thereby give us a little better picture of the situation of Tamang in Nepal. The 1981 census reports a total drop of 32,640 speakers of Tamang in ten years. In the nine districts of densest Tamang residence (see Table 1), the population of Tamang speakers is recorded as having dropped some 69,173, which is more than 17 percent of the 1971 population. Independent estimates by Frank (1973, 1974) would indicate that the 1971 figures of Tamang speakers are closer to the actual numbers of people called Tamang, even though they are also underestimated.

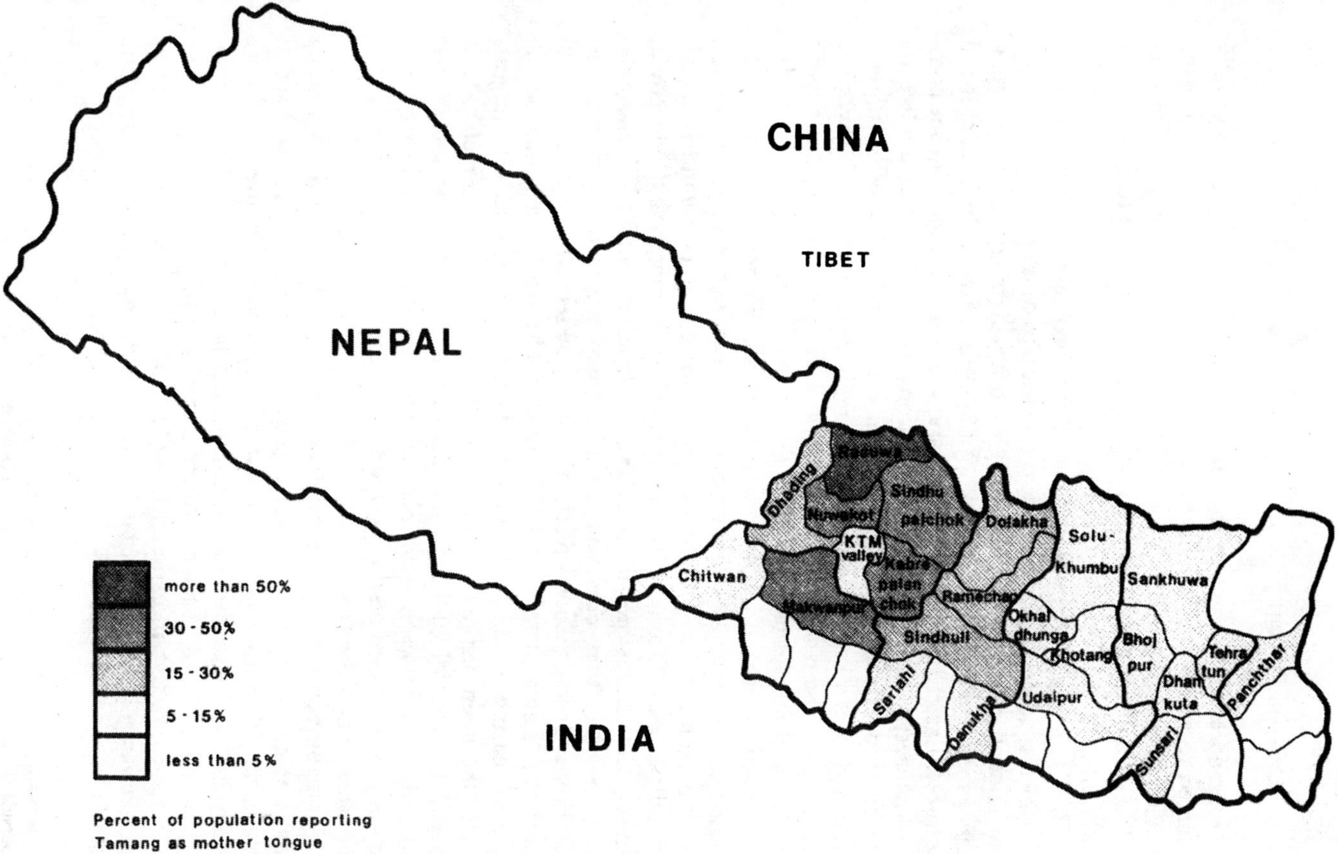

Map 2. Population density of Tamang in Nepal. Data from HMG (1975).

Tibetan-speaking groups in the far west of Nepal and groups usually referred to as Thakali are listed as Tamang in the government census (HMG 1975), and both are known to identify themselves as Tamang (Fürer-Haimendorf 1975:234, 1966:142) as are people in Karmarong and Langthang (Höfer 1979:149).

The "Tamang" label poses some further problems. Not only does it lack historical depth and statistical precision in censuses; it does not, as the Thakali case shows, necessarily encompass groups of people who always share a self-identity or a set of empirically established cultural features. Eastern and western Tamang are not conjoined into a common society, and intense social relations among Tamang tend to be confined to a circle of natal and affinal kin in a small radius of villages. Although ties between peoples in a region like that of the western Tamang can be traced like the links in a dialect chain, as one travels farther and farther from a village direct ties diminish until only fictive kin relations can be invoked or none at all. Western Tamang in the region of this research call everyone to the east of the Trisuli River and to the south "Shar-pa" or easterner, including populations usually called both "Tamang" and "Sherpa" in ethnography. Moreover, among themselves they distinguish *gle* (Nepali *ghale*) and Tamang despite the fact that outsiders consider them the same. According to Clarke, a primary social distinction in the Helambu region is made between "Lama people," and "Tamang." The wealthier Lama people are increasingly calling themselves Sherpa to outsiders. He suggests that "the main distinction between Lama and Tamang in Helambu is based on control of land and that the major differences of social organisation between them are best explained by a change from a corporate life based on the lineage and kinship over to one based on the household and the temple" (1980:84).

Tamang peoples' current tendency to see a greater affinity among themselves as one people with a common origin, history, and set of clans, is, I would argue, a recent phenomenon. On the one hand, Tamang have accepted state definitions, and on the other hand, emigration and mobility have brought Tamang from diverse regions into greater contact.[16] In general, however, the term *Tamang* acquires its primary significance in legal titles to land, tax rolls, censuses, and ethnographic literature.[17]

[16]Thomas Fricke in a personal communication has noted that when marriage occurs outside the usual range of marriages, as it occasionally does, those with other Tamang are considered differently from those with other castes or ethnic groups.

[17]Legal last names among western Tamang are for the most part Tamang. Villagers rarely use these legal names in local parlance but use instead kin terms or nicknames.

It is in the frame of recent national politics—in patterns of ethnic and caste strategizing common to greater South Asia—that a pan-Nepal Tamang identity is beginning to be more forcefully asserted.[18] In the late 1970s, a national Tamang conference was held in Lalitpur. A story from the *Rising Nepal*[19] reported among other things that "altogether two thousand five hundred persons were present at today's conference which was participated in by six hundred representatives of nineteen districts of the country. The six hundred representatives who participated in today's conference are from Kathmandu, Lalitpur, Bhaktapur, Rasuwa, Dailekh, Ramechhap, Sunsari, Sindhuli, Makwanpur, Bhojpur, Okhladunga, Solukhumbhu, Dhading, Ilam, Jhapa, Chitwan, Kavre, Dhanusha, and Sarlahi districts." Leaders of the conference called for "equal opportunity" and decried the "backward" condition of Tamang.

Linguistic evidence underscores the arbitrariness of ethnic distinctions in Nepal. According to Glover's (1974) classification based on lexical affinities, the Tamang language is of the Gurung family, classed along with Gurung, Thakali, and Manangi. Glover finds as great a difference between eastern and western Tamang as he does between Tamang and the other languages of the family. Mazaudon stresses the linguistic variance of eastern Tamang from western Tamang and Thakali in the following terms: "The Tamang zone is vast and if intercomprehension is constant from village to neighboring village, it is nearly absent between persons taken from the two extremities of this zone. Oddly enough the Tamang of Risiangku [a village in the eastern area] show correspondences with the Thakali yet differ from the Tamang of Sahu [a village in the western area] who are geographically closer" [my translation] (1973:37).

Such anomalies are not confined to linguistic evidence. People from one village can cite nuances of custom even in neighboring villages, and as one moves across the range of Tamang habitation—for instance, from eastern to western Tamang—major differences are discernable. For example, patterns of women's dress vary markedly within the western Tamang region and between the western and eastern Tamang. Where women's weaving along with lamaic writing figure elementally in western Tamang identity, they appear less important in more easterly zones (March 1984). Song styles and genres between eastern and

[18]For a recent discussion of the Newar movement see Gellner (1986). Caplan (1970) has reported on Kiranti movements. There are parallels among Gurung.

[19]Unfortunately the clipping of the *Rising Nepal* sent by a friend is missing the date but it is probably 1978.

western Tamang suggest that they are from different cultures.[20] Although similarities can be discerned across the range of Tamang habitation and we cannot dismiss some commonality between regionally separate groups of Tamang, similarities can also be discovered as one moves across ethnic boundaries.

Tamang ethnic identity, then, derives not from common culture but in contrast to the ethnic identities of other Hindu and Tibeto-Burman groups. The distillation of groups of people as Tamang occurred with the consolidation of the state, and "Tamang" as a label took on a particular meaning in the worldview and legal codes of the reigning elite. Moreover, in the genesis of centralized authority, Tamang were affected in significant ways. The legal codes of the nineteenth century reveal in condensed form an official ideology that in large part reflects popular constructions by Hindu groups of Tibeto-Burman-speaking populations such as Tamang. Hindu schemes, though, are not the only schemes at work in Nepal and differ from those of the Tamang themselves. There is not one overarching and integrative version of groups in Nepal shared by all but several; it is with recognition of these complementary reconstructions that the social fields of Nepal must be approached. Relative power, though, has enforced one view over others in many encounters and has contributed to the cultural enclosure of Tamang and the creation of local socioritual forms.

Brahmanical Social Schemes and the Formation of Tamang

Francis B. Hamilton wrote the following account of the Murmi—peoples now called Tamang—after fourteen months' residence in Kathmandu and its environs in 1802–3 and an additional two years' along the frontier of India and Nepal:

> In the more rude and mountainous parts of Nepal Proper, the chief population consisted of these Murmis, who are by many considered to be a branch of the Bhotiyas, or people of Thibet; but, although in religion and doctrine they followed the example of that people, and all their priests, called Lamas, studied its language and science, . . . it seems doubtful, whether the two nations had a common origin; but this will be best ascertained by a comparison of the languages. . . . The doctrine of

[20]Striking cultural differences between eastern and western Tamang are impossible to ignore. Unfortunately I have not been able to include Steinmann's study (1987) of eastern Tamang in this analysis. I became aware of it after this book was in press.

> the Lamas is so obnoxious to the Ghorkhalese, that, under pretence of their being thieves, no Murmi is permitted to enter the valley where Kathmandu stands, and by way of ridicule, they are called Siyena Bhotiyas, or Bhotiyas who eat carrion; for these people have such an appetite for beef, that they cannot abstain from the oxen who die a natural death, as they are not now permitted to murder the sacred animal. . . . They never seem to have had any share in the government, nor to have been addicted to arms, but always followed the profession of agriculture, or carried loads for the Newars, being a people uncommonly robust. Their buildings are thatched huts, often supported on stages, like those of farther India. (Hamilton [1819] 1971:52–53)

This account of the Murmi is among the first by an outsider. It was made only thirty-three years after Prithvi Narayan Shah's conquest of the Kathmandu Valley in 1769 and subsequent consolidation of the state of Nepal (Stiller 1973; Regmi 1976; Höfer 1979; English 1985).[21] Embedded in this brief account are three facets of the Hindu perception of the Murmi that played in the historical formation of Tamang as a distinct group: they were incorporated into the state as a subjugated population; they were marked off from other groups in Nepal as the consumers of beef and particularly carrion beef; and they were associated with lamas and Buddhism. These attributes all point to a view of Bhote-Murmi or emergent Tamang as outside the fold of the nascent state order.

In the late eighteenth century, Thakuri overlords from Gorkha, a town to the west of the Kathmandu Valley, consolidated what was to become the present state of Nepal. Through conquest, alliance, and negotiation, they eventually brought the diverse groups and regions into a centralized administration based in Kathmandu. Prior to this consolidation, the central Himalayas had been composed of disparate principalities. These Thakuri people were Hindu in orientation and saw themselves as distinct from the Tibeto-Burman-speaking groups of the hills of Nepal and the Tibetan groups to the north. They were high caste and eventually thought of themselves as Rajput warriors (Höfer 1979:45), ritually superseded only by Brahmans. As they formed a centralized state they required both an administrative and economic infrastructure and a unifying ideology.[22]

[21]Other British officers mention the Tamang (see Kirkpatrick 1811); however, none gives more than a cursory description.

[22]See Höfer (1979) for a detailed study of the social dimensions of the legal codes of 1854 which embed this idealogy. His work not only reveals integral processes of social formations in Nepal but has wide-ranging ramifications for the study of greater South Asia.

Through the latter part of the eighteenth century, through the nineteenth century, and well into the twentieth century, a feudallike polity emerged. This polity was eventually controlled by one sector of the Thakuris, the Ranas, who ruled Nepal for all practical purposes as hereditary prime ministers from 1846 until 1951. Although the royal Shah dynasty had led the consolidation of Nepal, they played a secondary role during this era and reestablished their reigning position of influence only after the fall of the Ranas in 1951. Contemporary Nepal is ruled by the royal Shah family and administered through a system called "partyless democracy," a system that on the one hand cannot escape the legacy of Rana administrative structures and on the other reflects an attempt to develop a modern democratic nation-state.[23] During the early period of consolidation and through the Rana period, the Tamang as we now know them gained a specific role in the feudallike order and in Brahmanical social ideology. They occupied lands adjacent to the Kathmandu Valley, the center of the administration, and along important trade routes in and out of the valley. Control of agrarian resources and trade were crucial to the formation of the state. Bhote-Murmi (Tamang) became commensally, sexually, and legally separate from other groups in the official hierarchy of the codes and occupied a relatively low position. They became an endogamous caste in the perspective of the state.

The lands and labor of many people now regarded as Tamang were readily accessible and were appropriated early on to support the feudallike state. This process had serious ramifications for populations of Tamang through the nineteenth and twentieth centuries. This order is most strikingly revealed in the system of land tenure that took shape in the early nineteenth century and continued through the Rana regime (M. C. Regmi 1963, 1964, 1965, 1968, 1976). Four forms affected the Tamang. Their lands often became the income-producing estates (*birtā*; *jāgir*) of functionaries of the state (military, administrative, or noble) or the Tamang became tenants on these estates. Tamang rarely held such estates although cases are not unknown.[24] They also were brought under a corvéelike system (*rakam* and *jhārā*) whereby villagers retained usufruct over agricultural lands in return for compulsory la-

[23]See Burghart (1984) for an excellent account of the history of the concept of the nation-state in Nepal.

[24]Villagers to the west of the Trisuli reported that Tamang who resided on the northern borders with Tibet had been granted birta estates by the Ranas for assistance in skirmishes with Tibet. Likewise some eastern Tamang reputedly held birta estates. I was unable to confirm these reports, and they may have also been referring to *guṭhi* grants.

bor; in addition to this service they were also subject to several additional taxes. Rakam was particularly prevalent around Kathmandu and to the northwest of the Kathmandu Valley. A third form was *guṭhi* or land endowed in the support of institutions, particularly religious and charitable ones. Although as in the case with birta estates Tamang were often tenants on such estates, they were rarely allotted these estates themselves. The general extent of guthi grants to Tamang, however, is unknown. In areas around Trisuli, local Buddhist lamas complained that holdings they described as guthi had not been recognized by the Rana regime, but this was not the case in other areas where such holdings were recognized.[25] A final form of land tenure (*kipaṭ*) whereby the government recognized inalienable, ancestral land rights has been reported for the eastern Tamang (Fürer-Haimendorf 1956). All these forms with the exception of guthi have been abolished in recent decades among Tamang and converted to *raikaṛ*, a form of freehold in return for taxes.[26]

Prominent Tamang are of course not unknown, and in several places sectors of Tamang retained ascendancy over poor communities of high-caste Hindus. On the whole, however, Tamang were excluded from both all-Nepalese and regional domains of influence and held a status in the consolidating state below that of other Tibeto-Burman groups. Tamang were rarely allowed influential economic or administrative dominion beyond the village level as were sectors of other Tibeto-Burman populations (see Fürer-Haimendorf 1966; Messerschmidt and Gurung 1974). Furthermore, high-caste Hindus and favored sectors of Tibeto-Burman groups (notably the Gurung) were regularly granted land and administrative positions in areas traditionally Tamang. To the west of the Trisuli, Gurung were granted lands for villages and took over control of a regional cult closely associated with political authority. In some places to the east, whole Tamang villages were reduced to the status of tenants and in some cases slaves.[27] Immigration of high-caste Hindus and other groups into Tam-

[25]*Regmi Research Series* reports on several guthi endowments in eastern Tamang areas (1977, no. 6:81–85).

[26]Guthi remains important in many regions of Nepal and is the basis by which certain families retain large land holdings despite attempts at reform: "There were, of course, other factors in addition to religious sentiments which caused people to endow land as Guthi. Such endowments, once made, could not be revoked. Landowners thus could legally deter their heirs from alienating landed property by endowing it as Guthi. A small portion of the income accruing from the land was then utilized for religious and charitable purposes, while the balance was appropriated by the family of the donor" (M. C. Regmi 1968:12).

[27]Slavery was officially abolished in 1924.

ang regions was encouraged by the state; those who knew the ins and outs of the legalities of land tenure, who shared the language and culture of the central administration, and who had connections in the administration were able to take over both cultivated land and jungle in many Tamang regions. These processes are similar to those outlined by Caplan (1970) for the eastern parts of Nepal but without the special protections allowed to Limbu in kipat or collective tenure.

The Murmi-Bhote, though, did not become "untouchables" as one might expect in the Brahmanical encounter and incorporation of subjugated non-Hindu populations, even though they had several attributes usually associated with untouchables, notably beef eating. The legal codes of 1854 and other nineteenth-century codes classified the Bhote including Tamang as pure (*chokho*) (HMG 1966; see Höfer 1979). Although they were thus set off from untouchables—the *pāni nachalne jāt* or those castes from whom water is not acceptable—they were among the lowest of the clean castes; they were classed with alcohol drinkers (*matwāli*) and subject to enslavement (*māsinyā*). These attributes placed them below other alcohol drinkers like the Magar and the Gurung, who were not enslavable, and the high-caste Hindus, who wore sacred threads, did not consume alcohol, and could not be enslaved. Although the codes do not specifically relegate particular groups to specific varna (Brahman, Kshatriya, Vaishya, Shudra) or the encompassing caste groupings of Indic theory (Höfer 1979:118), the Bhote by these criteria emerge somewhat ambiguously like Shudras.[28]

The fact that Bhote-Murmi as well as the array of other Tibeto-Burman-speaking groups listed in the codes were given a "clean" posi-

[28]In its formation, the order that took form in Nepal followed patterns presaged in the greater social history of South Asia. As Dumont recounts, those who became Shudras in Indic varna ideology were originally conceived of as servants. "It seems that this fourfold partition of later Vedic society can be regarded as resulting from the addition of a fourth category to the first three, these corresponding to the Indo-European tripartition of social functions (Dumézil) and to the triad found in the first books of the Rig-Véda: *brahman-ksatra-viś* or: the principle of priesthood, that of *imperium*, and the clans or people. The Shudras appear in a late hymn of the Rig-Véda and seem to correspond to aborigines (like the *dāsa* and *dasyu*) integrated into the society on pain of servitude. It must be noted that the Brahman is the priest, the Kshatriya the member of the class of kings, the Vaishya the farmer, the Shudra the unfree servant" (1970b:68).

Tamang here might well be constructed like the aborigines of ancient Indian history. As is evident in their status as enslavable, they clearly enter the emergent state on pain of servitude, a function of their subjugation. Although high-caste Hindus in the Tamdungsa region are quite explicit in declaring that Tamang cannot listen to the sacred texts of Hinduism, Bennett reports that they are ranked as Vaishya by high-caste Hindus in her research area (1983:10). Tamang, however, more closely approximate the status of Shudra in a varna ideology than either Vaishya or untouchable. This kind of ambiguity remains the key feature of Tamang identity in Hindu eyes.

tion within the hierarchy must on one level be a function of the relative numerical and political prominence of these groups and the fact that they probably distinguished themselves from untouchables prior to consolidation. Although Tibeto-Burman-speaking groups are clean castes in the codes, other criteria separate Bhote-Murmi from other groups. Power has always played in the manipulations of the particular rankings in caste systems and reflects the historical reality of nineteenth-century Nepal. Because of their inclusion in the early Gorkha principality and their apparent service to the Thakuri rulers, groups like the Magar and the Gurung may well have acquired their special position in the codes as unenslavable. Bhote (including those now called Tamang) were conceived more as a subjugated population than as loyal and allied servants, a conception marked by their enslavability. Moreover, with few exceptions, many of those now regarded as Tamang lived in relative proximity to the valley of Kathmandu, which became the seat for the consolidating administration. This geographic, and thereby strategic, centrality in the new state tended to bring the bulk of the Tamang population more directly under the control of the state administration.

Within this general configuration, groups now called Tamang took on unique attributes in state ideologies. In the legal codes of 1854, Bhote were the only people who were marked as beef eaters (Höfer 1979:143). Throughout the nineteenth century and continuing until today, Tamang are known as beef eaters. A handbook on Gurkha soldiers noted the difficulty of recruiting Tamang into the military: "Though he is not permitted to kill cows in Nepal, the Tamang will willingly eat the flesh of a cow killed by accident. It is for this reason that the more orthodox Gurkha officer is prejudiced against the enlistment of Tamangs. There is little doubt, however, that the Tamang makes an excellent soldier" (Great Britain 1965:113).

Beef eating is charged with meaning in Hindu Nepal. In Nepal, as in India, respect for the cow is integral in the differentiation of social and religious groups, and Hindus regularly invoke behavior toward cows and the consumption of beef in interactions with Muslims, tribals, and other non-Hindus. Although stories of killing cattle for consumption abound among outsiders, I must emphasize that Tamang in the areas of this research respect the sanctity of the cow and even perform standard Hindu rituals of nurturance and devotion toward cows. Cattle are highly prized. Tamang never injure them and are careful not to provoke accusations of mistreatment. Local Brahmans, in fact, often stable their cattle with Tamang. Many villagers, particularly those who travel in circles wider than the village, have dropped the practice of eating even dried beef carrion to avoid the suggestion of cow abuse. The respect for cattle extends beyond cows to other bovine species (particularly female water buffalo) in conformity with legal requirements.

The association of Tamang with violence to cows, then, does not reflect contemporary Tamang practices; such attributions rather reveal a political agenda. It is not uncommon, for instance, for Hindu outsiders to confess that they feel as though they are in "enemy territory" when visiting Tamang areas. To this day, accusations of violence to cows are voiced when factions vie for political dominion on the local level. Rivals of one populist leader among western Tamang accused him of crimes against cows throughout his political career even though he was one of the few villagers who never consumed beef and went out of his way to show respect for cows.[29]

Historically the characterization of Tamang as beef eaters reflects a socioritual logic. Bhote-Murmi-Tamang were outside the emergent order. In the Hindu state, not only are cows divine but respect for cows and for Brahmans go together, and Brahmans have had special associations with cows since ancient times (Brown 1957). Among contemporary Hindus one of the most auspicious gifts that one can give to a Brahman is a cow. To respect cows, in high-caste perspective, implies acceptance of Hindu hierarchy: to honor cows was to honor Brahmans and by extension to participate in the culture of caste upon which the ritual authority of the formative state was based. In Hindu social logic, to accuse people of consuming beef is to accuse them of violating essential principles of order, including the political order. Cow slaughter was of intense interest to the administration of the early nineteenth century, and proclamations concerning cows and beef eating abound. A royal edict from 1810 announces the close association of reverence for Brahmans and abstinence from beef eating; King Girban directed the Gurung and Lama peoples to the west of the Trisuli (where this research was conducted) on the pain of fines to "revere Brahmans and refrain from taking the flesh of dead cattle" unless they supplied hides to the government (M. C. Regmi, ed., 1972). The historical exaggeration of carrion-beef eating both affirmed and enforced the separation of the Bhote-Tamang as enemies of the nascent state; contemporary

[29]The most recent incident was in 1977 when anonymous and false accusations were filed with police during election time that the leader had slaughtered a cow for feasting, a crime that, to say the least, invokes the strongest passions among Hindus.

Tamang, as we shall see, reformulate these attributions into their own version of group differentiation.[30]

Along with an exaggerated attribution of beef eating, Bhote-Tamang were associated with Buddhism. As Hamilton ([1819] 1971) had noted, "the doctrine of the Lamas" was "obnoxious" to the rulers from Gorkha. The lamaic doctrine in Rana ideology associated the group with a competing socioreligious order, a perception supported by affinities between some Nepalese groups and Tibetans. Moreover, the geographic proximity of certain sectors of Tamang and the historical inclusion of some Tamang in polities more closely allied to Tibetan forms than to Indo-Nepalese forms may well have inspired Rana fears. A continuing affiliation with the doctrine of the lamas could be read as potential resistance to the formative state. It is doubtful, however, that hill-dwelling Buddhists were subject to direct or concerted persecution as some Buddhists were at certain periods in the Kathmandu Valley proper.[31] The experience of local sectors of Tamang and Bhote probably varied considerably; in the area of this research, which was relatively close to the Kathmandu Valley and a considerable distance from the Tibetan border, local lamaic institutions, although not persecuted, were certainly not encouraged under Rana rule. Further to the north and in other parts of Nepal, they were quite definitely recognized. In both Rasuwa and Helambu districts, regional elite were granted estates in support of monasteries, many of which are maintained to this day (see Clarke 1980).

The association with Buddhism, coupled with the importance of regional elite in the real politics of Nepal, also had another side; it may have enhanced the position of the Bhote in the legal codes in the same way that association with heterodox and competing sects may well have played in the historical elevation of Shudras or the lowest of clean castes in Hindu ideology from outsiders to insiders (Dumont 1970b:284n.32). The links of the Bhote (Tamang) to Tibetan Buddhism and their regional prominence probably influenced the construction of Bhote as clean. In some areas, Bhote (whether Tamang or other)

[30]For documents on cow slaughter and respect for Brahmans in the early years of the nineteenth century, see edicts edited by M. C. Regmi (1969, 1979a, 1979b, 1979c, 1980, 1983).

[31]Rosser (1966:81) and Slusser (1982:219n.15, 270n.1) report that the early Rana regime was a time of persecution against Buddhists in the Kathmandu Valley. Slusser notes that this persecution was directed toward Buddhists, "at least the casteless Tibetan ones who posed a threat to the imposition on Nepalese society of the Ranas' extreme notions respecting caste" (1982:219n.15).

maintained powerful positions. The selective attribution of beef eating to these groups may have been as much an attempt at marginalizing as a reflection of actual marginality. The official introduction of the term *Tamang* in place of Bhote-Murmi-Lama in the 1930s reflects a process of inclusion of Bhote populations in the vicinity of Kathmandu into greater Nepal and elevation in status vis-à-vis other Bhote groups. That "Tamang" thus implies greater membership in the sociopolity of Nepal is indicated by the fact that other populations in Nepal, particularly in remote areas with more entwined ties to Tibet, often call themselves Tamang in a bid for some national identity.

Be that as it may, during the Rana period, Tamang were relegated ideologically to a position outside the Brahmanical order. Their lack of recognition of the Brahman, implied in the marking of both Bhote and contemporary Tamang as beef eating and Buddhist, contributed to their ambiguous status. They were abhorrent because they were separate, but their separateness is what gave them the power of inclusion as a clean caste. Contemporary Tamang clearly view themselves as a distinct religious society, one based on the authority of lamas as opposed to Brahmans; to this day they prefer to call themselves "Lama" to outsiders. In an ironic ethnic awareness, a Tamang exorcist attempts to drive off intrusive evil spirits from southern valleys by warning them that there are beef eaters in Tamang country, warding them off with lines like the following: "Leave our child alone. Go play with an airplane high in the sky, go play with the thunder people, the moon people. Go play in Calcutta, in England, in America, in the eastern rivers. There are beef eaters in this country! You will be contaminated, a pure one cannot carry sin! Patricide and matricide may occur here! The moon may be murdered! Friend will kill friend!"

Mythic Contortions of Caste

Competition, conflict, and expropriation of resources may well characterize the historical encounter of the nascent state with groups now called Tamang, yet, a social compatibility also existed between tribelike Tamang with their exogamous clans and the hierarchical Indo-Nepalese with their endogamous castes. These two opposed orientations allowed for communication and agreement despite the fact that they appear irrevocably dissimilar. Tamang society is formed on the basis of cross-cousin marriage, which results for the most part not in extensive alliances across a large population but in intensive alliances among a small set of patriclans residing in neighboring villages.[32] In the villages around Tamdungsa almost all marriages were either within the village, in neighboring villages, or in villages a few hours away. This constituted a circle of kin. Some Tamang areas show another pattern where alliances are formed at greater distance for political or economic reasons. Fricke reports that the most distant marriages in the upper Ankhu Khola area were arranged in order to exchange pasture rights.[33] Even these alliances, though, were regionally confined, and villagers did not forge links across greater social or geographic distance as is the case with at least Sherpa and Gurung.

Tamang society in the area of Tamdungsa is highly localized and turned in upon itself: "restricted exchange" of this sort is "an imitation of endogamy within exogamy itself" (Lévi-Strauss 1966:123). Thus, for Hindu ideology, as expressed in both the legal codes and in contemporary social interaction, to declare Tamang as an endogamously separate caste does not necessarily conflict with the historically autonomous order of bilateral cross-cousin marriage. In fact, the historical separation and containment of peoples called Tamang may have reinforced a regimen of restricted exchange and stifled internal motivations toward either generalized exchange or marriage alliances across regions and the generation of independent sociopolitical hierarchies; in this way, the formation of the state may well have effectively "tribalized" local Tamang societies.

Though Hindu notions of the pure and impure, which circumscribe the Tamang as an endogamously and commensally separate caste, could be made to conform with the social reality of hill Nepal, other distinguishing features of the caste system could not. Castes in Hindu South Asia are never discrete elements and can only be understood as part of systems governed by relationships within a whole (Dumont 1970b:65–91). Essential to caste ideology is the occupational specialization of each caste and systemic asymmetry such that each caste is proscribed from performing necessary occupations for itself. These functional asymmetries are attuned to the opposition of pure and impure, and occupations are ranked accordingly. In the formulations of an "ethnosociology" of Indian society, caste generates innumerable transactions that affect "code-substances" of groups (Marriot 1976; Marriot and Inden 1977). Caste societies thus differ from clan-based

[32]Hindus—with some exceptions—find cross-cousin marriage abhorrent, and these practices among Tamang contribute to their degraded status in outsiders' eyes. Cousin marriage, however, has been reported for ruling clans.

[33]Personal communication from Thomas Fricke (see also Fricke 1986a).

societies in which equal services are exchanged symmetrically. The solidarity of the Indic social system is idealized in the varna model of four interdependent caste groups and in a system of economic exchanges and ritual obligations among different castes (*jajmāni*). Although these models are never adequate descriptions of socioeconomic life in Hindu villages of South Asia now or in the past, they reveal the distinctive ideology of caste culture in contrast to clan-based social ideology. In Nepal, groups such as the Tamang did not embrace orthodox theory.

In Nepalese ideology, interdependency among different groups was rarely elaborated, and varna in the legal codes "remains without specific substance for the five caste groups of Nepal" (Höfer 1979:118). For their part, Tamang certainly do not envision themselves as a service caste vis-à-vis the high castes who wear the sacred thread and purity and pollution only operate in a temporary sense and are not permanent or systemic attributes of social groups as in Indian culture (Dumont 1970b:48). Interdependency is not an ideological fact among Tamang or Indo-Nepalese, nor is full occupational differentiation a social fact in hill Nepal. Villages are frequently made up of only one or two groups, and although service contracts can articulate relations among higher groups and untouchables, they tend to be highly truncated and individualized—a full system of economic exchange (jajmani) centered on a landlord is unelaborated. This situation is particularly true in those areas in which Tibeto-Burman groups are the prevalent population; in western Tamang regions, villages are usually composed only of Tamang and a small number of *kāmi* (Blacksmiths) whose relations, although castelike, are not attuned to a totalizing caste structure with Brahmans at the top and untouchables at the bottom. Although untouchable, Kami are part of the social order of most Tamang villages; they are never linked by ritual obligations as they would be in Hindu society; the same is true of Tamang relations with high caste Bahun (Brahman) or Chetri (Kshatriya). The relations between Tamang and Blacksmiths and between Tamang and high castes must be approached according to Tamang principles of exchange upon which an idiom of purity has been historically glossed (see next chapter). The outcasting of Blacksmiths, moreover, is a feature of Tibetan as well as Hindu society.

The divergence between caste ideology and that of the Tamang is apparent on another level as well. In a wide-ranging comparative essay, Lévi-Strauss contrasts systems that distinguish groups according to cultural differences (occupations) with totemic systems, which do so according to natural differences (species):

> In societies where division of labour and occupational specialization do not exist, the only possible objective model [of social differences] has to be sought in the natural diversity of biological species; for there are only two objectively given models of concrete diversity: one on the level of nature, made up by the taxonomic system of natural species, the other on the level of culture, made up by the social system of trades and occupations. (1963b:9)
>
> The symmetry between occupational castes and totemic groups is an inverted symmetry. The principle on which they are differentiated is taken from culture in one case and nature in the other. (1966:123)

Hindu occupational complementarities in particular are also related to the religious opposition of the pure and the impure, giving the Brahman a hierarchical ascendancy and ritual authority (Harper 1963). The Tamang, although not classically totemic in their social organization, more closely approximate totemic or tribal cultures than Hindu caste culture in their linkage of social distinctions to nature. Tamang organize the external complementarities of castes according to a logic by which they distinguish internal clans, thus inverting a process reported for some groups in India in which totemic groups are distinguished according to caste logic (Lévi-Strauss 1966:120–22).

Two indigenous accounts from the Tamang, one textual and relating to the naming of clans and the other a contemporary narrative relating to the origins of caste difference, demonstrate the logic of this transformation. The first, translated from a text, recounts how the eighteen sons of *Ldong chen po,* an ancestral hero of some Tamang, acquired clans or *rus*:

> As they themselves cannot say what are their *rus*, they come together to ask him. He leads them to the dead body of a *g.yag* [yak] and says: 'All of you, take hold of the body of this *g.yag!* I will give you as name whatever part you take hold of.' To those who seized the horns, he gave the name of Rva-pha. To those who seized the nose, he gave the name of Snar-pha. To those who seized the nape of the neck, he gave the name of Snya-shur-pha. To those who seized the tongue, he gave the name of Lce-pha. To those who seized the lungs (*blo-pa*), he gave the name of Blo-pha [and so forth through liver, blood, skin, tail, testicles, stomach]. (Macdonald 1980:201–2)

Here our concern is less the particular origins of specific clans—and the clans of this text are not those of the contemporary Tamang (see chapter 3)—but the symbols of social differentiation. Although Macdonald quotes another portion of the text in which the sacrificial division results in a division of labor among clans according to function, here the dismemberment and consequent differentiation of human groups moves forward without any reference to function in an occupational or ritual sense; it thus operates more like totemic classifications based on natural distinctions than like caste distinctions based on occupation. The contemporary Tamang practice of dividing meat, in certain contexts, according to clan relation is a ritual confirmation of the sacrificial logic expressed in the myth.[34] Likewise, the hierarchies of local polity—like those apparent in historic Tibet—are reflected in the practice of delivering the heads of sacrificial beasts to the house of the village headman in annual rites of political legitimacy.

A Tamang Rendition of Caste Origins

Another account commonly told by western Tamang—who as we have seen have a long history of inclusion in a Hindu state—applies the theory of clan differentiation in the myth above to caste distinctions in contemporary Nepal. An old man recounted this version:

"A Lama [Tamang], a Bahun [Brahman], a Blacksmith [untouchable] and a Thakuri [Kshatriya] were the four sons of one mother cow. These four later ate the meat of their mother. The mother told them, 'When I die, don't give my body to the crows and vultures; don't give it to the animals. I am dying now. You four sons must eat my flesh; you must drink my blood. After cleaning and washing my flesh, eat it.'

"They sent the Lama to wash the intestines, the lungs, and the stomachs in the river. While he was gone the remaining brothers said, 'How can we eat mother's meat. We cannot eat it.' At this time the other brother was at the river washing the meat and ready to return. While he was on his way back, the others cooked the heart, the liver, and the little and big chunks of meat that did not need washing. The eldest brother [the Blacksmith/Kami] tasted the broth and said, 'It is still mother's meat. What can we do? We must give it to someone.' The three of them [conferred and] hid [buried] their portions behind a tree. When the other brother returned they said, 'Why are you late? We ate our portions. Now eat yours too!' They gave him his portion. The eldest brother called out, 'Have you eaten?' The Lama answered that he had eaten one chunk. He ate a total of four chunks. After eating

[34]Stanner has shown the similarity between sacrificial and totemic ritual (1959–63).

them, the others cried out, 'Enough! Enough! You have eaten portions for us all.' The other asked, 'Where is the rest?' and they took it out and showed him. They told him, 'We did not eat our mother's meat. You are a mother-eating man.'

"The other became angry and said, 'Yesterday we were equal [we ate together]. . . . Today you have done like this to me.' In anger, he grabbed the intestines and with a swat threw them at the cook [Bahun]. The Bahun declared, 'I have obtained a sacred thread.' The Lama then grabbed the stomach and with a swat threw it at the youngest brother [Thakuri]. The youngest brother exclaimed, 'Oh! I have a scarf for wiping my mouth. He has given me this I am now a Thakuri; I am king.' The Lama then thought, 'What to do? What to do?' The eldest brother [Blacksmith] was examining the head and the hide. The Lama grabbed these up and started swatting the elder brother, who exclaimed happily, 'Oh! this head will be an air tube and this leather will be a bellows. I will take these. I have become a Blacksmith.' After taking these, the elder brother went aside; he took the head and hide on his own and not out of anger. He said, 'I have my share.'

"This left the brother who had eaten the meat. What did he do? He thought, 'The honeycombed stomach remains; the meat has been eaten; and the rest I have given to the others.' He called out to the others, 'Now we four brothers have this honeycombed stomach left. We must divide it into sacred texts.' After saying this, he divided it into four parts [and gave one to each of the brothers]. Then he said, 'Now we must perform austerities. . . . We together will live righteously; we will not sin; we will not be greedy.' They then performed austerities. [The Thakuri threw his text in the fire.] Later the Bahun lost his sacred text. It fell out of his shirt, they say [while he was washing]. After ten or twelve years a cow ate it. He searched and searched and could not find it, so he stole the Blacksmith's. He had left his sacred text on the shelf to keep it from burning while he beat iron. His own brother the Bahun stole his sacred text [while the Blacksmith was defecating].

"After twelve years went by, the four brothers decided to meet one time to see what had resulted from their austerities. The mind of the Blacksmith was burning because he no longer had a sacred text. He thought, 'What can I do? I can't tell them I don't have it.' He sat silently thinking, 'In the age of truth what can I do? Oh! Mother! What can I do now?' The others then called out, 'Hey! Why have you not told us how things have gone with your sacred text?' The Blacksmith said, 'I performed austerities but my sacred text is gone.' The others responded, 'Because you have said you have no sacred text the three times we have asked you must now sit outside [the practice of contemporary untouchables]. We will not drink water from your hand. We will not eat food from your hand.' . . . After stealing the sacred text, after becoming a thief, the Bahun said the small castes cannot touch or hear the sacred text of the Bahun or they will go crazy. . . ." (Alternate variant: "We who drink beer and whiskey are not allowed to listen to Bahun's rites. They say we will go crazy but what the Bahun say is this: 'Bellows, hammer, hammer, tongs SWAHAA! Bitter intestines, anvil, a Blacksmith's foot!' ") "Besides the sacred texts of the Blacksmith and the Lama, there are no other sacred texts. The sacred text of the Thakuri was eaten by fire and that of the Bahun was eaten by a cow. It all happened like that."

From Clans to Castes

This account transforms Hindu occupational differences into natural ones on the one hand and ritual ones on the other. Like clans in the previous textual account, castes are distinguished according to parts of a bovine sacrifice as in Figure 1. On the other hand, each of the bovine organs announces the occupation of the castes—the Bahun has a sacred thread, the Thakuri a kingly scarf, and the Blacksmith his bellows; the Tamang consumption of bovine flesh announces their exclusion from Hindu society. Another variant of this account is recorded in Northey (1928:258–59). Here the three brothers are "Brahma, Vishnu, and Mahasur, by name." Brahma and Vishnu likewise deceive Mahasur after successfully hunting a bison. The intestines became their sacred threads, and Mahasur was degraded and became Tamang.[35]

Although animal dismemberment lends itself readily to metaphors of organic solidarity (and some Hindu myths are an example), the Tamang account of caste stresses differentiation over functional articulation; Tamang social ideology denies the notion of a religious society based on complementary asymmetry, an asymmetry focused on the purity of the Brahman.[36] The collusive trickery of Bahun/Thakuri/Kami results in the formation of the Tamang as a separate religious society oriented metaphorically toward a distinct textual corpus and

[35]See also Landon ([1928] 1987:46) for fragments of another version and Great Britain (1968:111–12) for a longer version.

[36]One Hindu account has the Brahman emerging from the mouth of Purusha, the Kshatriya from the arms, the Vaishya from the thighs, and the Shudras from the feet (O'Flaherty 1975:27–28).

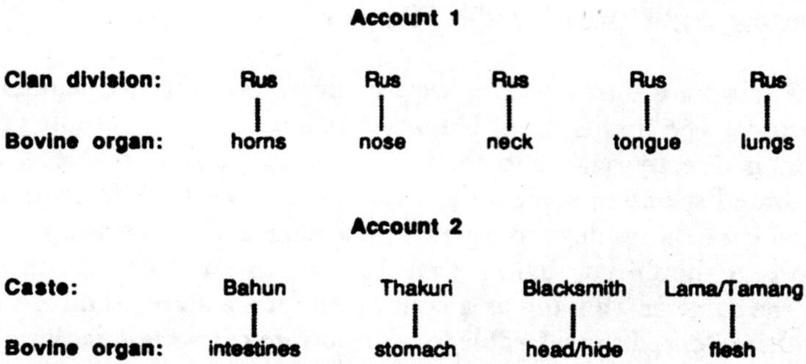

Figure 1. Mythic models of social differentiation

toward the lama, a Buddhist specialist, not the Bahun. From a sociocommensal continuity, the account relates the genesis of a hierarchy isomorphic with Brahmanical ideology. It then proceeds to make a travesty of this hierarchy by inverting the positions of untouchable Blacksmith (Kami) and Bahun. The Tamang become elevated and the Bahun reduced to the level of the Kami, an inversion that is repeated interactively in everyday life (see chapter 3). When the sacred texts are divided, the Lama/Tamang receive an equal and separate corpus. The pure Bahun (washing at the river)—the only other one to possess a sacred corpus—has stolen the text of the impure (defecating) Blacksmith.

This Tamang account, though, is more than a parodic contortion of Hindu caste order—a kind of compensation for Hindu dominance. It refracts Brahmanical ideology and social order according to a different symbology rather than participates in this ideology. In Tamang reasoning, caste position is not, moreover, a function of karma or the effect of prior births on rebirth and is not tied to a particular dharma or religious duty, the system of ethical values associated with Indic social theory. Although this Tamang mythic account of caste origins plays on Hindu constructions of order by juxtaposing the materials of caste interactions (commensality, the consumption of carrion, pure/impure, access to the sacred writing, the ritual ascendancy of the Brahman), Tamang translate this material into a different idiom. They seek an arrangement rather than an interactive theory of pure and impure. Tamang not only form a religious society that is their own but one that is, as we shall see, governed by a symbology that runs counter to rationalized theories of much of the Hindu-Buddhist world (O'Flaherty 1980; Keyes and Daniel 1983).

The Setting and History of the Village of Tamdungsa

From this long introduction, we can draw at least two significant conclusions. The first is that "Tamang" as a name for an ethnic group in Nepal is directly related to the formation of the state of Nepal as it incorporated specific peoples; the second is that caste difference takes on specific meanings depending on whose perspective one adopts. Furthermore, it should be obvious that Tamang as an ethnic group need not be the same as Tamang as a culture. In fact, a state administrative policy that allowed considerable local autonomy, a social ideology that enforced endogamy, and the demographic separateness of Tamang communities encouraged a cultural insularity on the local level and thus regional cultural variability. Much of the detail presented here is peculiar to Tamdungsa and its immediate environs and reflects the history of a locale; some of the detail may be specific to the village and it alone. Social and ritual organization in Tamdungsa, though, also show definite similarities to western Tamang of neighboring areas reported on by Höfer (1969, 1971a, 1971b, 1974, 1975, 1981), Toffin (1976, 1978, 1986), Fricke (1986a, 1986b), and Dobremez (1986).

Tamdungsa lies to the northwest of the Kathmandu Valley and to the west of the Trisuli River at the base of a massif, which rises to the high range of the Ganesh Himalayas and the borders of Tibet. Now part of the administrative district of Nuwakot, in the past it was part of Rasuwa and before that part of Panchsayakhola or the "five-hundred-rivers" region of the Rana administrative district known as "West No. 1." It is roughly a two-day walk to Kathmandu (or *yam̃bu* as the Tamang call it) and a half-day walk to the district center and a small bazaar town. The journey to Kathmandu can now be completed partially by bus, thereby truncating the journey to one long day. Few Tamang, though, find occasion to visit Kathmandu regularly; they make occasional trips to the nearby bazaar where they purchase salt, cloth, weaving thread, kerosene, and other items in the Newar and Muslim shops. Local administrative functionaries and politicians are an exception because they travel to the bazaar and nearby administrative offices to attend political meetings and to confer with cronies and judicial, administrative, and development officers.

The village of Tamdungsa proper sits on a mountainside at roughly three to five thousand feet above sea level (see Figure 2). Irrigated terraces lie below as low as two thousand feet along a river valley, and dry fields rise above to about six thousand feet. The village includes agricultural land, house sites, and common pasturage, forest, water

Figure 2. Tamdungsa houses and dry fields

courses, and sacred groves. Villagers also make use of high-altitude forests, which rise to twelve thousand feet directly above the village. House sites of clan-related families are clustered in neighborhoods amid the dry fields on the hillsides of the village. Those who own extensive wet fields usually keep a second house along the river. Villagers, however, prefer the climate higher on the hillside where they believe they are protected from malaria. Wet fields along the river at the base of the village and on the hillside depend on the summer monsoon rains for adequate flow of water. Those along the river support two crops, a monsoon paddy crop and a dry-season maize or wheat crop. Because paddy carries high ritual and market value and is a common feasting food, irrigated fields are prime land. Few households own enough such land, however, to produce enough paddy for profitable surplus and manage only to meet feasting and social obligations if that. Most Tamang whether rich or poor subsist for the most part on maize and millet intercropped in unirrigated dry fields high on the hillsides near their houses. According to local lore, it was not until recent generations that villagers cultivated rice in quantity at all and it was not until intensive contact with immigrant groups from the south that they learned the techniques of rice cultivation. This generation is the first that has not been involved in some degree in swidden cultivation. They supplement this basic diet with a variety of beans, vegetables, fruits, and occasional meat, dairy products, game, and forest products.

In 1977, Tamdungsa had seventy-two households of variable landholdings. Most households try to maintain some livestock, and in the past accumulation of wealth tended to be through livestock. Richer households maintained large herds of water buffalo and cows for the production of butter. These larger operations are rarely continued except in higher-altitude villages of the region. Some Tamdungsa villagers, though, farm surplus animals out to high-altitude herders in other villages. Today most households keep at a minimum some chickens and roosters necessary for sacrifice and social feasting. Many others maintain goats both for consumption and sale. Water buffalo cows are highly prized for their rich milk, which can be processed into marketable curds and butter, and the bulls are prized for their meat. Many keep cows in order to produce draught bullocks. Villagers also stable livestock for the manure they produce, which is essential for productive agriculture. Dry fields, in particular, do not have profitable yields unless villagers add compost. For this reason even those households that cannot afford livestock stable and feed cattle owned by others solely to use the dung.

Although Tamang have always been linked to a more extensive trade economy and Tamdungsa is opening more and more to wider socioeconomic networks, subsistence and closure still characterized the local economy in the late 1970s. All land in the village was owned and with a few exceptions worked by residents, some of whom owned plots in neighboring villages. Cash that was required for salt, cloth, thread, kerosene, taxes, and the like was usually acquired from the sale of grain, clarified butter, livestock, and other agricultural products, although the poorest households often had to search for cash employment in the environs of the village. In the late 1970s, every resident in the village was directly tied to agricultural production; however, as population and pressure on land increases, more and more families and individuals are migrating to other areas of Nepal and India in search of either land or employment. Most who seek income outside the community work on construction projects in other parts of Nepal and are recruited by local labor contractors (cf. Euler 1984). Others work in paramilitary police forces in Assam, and a few have been accepted into the British and Nepalese armies, breaking the pattern of historical exclusion.[37]

With the exception of a few households of the Blacksmith caste, Tamdungsa residents are entirely Tamang, and Tamang predominate throughout the district and the region. Nuwakot district according to the census of 1971 was 34 percent Tamang, and Rasuwa, which lies immediately to the north of Tamdungsa, was 83 percent Tamang (see Map 2). Tamdungsa Tamang, however, have had intensive historical relations with both greater Nepalese and Tibetan societies for centuries. The general region has probably been part of Nepalese political orders in varying intensity for the full two-hundred and some years of national history. Likewise significant ties with Tibet continued until the imposition of direct Chinese administration there in 1959 and the effective closure of the two sides of the border. The increasing involvement of Tamang in the state of Nepal as well as the immigration, particularly of Bahun, over the last hundred years has brought Tamang into greater and greater communication with Hindu society.

State Formation and Local Autonomy

Prior to incorporation into the political orders that evolved into the contemporary state of Nepal, the general region of Tamdungsa was

[37]Such patterns have intensified since 1977. At a count in 1987 over twenty individuals were employed in a way that played back into village economy.

part of Ghale (Tamang *gle*) principalities that held sway across north-central Nepal. Ruins of fortified "palaces" can be seen on strategic promontories in the region. The precise organization of these principalities remains obscure; however, they probably were governed by royal clans in association with various functionaries, in particular ministers and lama priests. This organization is vestigially reflected in regional lore (see Toffin 1969), a residual hierarchy between "royal" clans and others in contemporary social structure, and textual accounts (Stein 1961; Macdonald 1980). Although these principalities appear more Tibetan than Indic in form, they likely maintained significant communication with the Thakuri and Newar principalities to the west and the south, sitting as they did on significant trade routes. There also is evidence in the area of a regional sacrificial cult that may have reflected the old political regime; the sacrificial cult was, significantly, taken over by Gurung retainers of the early Shah state (see chapter 5).

Be these conjectures as they may, political domination of the Tamdungsa area by the Gorkha kingdom, which lay to the west, begins with the first half of the seventeenth century, when Rama Shah extended the dominion of the Gorkha kingdom to Dhading and northern Rasuwa (D. R. Regmi 1975:34–35; Kumar 1967:8). Whether or not this domain included the Tamdungsa area proper, which lies to the east of Dhading and to the south of northern Rasuwa, is not definitively established; however, one can presume that control was less than firm and even if the Tamang swore allegiance to the Gorkha kings and communicated tribute, they probably retained considerable autonomy. As late as 1739 a Ghale-Bhote force attacked Narabhupal Shah's troops on their way to Nuwakot from Gorkha (Höfer 1981:7; cited from Vajracharya and Shrestha 1976 [v.s. 2032]). The attack indicates something less than absolute and continuous control of the territory up to the Trisuli River, even though in 1742 the same Narabhupal issued a copper plate to legitimate the authority of the lords of northern Rasuwa (Macdonald 1973:6). It is clear, however, that when Prithvi Narayan Shah took over the Gorkha kingdom in 1744, his dominion extended to the Trisuli River in the east, including the locale of Tamdungsa. From Prithvi Narayan Shah's conquest of the Kathmandu Valley in 1769 and continuing throughout the nineteenth and twentieth centuries, western Tamang were more and more intensively enmeshed in a regional administrative order.

Beginning in the latter part of the eighteenth century and throughout the nineteenth, the villages in the vicinity of Tamdungsa were brought under rakam or the corvéelike system of compulsory labor. Government documents from 1855 (v.s. 1912) reviewed the following obligations and privileges imposed by Prithvi Narayan Shah, the first king of a consolidated Nepal:

> Since you live in a border territory, you have to fulfill both military and porterage obligations. Seize arms and ammunition, saltpeter, sulphur, being smuggled to Tibet, auction them, and hand over the proceeds to the royal palace. Capture any rebel who may try to escape to Tibet through that territory. Provide porterage services for Sirto supplies between Nepal and Tibet. Make regular payment of herbs and drugs, and other supplies due as Sirto from that territory. The inhabitants of ten villages, including Kharsa and Parcyang, shall provide Hulak services. The inhabitants of other villages shall work at the gunpowder factory. Provide assistance in the collection of Jagat duties on goods traded between Nepal and Tibet. Capture persons who create disturbances and hand them over to the royal palace. Hulakis [postal workers] shall be granted exemption from all tax and Jhara obligations. They shall enjoy security of tenure on their rice lands and homesteads. Inasmuch as this area of rice lands in your territory is not large, and you cannot maintain yourselves only through unirrigated hillside lands, you may bring salt from Tibet. The inhabitants of the ten villages who provide Hulak services shall be exempt from Jagat, Nirkhi, and Tak, or levies. Each household of those villages who work at the gunpowder factory may procure five manloads (of salt from Tibet). (M. C. Regmi, ed., 1975)

This proclamation confirms the early integration of the Tamdungsa region into the infrastructure of state productive and administrative estates.

Several forms of compulsory labor were instituted in Tamdungsa and adjacent villages toward the latter part of the reign of Prithvi Narayan Shah (1744–75). The ancestors of Tamdungsa Tamang worked in a black gunpowder factory, established by Prithvi Narayan Shah in the town of Nuwakot (M. C. Regmi 1979:37). Every household was required to contribute a total of sixty person days of labor in order to maintain its agricultural lands. Compulsory labor in the munitions factory was converted to taxes in the 1890s, when the procurement of modern machinery made local production of gunpowder obsolete (M. C. Regmi 1976:158–59). M. C. Regmi reports that the five-hundred-rivers region became the income-producing and administrative estate for the commanding general of the eastern zone in 1897 (M. C. Regmi, ed., 1983). Neighboring villages were engaged in labor relating to state herding and dairy operations, the postal system, paper production, and timber cutting, all of which continued until the 1950s when the first attempts to abolish compulsory labor were made, and some continued until 1963 when it was finally abolished throughout Nepal.

In addition to labor obligations, villages in the region were subjected to other taxes throughout the Rana period (1846–1951). These included taxes on wet and dry fields, houses, and threshing floors. Each village was also required to cultivate wet fields, the produce of which was used to feast touring government officials. According to local lore and official documents, Tamang villages were also required to supply hides to the military beginning in the early nineteenth century (see M. C. Regmi, ed., 1979a). Tamdungsa and neighboring villages, lying near the main route to Kyirong Tibet, were also often impressed into porterage duties during two wars with Tibet and were expected to contribute stores of grain to the troops when needed. With the collapse of the Rana regime in 1951 and compulsory labor shortly thereafter, Tamdungsa villagers gained freehold over their lands, which they retain in return for taxes. Attempts at land reform in the region have had little effect on local agroeconomy.

Along with a system of land tenure, the state instituted a system of local administration, which had important effects on the development of local sociopolities. The overall trajectory of the administrative history of Tamdungsa parallels that of much of hill Nepal as one of greater articulation with the expanding state, but this evolvement in itself implies a countervailing effect and contributed to insulating Tamdungsa. As M. C. Regmi observes, early Gorkhali administration had a "dual foundation," a combination of "centralization of political authority and decentralization of administrative functions," which resulted in a situation where "actual administrative power at the local level was exercised by officials and functionaries who derived their status and authority from the central government in Kathmandu, but who at the same time, enjoyed a large measure of freedom or autonomy in matters of local concern" (1979:18).

Although Tamdungsa was fully incorporated into the feudal order of Rana rule, local justice, tax collection, and administration devolved on headmen in the village. From the time of early consolidation of the state through the Rana period and until the present, headmen have been local Tamang and they have been the descendants of the prestate headmen or *pompo*, allowing the continuation in a new form of a local sociopolity that was subject as much to specifically Tamang patterns of interaction as to central power. According to local tradition, villages were headed by hereditary headmen until the mid-nineteenth century and the ossification of Rana administration. Rana administration designated two different types of local officials, both of whom were referred to by the general village term *mukhiyā: jimiwāl* collected taxes on wet fields and *tālukdār* on dry fields. In addition to these functions, local headmen organized villagers for communal labor and settled local disputes; the jimiwal proper had an ascendant status in the village and was the final authority in local matters. The jimiwal could apparently call on local labor for the cultivation of his fields as could the ascendant village lama. Toward the end of the Rana regime, one of the more powerful local headmen also contracted for the rights to be *dwāre*, an official who performed administrative and judicial functions throughout the region on behalf of the Rana overlord. He was eventually murdered by rivals to the north.

These headmen mediated between the state and the local community and thus were regarded somewhat ambivalently by other villagers. On the one hand, they dominated villagers and, on the other, they were able to act as intermediaries in problems involving contact with outsiders; they acted as patrons. Because their local influence derived in part from connections to the administration and familiarity with the legalities of the state, these headmen were able to consolidate property to a greater extent than their neighbors. Some converted communal watercourses and pasturage into valuable wet fields by extracting labor, and some appropriated the property of other villagers through money lending. These headmen were ascendant in village matters but rarely had influence beyond its confines.

Although their power emanated from relations to central authority, the headmen were excluded from entrance into the ruling elite; in Rana rule kinship and polity were in large measure coextensive, and Tamdungsa Tamang could not contract marital links into the higher echelons of Nepalese society. Tamang headmen were tied to a local system of marriage and a local system of authority. Headmen like others married their cross-cousins, and thus all Tamang submitted to an ethos of symmetrical reciprocity and were bound into a nexus of crosscutting ties; this generated a restricted and insular—and, from the perspective of greater Nepalese society, endogamous—sociopolitical domain. Although headmen could create supplementary alliances through polygyny, the practice tended as much to diffuse obligations as to consolidate power. In contrast to other parts of Nepal, Tamdungsa society unfolded with little formalized hierarchical transformation. Headmen did not form a unique class in the marriage system and were bound like all Tamang into a society based on the logic of equality and symmetrical exchange. The hierarchy of the Gurung endogamous divisions of the "four" and the "sixteen" clans is absent among the Tamang, and there is no evidence of marriage alliances among the wealthy and powerful across large geographic and social distance as is the case with the Gurung (Pignède 1966; Messerschmidt 1976a) and the Sherpa. The division of the Tamang into the "eighteen" and "twelve" clans, reported for eastern Tamang (Fürer-Haimendorf 1956), was known but played no part in the structure of western Tamang society. According to Tamdungsa Tamang, this division refers to pure Tamang and Tamang who have intermarried with other ethnic groups. These internal hierarchies appear to reflect specific historical relations between the Gurung and the eastern Tamang with greater Hindu polity and society; such divisions into numbered sets of clans is common in India (see Dumont 1970b:121–22). Thus headmen may have "walked like kings" as villagers report, but they were also subject to an ethos of reciprocity.

Ideally in Tamang perspective headmen are patrons who command service and goods but who are also required to be generous in return; their power in fact results in great measure from the fact that because they have more than others they can give more and thereby place others in subservient positions of obligation. Although the Rana polity provided opportunities for the accumulative tendencies of local elite, this development always remained within bounds; if headmen went too far in their violation of an overarching ethos of redistributive reciprocity, they were subject to vilification as the embodiment of evil and their local authority was undermined. To this day, headmen, as the exchanges in the political rites of the national festival of *dasaĩ* reveal, return protection for gifts or service according to a redistributive logic. For the nine nights before the feast day of Dasain, villagers gather in front of the headman's house, where they offer songs to the Buddhas for the honor and prosperity of the headman and the village. On Dasain proper, villagers used to arrange in front of the headman's house the heads with tails in mouth—here symbolically suggesting the whole animal—of all the buffalo sacrificed, and men and women of the village to this day receive blessings of protection from the headman in the form of stalks of grain seedlings and a *ṭikā* or forehead mark.

Although the administrative system changed after the demise of the Rana regime in 1951 and was replaced by the *panchāyat* system, which has known a variety of incarnations, the old order perdured in effect if not in name; the rivals for power in the village in the 1970s remained the direct descendants of the most prominent headmen of the Rana era. At the time of this research, Tamdungsa, along with a small Gurung village, formed one ward of a nine-ward administrative village. Although Tamang are a prominent population in the administrative village, they are brought into interaction with local Bahun (Brahman), Jaisi Bahun, and Chetri on the local level. Tamang, however, had played a major role in administrative affairs until 1977, and either the head of the village council or the representative to the district council had been Tamang; a man from Tamdungsa had been head of the village council for seventeen years. This pattern was changing as minority high-caste Brahmans (*upādhyaya bāhun*) increasingly manipulated the local system in their favor.

The play of local politics in the 1970s, however, did not concern most villagers, for they did not fully understand the contemporary administrative and development system, which like preceding orders appeared as an imposition. The administrative system requires the exclusive usage of Nepali language, which automatically bars large sectors of the Tamang from active engagement; even those with good colloquial fluency in Nepali are at a loss with the Sanskritic idiom of administrative discourse. Moreover, the low opinion many government officers held of Tamang did not encourage intensive involvement.

At the time of this research, villagers remained suspicious of administrative outsiders, and when they had to deal with the administration they continued to do so through local headmen who carried influence. Villagers not only understand the language of their village headmen, they are linked to them in overlapping ties of social affinity; headmen remain mediators between villagers and the state as in the past. Local headmen, whether officially recognized or not, continue to approach the government strategically, even though an expanding "development" bureaucracy and political campaigns bring villagers into more intensive contact with government officers. Direct intrusions from outside are uncommon; police rarely visit Tamang villages, and disputes, except for major land or political issues, rarely reach district courts or, for that matter, the local official administration. Threats to take cases to court, though, often encourage the settlement of disputes locally. Local headmen along with other senior arbitrators, including women with no official status, still settle most disputes. The main exception is fights among the headmen themselves.

Involution in Tamang Ritual and Social Life

Tamdungsa history from the eighteenth century through the nineteenth and the twentieth, then, is one of greater and greater articulation to a polity controlled by the Indo-Nepalese and ultimately based in Kathmandu coupled with a retention of significant autonomy and insularity. In this separation, supplemented by caste endogamy, a local society and ritual system developed. Tamdungsa may have been conjoined to an administrative polity based in Kathmandu, but as we have seen Tamang were not included within greater Hindu ritual society; they retained Buddhist rites as opposed to Brahmanical ones.

Tamang trace their origins to sacred Buddhist centers in Tibet. The *gombo* or temple of Tamdungsa and the images that it housed (now stolen) are linked to an encompassing sacred geography that extends from Tamdungsa through northern Nepal to Kyirong, Lhasa, and *bSam yas* in Tibet. These links had economic and institutional correlates that persisted until the establishment of direct Chinese dominion in Tibet, which effectively severed intercourse between Tamdungsa Tamang and Tibetans. Until then, each year members of every household in Tamdungsa hiked the five days to Kyirong to exchange grain for salt, and during the dry winter season impoverished Tibetans descended into Tamang territory begging grain.[38] Moreover, the lamas and gombo in Tamdungsa continued ritual connections north at the same time that political power was consolidating in Kathmandu. Village lamas often sought their religious masters in the monasteries of Kyirong, and many passed several years residing there. Lamas from Kyirong would also come regularly to Tamang villages to supervise rituals and to initiate local lamas.

While relations with greater Nepal intensified, direct ties north with other Tamang and with Tibet diminished. The Buddhist gombo in Tamdungsa, which was until recently the only one in the region, was reputedly held in the past by local lamas under a seal of authority from a monastery in Kyirong, Tibet. The oldest line of lamas in the village also claims that its ancestors held their land under nontaxable religious tenure until Rana rule. During the reign of Jung Bahadur Rana, how-

[38]The government order quoted above allowed Tamdungsa households "to procure five manloads of salt" free of tax. Although most households could manage to acquire enough salt to meet their own needs, some were able to get a surplus, which they would sell in Kathmandu for a small profit. One villager shrewdly lent money to others who paid back the principal and interest with their salt. The same man also lent money to Bahuns for their marriages and amassed considerable wealth by local standards. See also M. C. Regmi, ed. (1979, no. 7:104–5).

ever, border wars with Tibetans brought western Tamang loyalty to the Rana polity into question, and, again according to local lore, the religious tenure of land by local lamas was abolished.[39] Lamaic authority and training developed an increasingly local and uniquely Tamang character. Religious masters, by the 1970s, were all from the local area. Tamdungsa people were no longer at the limits of a Tibetan ecclesiastic order but were a population unable to form linkages larger than sets of villages allied through crosscutting marriage relations. In this social environment, the cultural forms we think of in connection with the contemporary Tamang took form.

The ritual authority of village lamas did not dissolve with the loss of official government sanction. Lamas continue to occupy an ascendant and honored position in village life. They hold a position complementing that of the local headmen and supervise the most extensive of Tamang rites. Villagers plowed and planted the fields of the head lamas of the village until the mid-1950s under an unofficial corvée just as they provided special labor services for headmen. The dual ascendancy of lamas and headmen was homologous in form to patterns associated with the polities of greater Tibet. The village in many respects formed—to follow Hocart's description of Indian villages (1950; Marriot 1955:190)—as a "degradation" of a "royal style." The local lords "walked like kings" and villagers accorded lamas the honors due the Buddhas themselves; both of them presided over ritual pageants homologous to the monastic pageants of Tibet, and the village took ritual form as a contained polity. Even though local lamaic practices took shape in relative separation from greater Buddhist institutions, villagers clearly linked themselves into a greater Tibetan Buddhist geography. In songs still sung at most lamaic rites, villagers situate the village gombo in relation to the gombo of villages up through northern Nepal and into greater Tibet.

In sum, the consolidation of Nepal may have led to an isolation of village communities within a feudal state, but the eventual severance of Tamang relations with Tibet did not entirely reduce Tamdungsa to the acculturative forces of Sanskritization commonly assumed in the ethnology of "tribe" and "caste" in South Asia. Social and regional containment fostered an evolvement of localized socioritual orders among the Tamang in which Buddhism became enveloped in a cultural system

[39]It is of course impossible to verify these events absolutely; however, it appears to be more than mere coincidence that the ascendancy of Jung Bahadur Rana also saw the redirection of Tamdungsa taxes and tribute from northern principalities to Rana military officers. Tamang still refer to a set of fields in the village as the "lama seal fields."

associated with a clan-based social organization. In their exclusion and relative insularity, Tamdungsa Tamang refracted Buddhist ideology into an ethos of measured exchange among exogamous clans. We have examined the place of Tamang in Nepal and the history of a local community in the state; we now turn to a perspective on Tamang society from within Tamang culture.

3 A Culture of Exchange and Its Paradoxes

The incest prohibition is at once on the threshold of culture, in culture, and in one sense, as we shall try to show, culture itself.

Claude Lévi-Strauss,
The Elementary Structures of Kinship

Intrinsic to the forms of western Tamang life are exchanges; particularly pronounced are those between affines. The marriage system of the Tamang is one of restricted exchange, and the values that govern marriage are one expression of ideals of balanced reciprocity that extend to all aspects of life and frame experience in general. As we have seen, Tamang emerge, from the perspective of the expansive state, as insular and endogamous, but they take form, from the perspective of village patriclans, as open and exogamous. In the mythic account below, the Gorkhali state appears only at a remove and specialized distance. Ideally, social and cosmic order unfolds for Tamdungsa Tamang in a contained flux of giving and receiving. They strive—impossibly—to make exchange encompassing among themselves and to control events by binding beings, human and extrahuman, to its power. The most common interchanges among Tamang as well as the most formal are framed in this give-and-take.

According to one account of the origins of the focal exogamous groupings of Tamdungsa, *dong chhempo*, an ancestral hero of Tamdungsa Tamang, fled into Nepal with his immediate kin after assassinating *gyalbo lungdar* (Tibetan *gLang dar ma*), an evil, anti-Buddhist king of Lhasa, Tibet. Dong Chhempo and his kin who traveled down alone from Tibet apparently had difficulty locating proper marriage partners, for first they tried exchanging in marriage with *tsen*—spirits who now reside between earth and sky—and then with *lu*—spirits who inhabit water and soil.[1] Both these marriages ended disas-

[1]Some versions of this account say that four clans descended at this time, but the one I recorded recounts only one. Other versions of the history of clans also exist.

trously. Marriage with tsen led to dumb children with bulbous goiters and marriage with lu yielded reptilelike offspring. After these frustrated attempts to marry out and Dong Chhempo's death, the descendants of Dong Chhempo, who constituted the *ḍimḍung* clan, engaged in two incestuous marriages, which resulted in the division of two additional clans. First, one son committed incest (*himri bāba*) with his mother's sister yielding the *mhamba* clan. Then, as they continued their descent into the midhills of Nepal, they settled at Sangam (Nepali Salme), where they built a house and planted grain; there, a brother and a sister got caught up in a poetic song exchange that led irreversibly to their union and the creation of another clan, the *himḍung*:

> While staying there, older brother *ṭhipsang* went with his wife to harvest the first maize. Younger brother *ingkyal* went to meet with younger sister *tikiri* at her house, where she was weaving. Her older brother [Ingkyal] played a song in the *tsherlu* style on a mouth harp. Then younger sister returned an answer to her older brother's song. At that time, the custom was that whoever won a song exchange could take the other off as a marriage partner. In this singing back and forth, the brother won and took his younger sister to live in Dangsing. When the elder brother's wife returned in the evening [she discovered that] younger brother and sister were not there: "Where have they gone? Where have they gone?" They did not know. Five months after this violation, younger brother sent a message asking if he would be allowed to come back or not. His older brothers replied, "You who have entered into your own line cannot possibly come here." Then all the other clan brothers met at a place now called Tamdungsa [not the present village site] in order to decide whether or not to allow him to come. For his part, Ingkyal went to Gorkha to get a royal seal and upon his return was going to prohibit his older brothers from staying there; he was going to chase them away. Then, the clan brothers, after meeting, decided, "No, what custom shall we give him [create for him]? What clan shall we give him?" They made the "younger sister custom" whereby [money and gifts had to be distributed to various kin]. . . . After giving like this, Ingkyal and Tikiri were given the Himdung clan *[himri bābi himḍung khor pin-chi*]. After saying, "*nhara koncho* can expel, can accept, can expel [the incest]," they gave this clan divinity to the Himdung.

For Tamdungsa Tamang, this account is about the construction of society and its paradoxes. It first poses two marriages with impossibly distant spirits and then with the impossibly close, a mother's sister and a younger sister. It concludes with the genesis of the primary and proper opposition of contemporary village life: exogamous patriclans between whom marriages that are neither too distant nor too close can occur. The account also points to the inherent power and valuation of exchange for the transaction of song, according to its own seductive momentum leads inexorably to marriage.

An Ethos That Implies Its Antithesis

In Tamdungsa, ordination is dependent on social differences and relations of reciprocity. The social order centered on the village and radiating through neighboring villages revolves around the two primary patriclans of this origination account: the Dimdung and the Himdung. The Dimdung are the descendants of Dong Chhempo and the Himdung the descendants of Ingkyal and Tikiri. Other clans in the village align with either of these two, structuring local society on its most extensive levels into two exogamous and reciprocal halves. From the perspective of Tamdungsa villagers, all the clans in neighboring villages fall into these two groupings, and these groupings structure actual obligations and rights of affines. Moreover, the exchanges established in the "younger sister custom," which succeeded Ingkyal and Tikiri's union, are those that continue today in the gifts that are given by a husband (and his patriline) to his wife's father and patrilineal kin in order to legitimate marital unions and the offspring of those unions. Thus, the account announces both an articulatory structure and a reciprocal ethos.

This ethos of exchange shapes not only marriage but most casual and formal sociality including eating, drinking, smoking, laboring, conversing, singing, and communicating among humans—siblings, spouses, affines, clan-mates, and others—and between humans and divinities and harmful agents. Productivity is directly tied to exchange, and the diminishment of wealth is linked in Tamang imagination with hoarding and the absence of exchange, possibilities hidden but nevertheless accompanying every transaction. According to Tamang lore, once, when two affines went hunting together in the high forest, the only game found was a tiny bird, which one of them secreted in his shirt. When the other asked whether there was any game, the one who had caught the bird replied that nothing had come. Later the deceived affine discovered that the other had selfishly kept the game, and he demanded that they divide and exchange it. At the moment that they butchered the tiny bird, it became so large that it took the two of them to carry it on a pole balanced on their shoulders. (For a complete account see chapter 6.) Not to exchange and share stifles well-being. To hoard, to leave out, to be tightfisted or closemouthed, to crave wealth, or to exploit without return for personal enrichment all are violations of the principle of exchange and are the traits of harmful agents who swarm the village groves and regional forests.

One cannot overemphasize the pervasiveness of this ethos *even in the contradictions of it in practice*. Tamang are far from a closed world of nonaccumulative reciprocity, and a tension between a reality of discrepancies in landholdings and a profitable commerce—more pronounced as Nepal transforms—and an ethos of reciprocity troubles village relations. As we have seen, the Tamang are an artifact of state formation and were bound into a feudallike structure, which generated discrepancies at the local level. Tamdungsa includes the well-off and the landless. Culturally and ritually, however, villagers retreat to an image of themselves and their villages as circles of kin caught up in rounds of exchange. Although the rich patronize the poor and asymmetrical tensions strain Tamang life, land-rich and land-poor households marry—in fact often must marry—generating alliances and hierarchies outside patronage or exploitation. Thus despite these discrepancies, which we will examine in greater detail, Tamang attempt to temper all relations within a structure of duality and an ethos of exchange. We must approach the values of exchange in light of this observation.

Exchange, thus, acquires meaning only in a semantic field of greater possibility. Not only does everyday life pose Tamang with contradictions to the practice of reciprocity, the potential for violation comes with, and is integral to, the declaration of a reciprocal order itself. The selection of reciprocity as the base of interaction between those who stand as "other" to each other in Tamang social consciousness implies more than a totalizing social theory that in practice generates communality (Mauss 1967; Sahlins 1972; Lévi-Strauss 1969; Hyde 1979). Tamang emphasize and elaborate exchange as a focal value not because it is necessarily a universal principle of human sociality but because it is but one possibility in human relations countered in Tamang imagination and experience by its antithesis (Meeker, Barlow, and Lipset 1986). That is to say, the announcement of an ethos of exchange silently enunciates the potential of its violation. Under, behind, between fixed points, veiled—and sometimes boldly out in front—to borrow Tamang idiom, are fearsome figures of disruptive, destructive, and degenerative excess untempered by the self-denial or restraint essential to continuing reciprocal relations. Ortner has described a similar tension permeating Sherpa life, where formalized exchanges mask hostility, competition, and an absence of relations (1978a:61–90). Tamang for their part preface every large social gathering, marked by the give-and-take between clans of food and service, with invocations to the divinities to protect them from bickering and fighting, which occasionally erupt in displays of bold hostility.

This chapter charts the forms of Tamang society premised on difference and exchange. By reviewing clan structure, marriage, and gifts associated with marriage, one can see how reciprocity creates bonds of obligation among individuals and social groups and constitutes the governing ethos of village life. Although this chapter concentrates on describing these elementary social differences and reciprocal relations among Tamang and their neighbors, the structure and events of Tamang sociality are not transparently unproblematic. Tamang reassert an ethos of balanced exchanges because it is tenuous and constantly threatened in the sway of human and divine affairs.

The ideal of regularity generates paradox and enables its antithesis. The ancestral figures of Ingkyal and Tikiri condense the contradictions of social difference and exchange: they are both siblings and spouses in an unresolved simultaneity, both the same (undifferentiated) and different in clan affiliation. The resonances of this contradiction reverberate beyond the abstracted conundrums of social difference and exchange—the creation of bonds through division—and relate to gender (March 1987). Social difference when combined with exogamy and patrilocal residence implies a special violence for women, a violence related to premises of the system. Women who are affectionately bound to their brothers and natal kin are separated from them in marriage; on the other hand, brothers are separated from sisters who stand as nurturant supporters to them. The account above mythically surmounts the socially impossible by equating sibling with spouse. It is, thus, as much about primordial contradictions in the play of gender and restricted exchange as about the origins of specific clans. Because the account unfolds within a context of positive rules of marriage, it suggests reexamination of theories of exchange that view marriage as the unproblematic transfer of women from one group of men to another (see Lévi-Strauss 1969; Rubin 1975; Van Baal 1975; Meeker, Barlow, and Lipset 1986). The play of order and intrinsic contradiction, as we shall see, relates directly to the ritual divergences of lama, bombo, and lambu.

Social Difference, Duality, and the Regime of Cross-Cousin Marriage

The most striking feature of greater Tamdungsa social order is its duality, which is expressed through rules of exogamy and cross-cousin marriage.[2] Tamdungsa proper includes members of seven different patriclans (*jāt* or *khor*). These patriclans in turn marry with (*ngyen brelba*) another nine in neighboring villages, making for a total of sixteen patriclans in the circle of kin (*mheme khorche*) focused on Tamdungsa. These sixteen clans are informally organized into two encompassing but unnamed exogamous groupings. This de facto dual organization regulates marriage and has implications for most interactions in village life: for any individual, any Tamang within the local area is either of his or her natal group or of the group with whom he or she can marry. Even when outside the immediate region, Tamang orient themselves toward other Tamang according to their clan affiliation and whether or not they are of one's own birth group or the other intermarrying one. All social intercourse among Tamang is modulated to this order. For most purposes, however, the various levels of Tamang social organization become conflated and focus on patriclan segments. These patriclan segments constitute the effective social units maintaining intertwined relations with a discrete set of patriclans in the local area. Duality here is as much a state of mind as an actual social organization.

These groupings, as I noted, are focused on the predominant clans of the local level, the Dimdung and the Himdung. The Dimdung were apparently the original inhabitants of Tamdungsa and the Himdung only became established locally when eight generations ago a sonless Dimdung man—the headman of the village—had his daughter's husband settle in his house and inherit his property. Other patriclans, although ancient inhabitants of other villages, are more recent immigrants to Tamdungsa. Each has become associated in village social order with either the Dimdung or the Himdung.[3] In addition to the Dimdung who were represented by forty-two households in 1977 and the Himdung by fourteen households, there were three households of *pakhren* who were affiliated with the Dimdung, four households of

[2]For a full description of the western Tamang kinship system and kinship terminology, see Toffin (1986).

[3]In the past, the region around contemporary Tamdungsa may well have been characterized by single-clan villages, which through accretion, migration, and the formation of greater Nepal may have become multiclan villages.

yeba, two of *blenden*, and one of both *galden* and *gole* who were all affiliated with the Himdung. In neighboring villages there were also Mhamba and *mokten* who were associated with Dimdung and *phyupa*, *tsoten*, *loptsen*, *gyadso*, *gyaba*, *thokra*, and *gongbo* who were associated with the Himdung. *Gle* (Nepali *ghale*), who do not fall into this dual relation, also live in northerly villages and on one rare occasion married with a Himdung in Tamdungsa. Segments of these clans are found in various combinations in a set of some fifteen villages in the vicinity of Tamdungsa and together constitute an effective local society. These clans are organized not only into two larger exogamous groupings but also into subgroups according to protective divinities (*tembe la*). Those clans sharing a common protective divinity cannot exchange spouses; apart from this prohibition there are no formal connections among clans sharing protective divinities. In fact, clans never organize corporately to celebrate their divinities; Tamang recognize protective divinities exclusively on the household and individual level. The only collective rites that seem to have been oriented toward clan divinities were rites celebrating the clan divinity of the Himdung. Every year in a ritual that had significance not only for the clan but for the village, Himdung men and women were required to joke back and forth incestuously, recalling the origins of their clan. The village headman, concerned with the image of the Tamang to outsiders, who already considered them incestuous because they married cross-cousins, halted the annual performance.[4] In fact, patriclans as total units across several villages never conduct rites or combine in action for any focused purpose. Along with the tendency to associate into larger units for the regulation of marriage, large patriclans like the Dimdung also divide into named segments.

No continuing hierarchies or asymmetries exist among patriclans in the exchange of marriage partners, and the ascendancy of one over another in particular exchanges is transitory. Discrepancies in wealth and power, however, are evident between the Himdung and other clans. All households with surplus land, with the exception of one, are Himdung. Himdung also have held all positions of official power for eight generations ever since the Himdung son-in-law of the Dimdung headman usurped the headmanship when his ailing father-in-law was unable to journey north to receive a turban legitimating his position. This ascendancy is reflected in the Himdung claim to be "clan lamas"

[4]A nearby village with important sectors of the Mhamba clan reputedly continued to perform rites celebrating their incestuous origins.

(as opposed to "studied lamas"). In the local nicknaming system, Himdung men all have "lama" as a last name and women "lhamo," whereas Dimdung are "rhong" and "wati."

These patterns of patriclan associations are characteristic only of the circle of kin focused on Tamdungsa and are not replicated in other western Tamang areas nor among the Tamang at large. The linkages of specific clans into exogamous units ceases as one moves beyond the local area. For example, even though Himdung and Blenden are not supposed to marry in the circle of kin focused on Tamdungsa, a Himdung man had married a Blenden woman; this woman, however, came from a village at great distance from Tamdungsa and outside the confines of local, intensive society. Thus, the marriage did not upset the proper order of exogamous groupings.

As one moves out of western Tamang areas, the divergences among groups called Tamang become even greater. Although lists of western Tamang patriclans (see Höfer 1969:21; Toffin 1976:40–41, 1986:24) intersect at some points with those of eastern Tamang (Fürer-Haimendorf 1956; Lama 1959), this observation reveals little because the patterns in specific areas vary considerably. Divinities of these clans reflect the vagaries of local history and thus cannot be used to trace relations among geographically distant groups of Tamang. For instance, a local sector of the Mokten clan, whom Tamdungsa villagers married, shares a clan divinity with the Dimdung because the local Mokten trace descent from a man who was brought up as an orphan in a Dimdung house. His descendants adopted the clan divinity of the Dimdung.

Despite these significant differences, a system of bilateral cross-cousin marriage appears common, if not the rule, across greater Tamang society. The system rephrases Tamang principles of duality and exchange. To marry either a mother's brother's or a father's sister's child assures continuing "restricted" exchanges (Lévi-Strauss 1969) between patriclan segments on one level and exogamous units on another. Although a bilateral system in practice, Tamang sometimes express a preference for a patrilateral cross-cousin marriage (or marriage of a man with his father's sister's daughter), a preference that when reported for the Gurung has generated considerable controversy and perhaps misunderstanding (Oppitz 1982). In Tamdungsa a man is said to have "rights" (*hāk*) to his father's sister's daughter despite the practice of bilateral cross-cousin marriage. To explain this anomalous expression (and perhaps also anomalies in the Gurung data), we need look no further than the ethos of symmetrical exchange. Rather than a prescriptive rule of patrilaterality, the rights of a man to his father's sister's daughter reflects the indebtedness of the father's sister's husband's patriclan segment to his wife's patriclan segment or to the patriclan segment from whom they have received a woman. Tamang want to clear exchange ledgers and erase implicit asymmetries in the world of actual exchanges and social relations. Those who have received wives are indebted (and must ritually serve) those who have given (cf. Sahlins 1972:222–23). As Lévi-Strauss has remarked, "Marriage with the father's sister's daughter, like marriage with the sister's daughter, represents from the logical as much as the psychological point of view the simplest and most crudely concrete application of the principle of reciprocity" (1969:448). Moreover, Tamang equate father's sister's husband with mother's brother and mother's brother's wife with father's sister, which obviates the matri- and patrilateral distinctions.

This stress on perduring exchanges among affines is nowhere more apparent than in the efforts the Tamang make to have the reality of all marriages conform to the ideal of cross-cousin marriages. Roughly one-third of all marriages in Tamdungsa were contracted with cross-cousins—23 percent with patrilateral cross-cousins and 13 percent with matrilateral cross-cousins (March 1979:209). Although the other two-thirds of marriages respected the strictures of exogamy, they were contracted with relatives other than actual cross-cousins, though many of these were between people who referred to each other with cross-cousin terms. The valuation of cross-cousin marriage retained its force however; after marriage, the partners and their respective kin treat each other and refer to each other as though the partners had in fact been cross-cousins, giving greater weight to the cultural ideal than to statistical practice. Within the marriage rites proper, significant categories of kin formally announce their new terms of reference.

All these marriages occur within a limited geographic range. Roughly one-third of all marriages of Tamang men were village endogamous and the other two-thirds were with women from villages in the immediate vicinity of Tamdungsa. Tamang women rarely marry into villages farther than a few hours walk from Tamdungsa. These marriage patterns generate a tightly bound and geographically restricted social order. The values of exchange appear vividly in the formalities of Tamang marriage, where the opposition of affines and the laws of reciprocity are declared repeatedly.

Marriage: Exchange, Seduction, and Abduction

Although marriage rites do not compare in importance with death rites in the expression of the values and structure of the Tamang social world (see chapter 7), a marriage initiates specific relations between individuals and patriclan segments that radiate throughout Tamang life. Marriages are usually monogamous, although it is not uncommon for men with means to marry more than one woman. (There was also one household in the village in which two brothers shared one wife.) Tamang finalize divorce without great difficulty and do so often in Tamdungsa, where about one-third of all men had been married more than once.[5] Divorce does not alter the prospects of remarriage for women among Tamang as it does among neighboring Hindus.

There are several paths to marriage, all of which incorporate the same cultural themes in somewhat different ways. The proper form of marriage is between cross-cousins and is arranged by the parents of the prospective couple; bride and groom can also conspire to elope from a festival, in a form of mock capture; in some instances brides can be captured with or without their consent. The former style accentuates reciprocity and negotiation, and the latter two, seduction and capture, respectively. Capture is and was very rare and is more the subject of stories by men than practice. Reciprocity ultimately takes the symbolic foreground in all types of marriage but never to the exclusion of the potential irruption of unrestrained eros and coercion. Even in the formal movements of negotiated marriages hints of capture abound. Exchange resonates through negotiated marriages in tension with other motifs.

Few marriages in Tamdungsa follow the formal procedures of negotiation, but all marriages eventually conform to the ideals of negotiated exchange; the seductive and forceful undertones of elopement and capture are overlaid in the finalizing themes of measured reciprocity through post facto exchanges. Almost all the marriages that occurred in Tamdungsa during my stay were mock captures. A woman and man (usually with the tacit consent of significant kin) arranged to return from a festival together, or the groom and his companions brought a woman down from her home village in the dark of night. Tamang place less ritual emphasis on exchanges at the initial stages of these marriages than they do on exchanges between sets of affines that occur months, if not years, after bride and groom have taken up coresidence.

[5] Not all these marriages, though, succeeded divorces.

These exchanges infix the marriage into a continuous structure and, most important, legitimate the offspring of the union. In the end, all courses of marriage partake of the others.

Full-scale negotiated marriages[6] tend to be contracted between cross-cousins and thus reflect the momentum of previous exchanges. This is not necessarily the case, though, because such negotiations can be the basis for the establishment of new alliances. Negotiated marriages begin with a formal request by a party representing the groom (and usually including the groom's father), who travel secretly at night to the house of the bride, thus avoiding detection should their suit not succeed. Upon arrival at the bride's home, the groom's party offers three flasks of whiskey to the senior woman of the house. If she accepts, formal marriage rites will occur within the year.

Exchanges also frame each stage of the marriage rites. At the wedding proper, the groom's party sends a messenger with gifts of whiskey, curds, and the top of a sugarcane to the bride's house, where he informs the bride's kin of the size of the groom's party in highly exaggerated terms. When the party arrives, they are ritually impeded by the bride's parents or brothers, who then serve them whiskey and a snack, juxtaposing a mock breach with the union of commensality. If the bride's family is wealthy, they serve the entire groom's party a feast of rice and meat; if not, they simply serve a few principals in the groom's party.

Exchanges not only mark the interchanges between prospective affines, they also structure the relationships between bride and groom and between the bride and groom and the respective parents-in-law. At the wedding feast, the groom gives three separate pieces of cloth to the bride along with either gold or money with which to buy gold. As the rites progress, the groom also conveys gifts of cloth, money, and whiskey to the bride's mother (the groom's "father's sister" in Tamang terminology), who in turn gives him a white turban. Then, beginning with her parents, the bride's patrikin give the couple money and blessings and the couple bow to the bride's natal kin, who now stand in an ascendant position to the groom and his immediate kin; they have become "wife-givers." After the conclusion of these exchanges at the

[6]Tamdungsa Tamang referred to two distinct patterns of formal marriage, the older-grandfather and the younger-grandfather custom. My information is on the older-grandfather custom, and the people I asked were unable to tell me what the younger-grandfather custom was. I witnessed only one marriage of the former type and only partial segments of it. This description is a reconstruction from conversations with, and comments of, Tamang villagers.

bride's home, the bride's brothers pick up their sister and bodily hand her over to the groom's brothers, who carry her to the groom's village on their backs.

Upon arrival at the groom's village, a similar give-and-take unfolds. The groom's household and immediate patriclan kin ply the party accompanying the bride (which never includes her parents) with the customary whiskey and food. Then, after a lambu (or lama) briefly invokes divine protection, the groom's father presents the couple with milk and the mother serves them meat; this ritual nurturance marks the incorporation of the bride into her husband's home. The groom's clan sisters give him another white turban, reaffirming important and perduring ties between brothers and sisters. Finally the bride and groom emerge and serve more whiskey and meat to the bride's party, who have already been treated with a feast of bread, meat, and whiskey. The married couple again bows to those who now stand in an ascendant relation to the husband. The bride conveys a final offering of whiskey to her brothers as they depart for their homes, announcing her continuing bonds to her brothers. Three days after the wedding, the newly married couple, with a small party that must include the husband's father, returns to the wife's home with offerings of bread and whiskey and stay for one night.

To avoid the expense of these elaborate feasts at negotiated unions or the potential refusal of a formal suit, grooms can elope with a bride either from a festival or from her home village. In unions resulting from such mock captures, the essential exchanges that legitimate the marriage occur after the bride begins residing in the groom's house, not before as in negotiated unions. Mock captures often occur with the knowledge of the parents, though their complicity is not necessary until after the fact. Mock captures always take place within the circle of kin and conform to strictures of exogamy; couples are often classificatory cross-cousins. Such marriages not only avoid elaborate feasts and negotiations, they provide a way around complicated situations. For instance, it is thought to be improper for younger sisters to marry before older sisters; if opportunity or desire motivates a younger sister to marry her only choice is to elope.

Mock capture is also a poetic favorite, infusing the formalities of exchange with eroticism and vice versa. Exchange and seduction go hand in hand. Mock captures at regional festivals or at large social rites like memorial death feasts begin with song contests. At such events, pairs of young women and young men dressed in their finery (see Figure 3) face each other and exchange lines of poetic songs and some-

Figure 3. Young Tamang women in festival finery

times dance back and forth. One pair sings a line and the other parries with a fitting response. Theoretically the pairs exchange verses until one or the other runs out of responses. Then the pairs exchange gifts; young women give men crocheted scarves, and men give women small baskets, combs, or weaving implements, all made from bamboo. At the beginning of the festival, young men and women parade back and forth, displaying their exchange goods to attract potential exchange partners. When they return to their villages after the festival, the young men and women prominently exhibit the scarves and bamboo items they have accumulated. An individual can participate in several exchanges during any festival. Most singing bouts end with such exchange, but some lead to more directly sexual encounters and sometimes to continuing amorous liaisons. At every major festival hundreds and hundreds of pairs sing back and forth and dozens do at other events.

These song bouts can also lead to elopement. With advance planning, a young man's friends will surround a young woman who has agreed to be "captured" and return her as a bride to the groom's village, where, after hasty invocations by the lambu, they are wedded. Potentially all song exchanges can lead to marriage, and the opening lines of the songs usually reveal the clan affiliations of the partners so that incestuous exchanges go no further. Moreover, Tamang like to point out that theoretically the pair that wins the exchange is free to take the others as spouses. Such an exchange led Tikiri and Ingkyal irreversibly into the incestuous union that generated the split between the Himdung and Dimdung clans.

Although most mock captures occur at festivals or rituals, they can also happen in other contexts. A young man and his companions can make their way in the dead of night to the bride's village, carry her back, and complete a brief wedding. True capture is rare but not unknown. One marriage in the village resulted from the forced detainment of a woman who had come to visit her sister. Villagers spoke of another marriage by strength (*balsing*), which had occurred when a local clan segment was refused a woman over whom they had asserted rights.

In the same fashion that negotiated unions hint at capture when the bride's parents ritually impede both the entrance of the groom's party to the village and their departure with the bride, mock capture and true capture convert to negotiated unions upon the completion of certain exchanges—exchanges that domesticate the seduction of song and coercion in the measured play of reciprocity. After the bride has begun to live in her husband's home, the husband's patrikin send a flask of whiskey to the bride's father, informing him of the marriage; this is the post facto equivalent of the flasks sent in request for a negotiated union. After the bride's natal kin have accepted this offering, the bride, the groom, and the groom's father all make a trip to the bride's home with offerings of bread and whiskey just as they do following the feasts of negotiated unions.

Tamang, however, place greater emphasis on exchanges that occur after these preliminary rites of marriage. Although negotiation, elopement, or capture can all initiate a union, a marriage is not complete until the husband and his natal kin formally convey customary gifts of bread, chickens, fish, cloth, and money to the wife's natal kin. Villagers explain that these exchanges, known as *wangde khonsrong* or *pe rhimba*, are to legitimate children of a union and to give them a clan affiliation; they must be performed even for children born out of wedlock. These exchanges, which notably do not focus on the transfer of women, are felt to be the most crucial in the sequence of events finalizing a union. Like much of marriage custom, these exchanges became formalized when the incestuous union of Tikiri and Ingkyal was resolved. There is no set timetable during which villagers complete these exchanges; however, they must be performed before a son's tonsure ceremony (usually at three, five, or nine years of age) and a daughter's wangde khonsrong ceremony. If a woman has no male offspring, the customary exchanges can be delayed until her death rites. These exchanges are often, but not necessarily, the context in which a wife receives property from her natal home. All women receive a hoe, sickle, and bronze bowl (see chapter 7) and, depending on the wealth of their natal households, varying amounts of movable valuables, the meaning of which we shall return to below.

Specific unions both respond to and generate particular relations of obligation among individuals and patriclan segments, and because kinship and society are for most purposes coextensive, the elementary structure of these relations shape all aspects of life. Although the positions and perspectives of men and women in this structure diverge, one can describe this structure preliminarily as tripartite. A man is a member of his own patrilineal group (*gyut* or *santān*) and has important relations to two sets of affines: his *ashyang-shyangpo*—a collective referent for mother's brothers and wife's brothers—and his *mhā*—a collective referent for sister's and daughter's husbands (See Figure 4). Although this formal order appears to be triadic—mha/gyut(santan)/ashyang-shyangpo—it is in fact a doubling of the mha/ashyang-

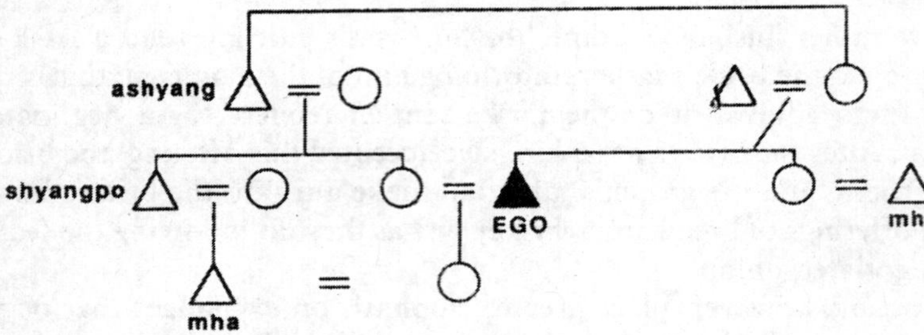

Figure 4. Elementary affinal relations among Tamang

shyangpo relation, revealing a system based on duality. For Tamdungsa Tamang, the opposition of Himdung and Dimdung elevates this affinal opposition to the structure of the whole village.

The arrangement among individuals of these opposed groups is not equal but hierarchical, countering the values of everyday transactions—the giving and receiving of casual hospitality, labor, conversation, and companionship—which result in no permanent gains or losses as individuals oscillate from the position of giver to that of receiver. Mha must deferentially approach their ashyang-shyangpo and honorifically serve them; ashyang-shyangpo assertively call on their mha to help in field work in times of labor shortage, to act as messengers, and to provide service at all ritual occasions. At death, when these relations are most obvious, mha fulfill all polluting tasks from carrying the corpse to cleansing the house, and they show deference to their ashyang-shyangpo throughout the death rites. Of course every mha is also someone's ashyang-shyangpo and receives similar services, often from some of the same clan that he serves. Thus, no perduring hierarchies between patriclans take form, a characteristic of systems of restricted exchange based on bilateral cross-cousin marriage. Moreover, through several generations, relations between patriclan segments that stand as mha and shyangpo to each other will oscillate.

Accumulation and the Contradictions of Reciprocity

Properly, all relations within the local community should be subsumed within this overarching ethos, but balanced reciprocity is contradicted in at least two spheres of everyday life. First, processes of state formation entrenched several households in an ascendant politicoeconomic position within the village, a situation aggravated by general pressure on land over the last two generations. The same history that contributed to Tamang insularity as a community of restricted exchange, thus, also produced discrepancies within local communities. But these inequalities do not generate hierarchy in marriage relations. The powerful and wealthy did not necessarily marry with the powerful and wealthy of neighboring communities.[7] Whereas alliances across great geographic distance characterize the marriage patterns of the elite of Sherpa and Gurung societies and reflect hierarchies within those societies, such alliances did not prevail among Tamdungsa Tamang, who confined their marriages to the local community and often without direct regard to comparable wealth. Inequalities, though, pose contradictions and foment tensions. Accumulation and consolidation of resources violate values of equality. A second contradiction to the ethos of balanced reciprocity is, of course, that Tamang are engaged in a range of relations with non-Tamang. Such relations do not fall within the same parameters as those among local kin, a subject taken up in the next section.

The smallest productive unit in Tamang subsistence is the household or *dim* (see Fricke 1986a), usually composed of a man, his wife, unmarried sons and daughters, and often one or more married sons and their children. Tamdungsa had sixty-seven households of Tamang and five of untouchable Blacksmiths (*kāmi*). Of these seventy-two households, five had a substantial surplus of land that produced more than enough grain for subsistence, six had adequate holdings, and the rest had variably less than enough for subsistence, although many of these were near subsistence levels. Of the latter, eight, including the five households of Blacksmiths, were essentially landless.

The majority of the households in the middle range of this continuum formed exchange labor groups, and Tamdungsa tended to form itself as a closed economic community based on principles of symmetrical reciprocity on this level. Unable to hire day laborers and often short of sufficient draught animals, these households share agricultural labor and resources. Although most often these exchanges relate to person days of labor, conversion of labor into oxen teams with plows occurs frequently. The system of exchange labor articulates well with local ecology. Differential altitude, sun and wind exposure, and soil conditions converge to structure remarkable variation from plot to plot in

[7]For a more detailed examination of wealth, domestic cycles, and marriage and a discussion of egalitarian ethos and discrepancies in wealth, see Fricke (1986b).

most highland villages. Growing seasons from the higher dry fields may vary as much as a month on either end of the agricultural cycle. Thus, communal labor teams can efficiently plant and work fields by moving from higher to lower plots at the time of planting and lower to higher plots at the time of harvest. Exchange labor, of course, is not just more efficient but also more pleasurable for villagers who enjoy the exchanges, songs, and banter of joint efforts in what is backbreaking work.

Even the land rich join these labor teams as their labor resources allow. In most circumstances, however, they do not have enough labor to fulfill exchange requirements and must resort to hired labor, thereby opening the closure of exchange on both ends of the economic continuum: the land rich are labor poor and become grain rich, and the land poor are comparatively labor rich but grain short. The land rich need to hire day laborers either from Tamdungsa or neighboring villages to plant and harvest their fields. One land-rich household needed to employ ninety villagers for a half day in order to get its paddy fields planted. The land rich have several other options in terms of tenancy, in which the landlord and tenant split the produce, but tenancy arrangements have become unpopular since land reform laws of the 1970s gave rights to tenants.[8]

Most of those who were land short could make up their deficiencies by working at peak labor times for the wealthier households or would supplement agriculture with some animal husbandry, petty trade, weaving, and the like. The poorest Tamang would usually become retainers or herders for the wealthier households in return for food, clothing, and, depending on the arrangement, some money.[9] Some land-rich households gave usufruct over fields to poor families in return for regular labor service. The land rich tended to go beyond the village for labor only at peak times. No one in the village went without food or shelter, and villagers were careful to make sure that even the

[8]The two wealthiest households in the village used different strategies for planting their extensive holdings. One planted its entire holdings in one day, using labor from the village. The other let out large sectors of its land to tenants and planted the rest over a long period, using occasional day labor. Three types of tenancy were practiced in Tamdungsa: (1) *adhiyā*, in which the tenant and landlord split the produce equally; (2) *kud*, in which the tenant gave a set amount of grain to the landlord no matter what the total yield; and (3) *bandāki*, in which the tenant acquired usufruct of land as interest on a loan.

[9]In Tamdungsa, the poorest households included two landless widows with no sons or brothers to support them. They were given land for a house site and regularly supported by wealthier households. House labor by the poor was often in return for loans and usually took the form of the debtor placing one of his children in the lender's house for a certain period of time.

poorest got a share of what they had; not to include all and to allow some to go without would open one to danger.

The grain surpluses of the land rich and the deficiencies of poorer Tamang also open the village to the surrounding regional economy in direct ways. The grain-wealthy households sell or barter surpluses of rice in the bazaar town to the south or to the rice-deficient regions to the north. Tamang regularly barter grain for materials and commodities not available in Tamdungsa. Village rice, maize, and millet are traded for high-altitude timber and bamboo, wool blankets, radishes, beans, potatoes, dogs, fruits, forest foods, medicines, and the like. Poorer Tamang likewise hire themselves out seasonally as masons or porters in neighboring villages or engage in petty trade in grain, hashish, manufactured goods, and livestock. Some hire themselves out for longer periods as coolies on construction projects in the far reaches of Nepal and in India. All households require some cash for taxes, cloth, lamp oil, thread, soap, salt, and incidentals, and individuals must either pursue wage labor, sell some produce, or, if they have capital, lend money for interest.

Whether or not Tamang transactions are always symmetrical, an idea that the world should be governed by reciprocity prevails and structures their social imagination; thus contradictions in wealth are constructed ideologically according to principles of exchange. Two of the richest and politically dominant households at the time of this research are cases in point: both had been subjected to gossip and accusations about their characters. One of the households, through connections with politically dominant outsiders, could harshly extract deference and service from other Tamang households. This household was reputed to hold two grain measures, a large one for receiving payments and a small one for doling out loans in kind; more important, other villagers constantly whispered that they were poisoners (*mengko*). People were cautious about eating with them, thus shutting them off—as they shut others off—from important commensal exchanges. The other prominent household made much greater attempts at open and symbolic redistribution of wealth, and the headman of the house was a populist political leader who was known for his fairness and generosity. This, however, was not true of his grandfather, who had originally accumulated wealth through loans and petty salt trade; villagers murmured that he had kept a *bir*, an animallike familiar that consumes the well-being of other households in order to enrich the household of its master.

Other non-Tamang are treated in a more strictly exploitative vein.

But even those relations that are marked as castelike in Tamdungsa are perhaps better understood within the idioms of exchange than those of purity and impurity. In fact, the comparative idiom of exchange may be the best language for understanding relations across cultures in Nepal.

The Boundaries of Reciprocity

Social relations for Tamang are not confined to the circle of kin. Every Tamang village in the region, including Tamdungsa, had at least a few households of the Blacksmith caste. Nearby there were separate hamlets of Bahun or Brahmans—*upādhyaya bāhun* of the *kumāi* branch and Jaisi Bahun or widow-remarrying Bahun, all of whom Tamang refer to along with Chetri or Kshatriya as *jarti*. All these groups are farmers. A small Gurung community immediately adjacent to Tamdungsa traces its origins in the region to land grants made to its ancestors by the early kings of a unified Nepal. There were also scattered houses of Chetri, Newar, Khatri (offspring of Jarti fathers and Tamang mothers) and *nagarkoṭi* (offspring of Newar fathers and Tamang mothers) in the locale. Tamang also had ties with Damai (Tailors) and Sarki (Leatherworkers who keep pigs) from the region—both of whom, like Blacksmiths, are untouchables. In some Tamang villages there were *gle* or Ghale clans; however, these clans did not constitute a separate group but a subdivision of the local Tamang. Tamang clans and Gle clans intermarry and speak the same language. Trips to the bazaar town or to Kathmandu and ventures to more distant regions in search of employment bring Tamang into contact with the full range of Nepalese groups and those of greater India and Tibet. More influential Tamang have regularized economic and political ties to individuals of other ethnic groups. Tamang, like all Nepalese, also ritually create fictive siblingship with individuals of other groups (Okada 1957); these ritual siblings, known as *leng* and *lengshya*, are contracted between men and between women, respectively. They allow Tamang to enmesh relations with outsiders in patterns of kinship.

These ritualized kin relations are forged precisely because transactions with individuals of different groups and with distant Tamang are governed by an ethos in direct opposition to the tempered play of reciprocity that regulates local Tamang intercourse. This absence of reciprocity is readily apparent in the relations of Tamang with Blacksmiths who live among them and with whom Tamang have embedded ties spanning generations. Blacksmiths reside in separate clusters in the village, where they operate their forges. Blacksmiths are virtually landless and earn grain by providing ironworking service and performing day labor for Tamang households. Following greater interactive patterns in Nepal, Tamang treat Blacksmiths as untouchable, or those with whom one will not share water. Blacksmiths may not enter Tamang houses; Tamang will not receive food or water from their hands. Tamang and Blacksmsiths do not share tobacco from the same hookah; Blacksmiths sit on the ground in the presence of Tamang and are often treated brusquely. Direct physical contact was not strongly restricted, however, and it was common to see Tamang and Blacksmith youths arm-in-arm, particularly girls.

Although integrated in the local economy, Blacksmiths reside on the margins of a closed Tamang society. They are fluent in Tamang, but speak Nepali at home and have a secret language, which they sometimes speak when in the presence of bilingual Tamang. Although ever present at the peripheries of Tamang ritual feasts and given food, they pursue distinct ritual practices linking them to other Blacksmsith communities in the region. They do not respect lamas or join in Buddhist rites. Blacksmith shamans, however, often supplement their skills with training from Tamang masters.

Although Tamang/Blacksmith relations are usually approached in the idiom of Hindu caste, their relations are only superficially castelike in the Hindu sense.[10] Caste ideology, structured in orthopraxic expression by an opposition of pure and impure, is a secondary aspect of their relations. These relations, like those throughout the Tibeto-Burman and Tibetan worlds where there are untouchable Blacksmiths, are governed by different values. For Tamang, bodily secretions and death, though polluting, do not generate a ritual hierarchy based on permanent purity and pollution, and thus they do not replicate Hindu values. All pollutions in Tamang terms are readily cleansed. Relations with others are governed by principles of exchange, which are logically prior to the attribution of relative purity and pollution.

Tamang unremorsefully exploit Blacksmiths in a way they would never exploit their kin. Tamang/Blacksmith interactions are accompanied by a continual haggling in which Tamang try to extract the most from Blacksmiths and give up the least and Blacksmiths plead for the most and offer nothing in return. Relations are never modified by

[10] They are "hybrid" in the terms Dumont applied to the Pathan scheme (1970b:208–9; see Barth 1965).

the encompassing reciprocity that governs relations among affines or between rich and poor Tamang. Blacksmiths are the other, outside the world of bounded exchange. This relationship allows a more purely accumulative economy to reign tempered only by Tamang power on the one hand and the Blacksmiths' unique ironworking and labor service on the other. These relations constitute a "negative reciprocity" in direct contradiction to Tamang ideals. As Sahlins has noted, "Negative reciprocity is the most impersonal sort of exchange. In guises such as 'barter' it is from our own point of view the 'most economic.' The participants confront each other as opposed interests, each looking to maximize utility at the other's expense" (1972:195). Blacksmiths are outside insiders. Exploitation and unmitigated accumulation is allowed because of difference, and difference is perpetuated because of exploitation.

Thus, Tamang and Blacksmiths do not share a culture of symmetrical exchange, nor do they share the culture of asymmetrical exchange that regulates Hindu interactions according to a hierarchy of pure and impure. Rather, their interrelations are formed according to presumptions of total difference. Within the bounds of Tamang society, goods are potentially infinite in amount and can theoretically be continually divided so that all receive their due portion; outside these bounds, and particularly in interactions with Blacksmiths, goods are finite in amount and there is a final scarcity: Blacksmiths do not receive their just portion. They define the limits of inclusion. They become in their exclusion the antithesis of reciprocating and generous affines. Tamang pay a psychic price for this exclusion. As those who are left out, Tamang imagine Blacksmiths to be always demanding, hungry, waiting at their stoops, begging, pleading, hovering at the margins of their feasts, and, above all, subject to intense jealousy. With a glance at a milking buffalo, a plate of food, a stocked granary, a healthy child, or fine dress, Blacksmiths can ruin well-being, infecting it with a degenerative, consumptive force that is fueled by their want. Blacksmiths, especially the women, are frequently accused of being witches (*bokshyi)*, and the spirits of dead Blacksmiths and other untouchable women are believed to capture the shadow-souls of children, thereby making them ill. Their craving, like that of other evils, accompanies and threatens any prosperous production.

The place of other castes or groups is more ambiguous than the Blacksmiths' and must be approached contextually. For instance, Tamang relations with neighboring Gurung are marked by an equality of symmetrical exclusion. They share each other's rice and maize mush (cf. Höfer 1979:26) but will not share millet mush; they also will not share a common hookah stem. Status appears to be fluid and strongly affected by wealth. Most local Gurung are relatively impoverished and tend to be subservient to wealthy Tamang, often laboring for them.

Relations with high-caste Hindu groups, like those with Blacksmiths, are irreducible to either Tamang or Hindu social theories and are best approached through patterns of exchange which allow us to translate both systems into a common idiom. Although Tamang lump all high-caste Hindus together under the rubric of jarti, there are several significant sectors of high-caste Hindus in close contiguity to Tamdungsa, and Tamang have in general somewhat distinct relations with each. Upadhyaya Bahun and Jaisi Bahun communities reside in nearby hamlets of related kin, separate from Tamang villages. There were a few Chetri houses but these were insignificant. Both Upadhyaya Bahun and Jaisi Bahun groups had moved into the region in the last two generations. Nearby Upadhyaya Bahun, although numerically insignificant (numbering only five or so households), have come into prominence in the system of local councils (panchayat), a new regional school system, and have incrementally acquired more irrigated lands (often by legal manipulation). There are also more established Bahun communities a bit farther away. These communities took root during the Rana period when they were granted estates and administrative positions in the region. The familiarity of Bahun with the language of the state and their ties to kin in the district center and Kathmandu allowed them the resources to carve a position rivalling and increasingly superseding that of Tamang headmen. They are taking an ascendant position vis-à-vis Tamang directly opposite that occupied by Blacksmiths. The increasing political dominance of Bahun in the locale is encouraged by gerrymandering of local administrative units to the effective exclusion of popular Tamang leaders above the ward level.

The attitudes of Upadhyaya Bahun toward Tamang are framed primarily within Hindu ideology of purity and secondarily according to diet criteria. Tamang lack of recognition of Bahun as ritually superior and their consumption of meat, including bovine carrion, and alcohol make them formally low. Tamang for their part view Bahun as sharpsters, irrevocably corrupt and deceitful. Jaisi Bahun on the other hand are less influential and for the most part are poor farmers and herders who reside at higher altitudes, where their fields are meagre and often only marginally productive. They carry no outstanding influence in local political and economic life and have closer associations with Tamang. Jaisi Bahun often labor for wealthier Tamang households.

Although they deny it when asked, many speak Tamang language fluently.

Tamdungsa Tamang share no ritual ground with Jarti and do not employ Bahun as priests except in rare instances.[11] Thus, contrary to the patterns of caste relations usually reported for Indian villages, ritualized hierarchies paralleling other social complementarities are virtually absent. When less influential Tamang act with deference to local Upadhyaya Bahun, this courtesy reflects power not ritual purity, and Tamang do not conceive of themselves as integral in a system of asymmetrical exchange in which they respond to the purity of the Brahman. Hindu ideologies of gift giving, particularly as they relate to food, are a direct inversion of those of the Tamang. In many Hindu transactions, to give a gift to someone is to announce the recipient's ascendancy; in varna ideology Brahmans, like divinities, are described as the receivers of gifts and the lower castes as the presenters of gifts. In contemporary social transactions, this construction of gifts works in the hierarchies established in Hindu marriage, whether hypergamous or isogamous. In Nepal, the gift of a virgin or the primary marriage establishes relations in direct opposition to those among Tamang. The brother of a man's wife is considered to be lower than the husband, making givers inferior to receivers. Tamang are well aware of these discrepancies and regularly note that Hindu forms invert the proper order of things: Tamang honor and serve a wife's brothers; Bahun and Chetri practices place the receiver in an ascendant position.

Tamang and high-caste Hindus, of course, do not normally marry; if they do, they flee the locale. Thus these complementary constructions of affinal relations do not directly conflict. Tamang and Hindu, however, do frequently encounter each other, and their contrary valuations of transactions suggest new approaches to the interpretation of Nepalese diversity. Tamang custom requires hospitality; they treat visitors, beggars, travelers, and government officials generously. This generosity is usually expressed in offerings of food and drink. Among Tamang, sharing of whiskey, snacks, and meals is a primary medium for expressing social relations and generating obligations. This commensality encounters its inverse when Tamang attempt to treat Bahun, Jaisi Bahun, Chetri, or other groups who consider themselves of higher status. High-caste Hindus define social relations as much by rules of

[11]Twice in the last two generations a Tamang household in Tamdungsa employed a Brahman from a neighboring village to perform rites of prosperity. These two performances appear to be linked to the attempt on the part of the household to forge political alliances with neighboring high-caste Hindus and to gain legitimacy.

exclusion as inclusion and will in most circumstances refuse to eat food cooked in water from Tamang hands. Although local Jarti are usually very concerned about maintaining commensal distance from Tamang, villagers regularly relate stories of Bahun and Thakuri from Kathmandu who have eaten with them while visiting the village on government business. These officials, who eat with Tamang either because of modern, more egalitarian ideology or because they are out of their regular interactive environments (or both), end up tacitly supporting Tamang views of themselves as inferior to no other group. These transactions have made Tamang villagers, though well aware of the sensibilities of local Jarti, fond of testing them.

In some instances, these contrary commensal models encounter each other directly, as when Jarti end up staying overnight in Tamang households on their way to home villages. When this occurs, as it regularly did at the wealthier Tamang households, a play on views of commensality would be initiated by Tamang. As household members would gather around the hearth to eat the evening meal, the head of the household would invite the visitors, usually seated on the veranda, to join them. Of course if the visitors hailed from the city and no longer subscribed to commensal restrictions (at least in contexts where immediate kin could not observe), they would enter and eat. More often than not, however, local Jarti would politely refuse this hospitable invitation, claiming lack of hunger and perhaps the fear of losing caste. After several entreaties the hosts would give up but insist that the visitor eat something. They would prepare popped corn or other foods that can pass between Tamang and Jarti, or more commonly, they would give coals, cooking vessels and utensils, plates, and raw grain and vegetables to the visitors and direct them to a place where they could prepare their own meal.

These encounters are not competitive bouts of status assertion but rather plays of cultural difference. Jarti and Tamang have completely different understandings of the interaction, and both leave satisfied with the outcome of this commensal play. Jarti leave assured that their caste integrity remains undefiled and that their superiority is secure. Tamang for their part have also retained their dignity. Unbeknownst to the guests who have refused their hospitality, Tamang have equated them with untouchables by providing them with the dishes and pots they usually reserve for all outsiders, including untouchables. Conservative households never allow non-Tamang to eat off the bronze dishware required in intra-Tamang feasting. Thus, Tamang lump all outsiders together and ignore the subtleties of Hindu hierarchies. This equation of high caste and low caste plays out in practice the mythic parody of caste origins and textual traditions recounted in chapter 2, which associates Bahun with the texts of the Blacksmiths.

Relations among groups in hill Nepal must be approached with an understanding of the different semantic fields converging in the scenario outlined here. There is no final sociological denominator that can encompass encounters like these; however, an exchange theory affords a translatability of these differences. Tamang work from symmetrical exchange and Hindus from asymmetrical exchange, but these differences are of little concern to either participant, for each approaches the other—unless there are mitigating relations like ritual bonds—as subject to exclusion. The commensal play described here of course occurs in a domain where Tamang retain control. When interactions shift to spheres controlled by other groups, the Tamang can be confined to the constructions of orthopraxic Hindus. There are, of course, wide fields in urban and modernizing Nepal in which other modes of transaction unfold, but these must be viewed against the backdrop of differences like the ones described here.

Finally, these interchanges are plays on status and difference in which little is at stake. Where negative reciprocity and power converge, as they have in the historical domination of sectors of Tibeto-Burman populations or in situations similar to the Tamang oppression of Blacksmiths or impoverished Hindus, status formations have become more rigid. This process, however, cannot be understood from a formalist economic history; equally important to an understanding of this process are the cultures of exchange and reciprocity out of which Nepalese economies emerge—whether negative or positive, symmetrical or asymmetrical—which shape relations and generate tensions. In general, though, the evolvement of political hegemony in Nepal means that on the whole systems like that of the Tamang based on balanced reciprocity are likely to be increasingly undermined by the growth of accumulative strategies of economic practice, many of which are promoted as "development."

Exchange and the Powers and Vulnerabilities of Women

Most visions of marital exchange and its implications are created from an androcentric perspective. When one examines marriage systems premised on reciprocity (van Baal 1975) from the perspective of women, however, new dimensions to the theoretical problem of the "traffic in women" (Rubin 1975) come into view. In particular, what Meeker, Barlow, and Lipset have labeled the "double and divided claims of men over women" (1986:27) might better be conceived, especially in systems of cross-cousin marriage, from the perspective of women (March 1979, 1984, 1987). There are ways of seeing women as central as men in Tamang exchanges.

To describe a social system as a system of exchange (Lévi-Strauss 1969) implies nothing directly about the status of men or women as actors. The reduction of a structural theory of restricted exchange, though, into a strategic theory of alliance usually relegates women to the role of valued objects. This shift from a structural overview to a strategic model of social action neglects the powers and resources of women (van Baal 1975) readily observable among the Tamang on the one hand and the theoretical implications of gender and kinship on the other hand. Women are often accorded special possibilities for action in systems of cross-cousin marriage because they have wide-ranging and embedded ties in two groups and are strategically central. Concretely put, a woman's father-in-law is likely to be her mother's brother.

Furthermore, marriage exchange among the Tamang has as much to do with an exchange of children as with an exchange of women. As we have seen, the most important rites in the process of marriage legitimate children of a union (which in turn sanction the marriage) and announce ensuing relations between patriclan segments: a patriclan segment can only reproduce itself through the women of the other. The relative ease of divorce among Tamang and the fact that children remain with the husband suggests that Tamang value exchange in the abstract. In the symbology of marriage rites, the values of exchange prevail over others. Images of capture are expressed as much to exaggerate the supersedure of exchange as to represent values of capture qua capture. But the most compelling evidence for a reassessment of exchange theory and women is that women among the Tamang do not act as though they were commodities nor are they treated as though they were. Women, even very young women, can and do regularly resist marriages arranged according to the momentum of clan exchange and often make special demands; one young woman in Tamdungsa insisted on usufruct over land owned by her brothers before she would go in marriage to a poorer household. Women, even though they have been through the initial stages of marriage rites, can and occasionally do balk at changing their residence. Tamang women do not like to marry men from villages at great distance from their natal homes and most marry within a few hours' walk of their natal homes if not in the village itself; when they marry into other villages, they prefer to go where their sisters or other *ananenchon* or clan sisters have already married.

Equally important to an understanding of Tamang and the place of women, however, is that villagers do not imagine women as being absolutely transferred from one clan to another by marriage. When asked about clan affiliations of women, Tamang offer two responses: the usual one is that a woman's clan is her natal clan; however, some answer that a woman's clan is the same as her husband's—inconceivable within Tamang rules of exogamy—but when pressed change their answer to natal clan. Neither answer is wrong and this ambiguity reflects the dual affiliations of women, an apparent contradiction reveals an underlying reality. After marriage, a woman acts either from the relation to her brothers and her natal clan or from the relation to her husband. Although marriage implies obligations and privileges for a woman in her husband's household, her ties to her natal kin, especially her siblings, remain very strong. These links are much more extensive than in neighboring Hindu populations, where they are also important (Bennett 1983). The relations between siblings are demarcated by special terms: *busing* refers to a man's patriclan sisters; *acho-ale* refers to a man's or a woman's patriclan brothers; ananenchon refers to a woman's patriclan sisters. Relations between patriclan siblings, whether same or cross-sex, are extensive and important among Tamang. Sets of clan brothers or acho-ale not only usually retain close bonds among themselves (even though they can also be caught up in bitter disputes) but also with their sisters; brothers are responsible for supporting sisters should they return to their natal homes.

The mutually supportive relations among brothers and sisters are evident in a series of continuing ritual obligations, the expression of which begins at the time of a boy's tonsure. Further, every year sisters return to their brothers' homes at the time of the celebration of *tihār* (Tamang *tiwār*), when they assure the well-being of brothers through gifts of whiskey, food, and blessings; brothers reciprocate with offerings of money. Sisters who marry away from the village also must return once a year in order to offer sacrifices to a local earth divinity who can afflict those who leave the village. At death, moreover, sisters have special mourning obligations toward brothers and offer special gifts of food to their dead clan brothers and sisters; brothers for their part are sponsors for the memorial death feasts of divorced or unmarried sisters. Brothers are the first to light the cremation pyres of brothers and sisters.

Busing, ananenchon, and acho-ale affirm relations not only through common clan membership but through marital exchanges: their children should properly marry, and they are respectively parents-in-law for their siblings' children. Moreover, mother's brothers have special obligations to "expel" the grief of their sister's children at the time of deaths. March has described the importance of this relation among Tamang:

> The most crucial relation a woman must maintain is that with her brother(s). The tie between Tamang cross-sex siblings is the balance point from which all sociality hangs. In the relation between Tamang sister and brother are counterpoised the forces of patrilineality, which dictate clan membership, and those of cross-cousinhood, which determine potential marital relations. The bond between cross-sex siblings simultaneously stems from shared descent and foreshadows subsequent marriages. (1984:731–32)

Ritualized ties between brothers and sisters reflect principles of mutual protection and nurturance. Sisters, like mothers and daughters, care for their brothers and support them in an affection uncomplicated by cross-clan affiliations. One shaman, in a fashion similar to other men, regularly recalled the affection his sisters showed him when he was attacked by ancestral spirits and the special gifts they gave him to effect a cure when he was morbidly ill. Sisters regularly weave for brothers and are regular visitors to their homes. Brothers in return often aid sisters materially.

The dual affiliations of women to natal and marital clans receive symbolic condensation in the obligatory property that a woman receives from her natal home after marriage. As I noted, all daughters-sisters when they marry must be given a hoe, sickle, and brass bowl. The hoe and sickle are used by their husband's *mhā* (sisters' husbands) to clear her cremation site and the brass bowl is used by the woman to wash the faces of her dead parents and her siblings if the latter are daughterless. Thus, the hoe and sickle mark the transference of the obligation to perform her death rites from her natal to her marital clan, and the bowl marks her continuing obligations to, and associations with, her natal kin.

Women are empowered in significant ways through these dual associations and become mediators in most aspects of life, moving more easily than men across the formal oppositions of society. Women occupy a privileged position in negotiations and communications upon which all intercourse depends. Their centrality, though, is most obvious in the exchanges of food and drink which are integral in all aspects of social life. All hospitality is ritually managed by women who, as March recounts, honorifically serve food and drink:

> In general, hospitality is offered by the head woman of the household in her capacity as coparcener of the family's estate and exchange obligations. Her responsibilities are most explicit in formal hospitality and on ritual occasions, when she personally assembles and places offerings (whether or not she has cooked them herself) before the honored guests or divinities. The gestures, body movements, and language that accompany the hospitality are highly formalized, and they evoke some of the basic imagery of hospitality for both Sherpa and Tamang. In particular, offerings should be made with the right hand extended, the left hand touching the right elbow, body and head inclined slightly forward. Honorific, even archaic language should be used. (1987:360)

The prowess of women as brewers of beer, distillers of whiskey, and managers of commensality is highly respected and recompensed. All major social rites include the formal designation of a woman known as *chhangma*, who acts as official hostess and organizes the care of honored guests. Women are as much empowered as subordinated in their mediatory position. They act in the fulfillment of the ideals of exchange and thus cannot be reduced to objects of trade on the level of social action, even though the marriage system can be described as a system of exchange in which women move residentially between patriclan segments (March 1979).

Women not only derive power from their mediatory position, they retain a certain autonomy in their husbands' homes. Women often bring other personal wealth along with the obligatory hoe, sickle, and brass bowl. Although sons inherit house, fields, cash, and other major property, daughters receive variable amounts of movable property depending on the wealth of their natal kin: silver, gold, and bronze jewelry, copper and bronze housewares, money, cloth, chickens, goats, cows, and buffalo. Even when the gifts are minimal, women regularly recount how a small amount of traditional property or *dso* increased significantly under careful management (March n.d.). Moreover, wealth literally and figuratively "sits" with women once they become members of their marital homes. As a household accumulates cash, it is regularly converted to gold or silver jewelry. This wealth when added to that which a woman brings in marriage forms the capital reserves of households and is used as collateral when they secure loans. Women often control a household's capital resources, and even the village headman would beg cigarette money from his wife if he was, for example, heading to a meeting. Furthermore, women are coequal with men in the management of the household and have direct involvement in the consumption and distribution of household production. Labor is highly valued, and daughters are directly remembered for their labor with annual allocations of grain. Women after marriage are far from subsumed in the household of their husbands. It is often personality as much as gender that structures domestic dominance.

Thus, a view of women's social resources tempers an image of Tamang society as strictly patrifocal and concerned with patriclan continuity and an exchange among men. The reductive developments of alliance theory are inadequate even from an androcentric perspective. Although men never act ritually as members of their mother's or mother's brother's clan and accentuate their affiliations with clan brothers with whom they reside and share property, they retain relations to their *shyang* or matrilateral kin and have obligations of nurturance to their sister's children. Reexamination of women's positions and resources in systems of restricted exchange complements the patrifocal view outlined above: society is more than opposed patriclans, and cross-cousin marriage implies more than exchange—it announces for women (and to a lesser degree, men) dual affiliations that allow unique powers, vulnerabilities, and vision. Moreover, through women the incompleteness, paradoxes, and ruptures of arbitrary exchanges are exposed.[12]

Difference, Gender, and Ritual Structure

Restricted exchange implies more than a field of possibility for the mobilization of relational resources, which produce social formations that in turn empower women. Restricted exchange is not just a theory of social order; it is the underlying orientation of Tamang in an encompassing sense and relates directly to the ritual field that both reex-

[12]As Meeker, Barlow, and Lipset have pointed out, exchange theory must take into account the "double and divided claims [of men] over women" (1986:27), that is, the relations of men with both sisters/mothers/daughters, which they classify as "primordial," and with wives, which they classify as "secondary" and sexual. The doubling and dividing implicit in marital exchanges, however, need not be reconstructed through men; among Tamang it is more readily articulated through women and in terms that are neither exclusively nurturant nor sexual, though both play in Tamang symbology in important ways.

presses this order and deals with its paradoxes. For the Tamang, exchange should work toward social closure and a cohesive totality—yet exchange itself depends on the ruptures of social differences and exogamy. The account of Ingkyal and Tikiri with which we began, then, has a special poignancy for the Tamang because it condenses the problematics of order and alliance. Ingkyal is brother-husband to Tikiri as she is sister-wife to him. This mythic solution is not possible in practice, and the breaches of social life are focused on women who leave their natal homes, siblings, and parents for their husbands' kin. Women's sufferings in separation, then, come to represent the facts of breach inherent in Tamang unions.

We are now in a position to identify a relation between what would usually be described as a social system and what would usually be described as a religious or ritual system. Because difference and exchange are the elementary conditions of both order and paradox in Tamang life, they are linked directly to problems of meaning. It is these philosophical ramifications of difference, exchange, and gender that are the subject for the chapters that follow on cosmology and ritual multiplicities. Much of Tamang ritual—particularly the sacrificial and the lamaic—attempts to recreate primordial orders, whereas other aspects of ritual performance play with paradoxes in those orders. To elaborate on these metarelations in the Tamang ritual system, we need to turn to the rituals themselves, but first I must introduce the pantheon and cosmos to which they relate.

4 Panoramas of Cosmic and Temporal Orders

In the rituals we see cosmology in action.

S. J. Tambiah, *Buddhism and the Spirit Cults in North-East Thailand*

Tamang encounter innumerable extrahuman beings in their lives and attribute a range of experiences to the activity of powerful Buddhas, divinities, spirits, and harmful agents. They occupy and order the cosmos as villagers know it. Relations among these beings and between them and humanity are essential to cosmic order and are integral to ritual performances. Lambus, bombos, and lamas without exception include representations of, and invocations or adjurations to, these beings in their rituals. Moreover, all rituals minimally if not centrally entail the communications of offerings and words from humans to these beings and thereby transpose idioms of sociality, particularly those of reciprocity, from human to divine and demonic domains. Before we turn to these ritual forms, especially the sacrificial ones, a panoramic excursion through the Tamang cosmos and an overview of ritual cycles will allow us to contextualize succeeding chapters, which even in their detailed attention to the constructions of particular practitioners can provide only a partial view.

In the reconstruction of cosmologies, we usually imagine maps, sacred geographies, heavens, hells, and the beings who inhabit them. Above all, we think of a cosmology as a firm ordering of space and of the juxtaposition of orderings of space, humanity, and extrahumans, and the forces that order relations in and among these fields. Although Tamang have no single, consistent classificatory scheme for the array of beings who inhabit their worlds—no inclusive texts, no totalizing iconographic paintings, no final formalized lists of beings—it is possible to uncover a logical ordering of space and of the beings who inhabit it from the structure and placement of ritual spaces, iconographic representations, and the words and acts of specialists and nonspecialists.

All practitioners construct altars (*brangke*) housing images of the Buddhas, divinities, or evils depending on the rite. Kneaded *tormo* (white rice dough images) are forms and bodies (*go*) of Buddhas and divinities; *mhingo* (black millet images) and *linga* (rice dough images) are those of evils. In many villages *gombo* or permanent temples of the Buddhas house clay statues and paintings of the Buddhas. Lamas possess books, iconographic paintings (*thangku*), iconographic cards (*tsaklhi*), and small statues (*ku*) of the beings of the lamaic cosmos. Many of these beings have origination accounts (*ṭhungrap-kerap*), which are recounted in ritual recitations or colloquially in less formal contexts. Some are well known with graphic representations; others are vaguely known.

Classes of Beings

Tamang invoke an endless effusion of beings, some of whom they share with Nepalese Hindus, Tibetan Buddhists, and other Tibeto-Burman groups.[1] One of the dynamics of Tamang cosmology is its inclusiveness. Tamang practitioners attempt to incorporate all beings in their ritual attentions to make sure that none is left out; beings denied become, like humans, prone to hostile responses. The tendency to view the array of beings stratigraphically, that is, according to the historical origins of various beings, should be resisted. Many beings in the cosmos may have originated in the languages and cultures of neighboring groups with whom Tamang have had intensive relations over the past centuries. Yet to prestructure their cosmos in these terms suggests that it is fragmented into indigenous Tamang, Gurung, Newar, Hindu, and Tibetan sectors when it constitutes a whole governed by a distinctive cultural logic. Ghostly shades or village divinities are no more or less "Tamang" than regional "Hindu" divinities or "Tibetan" Buddhas; thus, the concretized entity "Tamang" reasserts its elusiveness.

The problematics of classifying beings according to criteria of origins

[1]For relations to the Tibetan pantheon see Tucci (1949), Waddell ([1895] 1972), Beyer (1973), and Nebesky-Wojkowitz (1975). The *sangkye* no doubt relate to the Tibetan *sans-rgya*, the *la* to *lha*, and the *noppi-nottsen* to *gNod sbyin* (Jäschke [1881] 1972:571, 598–99; Tucci 1949:717; Beyer 1973:293–94). Tamang include a host of other named beings shared with Tibetan groups like *tsen* or *btsan*, *du* or *bDub*, *lu* or *klu* (Nebesky-Wojkowitz 1975:605, 616, 625, 634; Tucci 1949:717; Beyer 1973:292–99). For relations to the Gurung pantheon see Pignède (1966), and for relevant Indo-Nepalese correlates of Tamdungsa *masān*, *bir*, *bokshyi*, and a host of other minor spirits and divinities, see Stone (1976:57).

becomes apparent when we look to the prominent village divinity *shyihbda*, a divinity whom Tamdungsa villagers share with many other western Tamang. Several different perspectives that confound syncretic approaches can be brought to bear on the meaning and origins of Shyihbda. Shyihbda undoubtedly relates to the *zhi-bdag* or lords of the soil of Tibetan tradition, but Tamang also call Shyihbda, *siwa* or Shiva, a focal Hindu divinity in Nepal; Tamang also use the gloss *nhakpo chhempo* for Shyihbda, which in Tibetan is an appellation for Shiva (Jäschke [1881] 1972:300). A further historical complexity is introduced when we examine the meanings of Shiva among Nepali-speaking populations. An embodiment of Shiva in Nepal near Pashupatinath, a celebrated Shiva site, is referred to as *kirãteshwār* or Kiranti god; Kiranti is a term applied to the Rai and Limbu of eastern Nepal and more generally to all Tibeto-Burman groups in highland Nepal (cf. Allen 1981).[2] Moreover, it is not a farfetched conjecture to suggest that Pashupatinath may have evolved into its present form from another autochthonous divinity. The historical origins of Shyihbda then are highly problematic and can only be understood in terms of dynamic transformations that are continuing in contemporary Nepal. The intercommunications across the Himalayas have obviously been complex, and to approach Shyihbda as one thing or another masks a more intriguing reality, which we shall take up shortly.

Although the meaning of the beings of the Tamang pantheon cannot be attributed exclusively to their origins, divisions in the pantheon do reflect the social complexity of the Tamang world. Just as Hindu Nepalese, Newar, Gurung, Tibetans, and other groups are part of their social field, likewise hosts of beings associated with other peoples are realities in Tamang ritual life. Divinities and harmful agents emanating from the south and associated historically with Indo-Nepalese or Hindu groups are addressed in Nepali; those from the north and associated with Tibetans are addressed by lamas in Tibetan; other beings are addressed in archaic or colloquial Tamang. All beings are accorded offerings appropriate to their associations.

Similarly, it is essential to avoid rigid distinctions between the Tamang cosmos and those of other groups who practice forms of Tibetan Buddhism. Following other studies of South and Southeast Asia (Dumont and Pocock 1959a; Obeyesekere 1963; Kirsch 1972; Tambiah 1970; Östör 1980), I am concerned less with conjectured disjunc-

[2] I am grateful to Harihar Acharya for pointing this out to me. The association is based on the ragged clothes and demeanor of Shiva, which are like the clothes of these hill dwellers.

tions between literate formulations and village ritual practices than with continuities between presumed levels. In other words, the Tamdungsa cosmos is not a garbled reflection of a pure Tibetan Buddhist pantheon, a pantheon that is itself often rendered as a degradation of original Buddhism. The particularities of the Tamang cosmos, in fact, suggest that it is very similar to those of the greater Himalayas and South and Southeast Asia. Neither history nor ethnography can present examples of religious systems that are purely Buddhist in the doctrinal sense nor of Buddhist cosmologies that do not include several types of beings. The multitude of beings recognized by the Tamang is an identifying mark of all forms of Mahayana and Vajrayana Buddhism in northern Asia as well as of Theravada evolvements of South and Southeast Asia. As Gombrich has remarked for Sri Lanka:

> Some Buddhists recognize this explicitly: one old monk said to me, "Gods are nothing to do with religion." Gods are powerful beings to be supplicated for worldly goods; Buddhism . . . is concerned with ethics, future lives, and release from worldly existence. An ordinary Buddhist layman is no more concerned to accept or deny the existence of some new supernatural being than a western layman is concerned to accept or deny the existence of some newly discovered type of nuclear particle or natural force. Both are just facts of life. (1971a:46–47)

Tambiah's (1984) study of Buddhist saints and cults of amulets points to a vibrant Mahayana-like dynamism in Thai religious life, one that has probably been true of Buddhism since its inception. This is not to deny that the Tamang have a different orientation toward the world than monastic renouncers of Tibet but rather to suggest that in the study of religious systems of the Nepal Himalayas it is best to avoid notions of a standard or a correct form of Buddhism or Buddhist pantheon and to recognize differences less as degradations than as variations.

Approaching the Tamang pantheon as a totality, one encounters all sorts of beings ranging from Buddhas who inhabit celestial heavens to nasty, stinging spirits who frequent local forests. These beings can be conveniently organized into several distinct types according to the ritual attitude Tamang assume:[3] *la* or divinities; *noppi nottsen* or harmful,

[3]Höfer suggests an alternative rendering of the pantheon as composed of an overlapping and hierarchical set of *la* and *lu*, *mán*, and *syimo* (1979:12). He positions *bir* and *màsā:n* to the side. The details of the Tamdungsa pantheon correspond well to his schema, but I have chosen to organize the pantheon according to ritual attitude.

harming agents; and *sangkye* or Buddhas (whom Tamang occasionally refer to as *la*). *Tsen* and *lu*, both ritually important, are, along with other comparable beings, intermediate categories and acquire particular inflection in Tamang imagination. Both embody characteristics associated with harmful agents and divinities. This is a tentative and heuristic classification based, as we shall see, on ritual orientations as much as on linguistic criteria. Although these categories overlap and there is considerable ambiguity, divinities and Buddhas are most often propitiated and harmful agents exorcised. Within these broad divisions are many subtypes, which we will consider. In ritual and common speech, Tamang most often use classificatory phrases like *la-lu*, *mhang-mhung*, and *shyingo-sanḍe*. The latter two are forms of what I have labeled *noppi nottsen* or harmful, harming agents, a classificatory term bombos use in invocation for evils in general.

These beings can be located in various spaces within the cosmos and give the cosmos affective form. From Tamdungsa, the cosmos extends out from earthly domains to removed heavens (*ne*) occupied by divinities, Buddhas, and harmful agents. Although Tamang ambiguously speak of divinities as occupying both their earthly sites and removed heavens, divinities have a clear linkage to worldly territories. These territories include familiar places in the immediate vicinity of the village as well as more distant valleys and peaks. Also tied to earthly domains are many types of harmful agents who, in contrast to divinities, roam freely but usually in circumscribed areas. Although the earthly domains extend in all directions, north and south (which correspond to up and down for the highland Tamang) are special reference points. Up and to the extreme north, over the high passes of the Himalayas, lies *ui same* "Same of the center" (Tibetan *bSam yas*), to which Tamang trace their ultimate origins and where many of the primordial events of Tamang lore took place. Down and to the extreme south of the Kathmandu Valley (*yambu*) lies India (*gyagar*)—also the home of mythic events and beings. Below this Tamang locate America and other distant areas that have recently entered their geographic consciousness. Specialists in particular are schooled in the recitation of place names along the trails north to Ui Same and south toward India, marking the sites of divinities and Buddhist temples.

Removed from the confines of earth are places especially linked to certain beings. Buddhas reside in celestial paradises far beyond the access of humans. Tamang also speak of places of the divinities (*lai ne*) that can refer either to sites on the earth's surface or to removed heavens in the high mountains. During rituals, bombos go to divine heavens, literally "go into the divine" (*lari ngyipa*) where they "reveal." The guardians of bombos and their ancestral spirits reside in heavens in the high reaches of the Himalayas referred to as *beyhul* or secret places. Although villagers encounter harmful agents on the trails and forest margins of the village, these agents are also associated with hellish spaces usually only accessible to bombos: places of the living, of the dead, and of confusion, distress, gossip, cannibals, closed mouths, and licentious sex.

The beings who inhabit these domains influence well-being, and thus villagers strive to retain relations with them all. Divinities and harmful agents intrude directly into everyday life and are responsible for well-being and misfortune, respectively. We will consider them first and then the Buddhas, who are less immediate in their worldly involvement but no less important. Although it is impossible to separate the forms of these beings from the rituals in which the forms are generated, this chapter concentrates on outlining their representations and their place in the cosmos.

Divine Domains

Tamang associate divinities with specific geographic sites extending from hearth and home, through neighborhoods, the village, regional hills and mountains, to distant, unknown regions. The most important divinities are those in the village and nearby hills and valleys. Other divinities, although named and occasionally propitiated, are less elaborated in Tamang cosmology. The divinities in two sites, *shyihbda* and *shyingmardung*, are thought to be most directly responsible for events in the village and are prototypical of divinities as a class of beings. They reveal their form and nature in large measure. Rites to Shyihbda include recitation of extensive lists of other divinities who are recognized with offerings along with Shyihbda. This confers on Shyihbda a superordinate position in the ritual recognition of divinities.

Village Divinities

Shyihbda and Shyingmardung are like royalty of Tamdungsa and reign over its immediate territory. They occupy separate groves in the village, which are protected from human disturbance and defilement. To cut trees, quarry stones, turn the earth, or contaminate these sites will unleash certain retribution in the form of disease or natural disaster for the violator or the village at large. The Shyihbda site is located on the upside of the village and the Shyingmardung on the downside. A relatively minor but structurally revelatory divinity, *kharta*, resides between them at a third village site.

In Tamang lore, once there was the earth, there was Shyihbda; Tamang refer to Shyihbda as the master-mistress of the soil. Shyihbda groves are found in most Tamang villages throughout the locale, and the permanent "staying place" of Shyihbda is a few hours' walk to the north of Tamdungsa. Villagers occasionally travel there to present sacrificial offerings through a privileged local sacrificer. Once before planting and once before harvesting, villagers transmit sacrificial offerings to the village Shyihbda. In the former, they urge Shyihbda to let showers moisten the soil so grain will blossom in profusion; in the latter, they request a bountiful harvest. Shyihbda governs natural forces that affect agricultural prosperity, suppressing earth, stone, and water, countering harmful agents, containing social discord, and, in general, protecting humans and livestock.

Shyingmardung, unlike Shyihbda, is tied specifically to residents of Tamdungsa and is not found in neighboring villages. If Shyihbda rules the earth and natural forces, Shyingmardung, although not divorced from natural conditions, is more closely linked to social stability. Thus it is invoked first at all large social rites. As one lambu remarked, "In all boys' tonsure ceremonies, in marriages, and in memorial death feasts, special offerings must be made first to Shyingmardung. . . . In one aspect, it is like a true-straight divinity; in another aspect, it is like a witch (*bokshyi*). It makes people shake, it makes people crazy, and it makes people vomit. If you make an offering of millet beer, nothing at all will happen." Shyingmardung also adheres to and troubles women who marry outside the village and others who have left the village for extended periods of time. These women must return once a year to offer sacrifices to Shyingmardung; other emigrants from the village make special pledges to this divinity before they leave. Unlike Shyihbda, who controls territory in the village and out to the farthest known parts of the region, Shyingmardung influences only natives of the village.

In the same way that Shyihbda and Shyingmardung relate, respectively, to natural and social orders in the village, they complement each other in other aspects. As I noted, Shyingmardung is down the hill toward greater Nepal, and lambus must invoke Shyingmardung in Nepali language. Shyihbda, although of the earth, is up toward greater Tamang territory and Tibet, and lambus call on the principle aspect of

Shyihbda in archaic Tamang and the secondary, female aspect in Nepali. Crude stones mark out the altar of divinities, and both sacred groves contain two distinct parts: the male, which receives *karche* or white offerings of milk, and the female, which receives *marche* or red offerings of blood. Shyihbda's male aspect is invoked as *la ngyingpo* and the female as *lai mhiktung rhemo* (meanings are obscure). Shyingmardung's female aspect is referred to as *jala kanyā devi* or "virgin of the waters" and the male aspect as *suna pang ki mhāddheu* or "the golden winged great god," linking Shyingmardung to water and air in contrast to Shyihbda, who is tied to the earth. Although both have male and female aspects, rituals focus on the male aspect of Shyihbda (who, though he does not take blood offerings, is not vegetarian and is offered meat) and on the female aspect of Shyingmardung. The former receives a black, barren she-goat and the latter a black he-goat. Both divinities can be protective or afflictive; however, Shyihbda is more predictable and protective and Shyingmardung more uncertain and afflictive. Although no explicit mythology links these two divinities together, it is apparent that they encode a set of contrastive features that articulate significant dimensions of Tamang experience (see Figure 5).

Kharta, the third village divinity, continues this structural logic—potentially interminable—by standing in complement to the very oppositions marked in the other two divinities. Kharta, whose site is geographically between Shyihbda and Shyingmardung, receives only white karche offerings, and villagers release sexless chicks unharmed as offerings.

The contrasts clearly evident in these focal village divinities are certainly extensive; however, they are not entirely inclusive. The pantheon as it continues down into the village and out into the region elaborates

SHYIHBDA	SHYINGMARDUNG
MALE (female)	(male) FEMALE
(karche) MARCHE	(karche) MARCHE
receives a SHE-GOAT	receives a HE-GOAT
UP the hill	DOWN the hill
EARTH (air-water)	(earth) AIR-WATER
ARCHAIC TAMANG (Nepali)	(archaic Tamang) NEPALI
PROTECTIVE (afflictive)	(protective) AFFLICTIVE

Figure 5. Structure of Tamdungsa divinities

other significant features. Moreover, new divinities are created, those of other peoples and regions added, and old ones transformed. This set of village divinities, though, exemplifies an attempt by the Tamang to temper the artifacts of experience—which are always on the verge of fragmenting—into a logical and measured order.

Neighborhood, Clan, and Household Divinities

Shyihbda and Shyingmardung may be prototypical of the divine, but they are by no means the limits of the Tamang pantheon, which, as I noted, ranges geographically and socially inward to neighborhoods and households and outward to the region and the greater cosmos as the Tamang know it. In Tamdungsa there were six neighborhood divinities all basically of the same form as Shyihbda and Shyingmardung and with male and female and karche and marche aspects. Only those living in the immediate vicinity of these sites worried about calendrical recognitions. In all household rituals, practitioners must also remember a set of divinities associated with the structure and the stability of the house. Lists vary somewhat, but one lambu invokes the following set:

> Let's offer incense to the outside gods!
> Let's offer incense to the inside gods!
> To *gomsri rāja* the door god,
> To *dādung ḍolmo* the pillar god,
> To *elen dewa* the hearth god,
> To *gunsro ḍolmo* the fire god,
> To the drying basket god,
> To *hosal bāri* the wood god,
> To *phintri lamo* the mainbeam god,
> To *kuman ḍolmo* the sky god,
> To twelve supports of the earth,
> To *tsara-nhara* the water god,
> To *eleng lengen* the rock god,
> To *damji ḍolmo* the air god.

Although some of these divinities apparently relate to nonspecific elements—water, rock, air, sky, and earth—they refer to specific manifestations in the house: water jugs, walls, the sky above, and the earth below. These minor divinities protect the house and assure its stability and productivity.

Invoked in the same lists as these divinities are the supporting divinities of the clan of the household head. In Tamdungsa most supporting divinities carry the protective paraphernalia of lamas—a future-telling book, a hand drum, a golden thighbone trumpet, and a clear-beaded rosary—and wear Buddhist headdresses and protective lamaic charms. All members of a clan share a common supporting divinity (*tembe la*), but these divinities are propitiated by households or individuals only with the first fruits of harvests.[4] Bombos call down the blessings of these divinities in a variety of contexts. Not all supporting divinities take the form of lamaic protectors. Some clans have a more fearsome protector imagined to be a hunter armed with bows and arrows.[5]

Regional and All-Nepalese Divinities

Tamang ritually attend to divinities of the four directions, all of whom have specific groves or temples in somewhat distant places but are thought to be influential in the village. Tamang can ritually attend these beings in the village either by constructing temporary altars or by traveling to the primary site of the divinities much as they on occasion sacrifice to the local manifestation of Shyihbda and at other times make offerings at the principal site. During the year, Tamang also sacrifice to Durga in the all-Nepalese festival of *dasaĩ*, and to Bhimsen and Kali on the occasion of small Dasain in March-April. In invocations, lambus and bombos list numerous other divinities of the high peaks of the Himalayas, low valleys of the region, and of greater Nepal and Tibet. Most of these are simply listed in chants and lack specific mythic or iconographic elaboration. Tamang list these divinities because of a ritual compulsion to be as totalizing as possible and to mark out in a sacred geography the whole of the world as they know it.

Some of these more distant divinities, however, receive direct attention as the objects of pilgrimages and festivals at which Tamang from throughout the region, sometimes along with other ethnic groups, congregate for revelries. Tamang regularly attend festivals in the immedi-

[4]There was one exception to this general pattern, the village celebration of the supporting divinity of the Himdung, which was less a celebration of the divinity than an elaboration of the themes of clan exogamy and incest (see chapter 3).

[5]These are called *ḍabla*, who in Tibetan formulations is the "'enemy god' . . . those deities who are believed to be especially capable of protecting their worshipers against enemies, and to help them to increase their property" (Nebesky-Wojkowitz 1975:318). According to Höfer, dabla among Tamang is "armed with bow and arrow, roams in the forest and since he is Lord of the game every successful hunter owes him sacrifice" (1971b:18).

ate area and try to attend more distant and famous festivals several times during their lives. Most important to Tamdungsa villagers were festivals on the hillock above the village, on a high peak and promontory in the region, one at the confluence of two rivers near the base of the village, one in the bazaar town, and one in a nearby Gurung village. Tamang attend these as much for the commensality, dancing, singing, and visiting that mark these all-night affairs as for other explicitly ritual ends. Several festivals in fact have no overt recognitions of divinities but bring villagers in contact with Tamang from throughout the region. It is from these festivals that couples commonly elope. Tamang also embark on pilgrimages to such famous sites as Gosainkund and Dubche in the mountains, Pashupatinath, Bauddha, and Swayambunath in the Kathmandu Valley, as well as other less prominent regional sites. On most of these occasions, Tamang accompany their own practitioners (usually bombos but sometimes bombos and lamas), and they ritually approach and thus incorporate regional and all-Nepalese divinities into their own symbology. Overall, however, these distant divinities are not active forces in local events. It is the divinities of house, neighborhood, village, and the immediate region who impinge on everyday life and constitute a divine society to whom Tamang have regular obligations.

Harmful, Harming Agents

Counter to the ranks of divinities who inhabit the world from hearth out through the cosmos range the banes of humanity, a society of harmful, harming agents who hamper, derange, sicken, and destroy at every juncture. They inflict villagers with everyday misfortunes and diseases. Like divinities, harmful agents hail from the various locales and social arenas that make up Tamang experience and reflect a diversity equivalent to that of the divine. These harmful agents, though, in contrast to the divinities—who can be made protective—are always and purely afflictive. There is some ambiguity, though, associated with the harmful agents just as there is with the divinities. Some harmful agents (*māpon*, tsen) can be protective. Moreover some of the evil spirits in Tamdungsa are divinities in other villages. This ambiguity is borne out when lambus mold white dough images (tormo) of some evils along with black dough images. In some villages, evil spirits can be upgraded and become like divinities. Harmful agents include the local shyingo or shades and the regional mhang-mhung or evil spirits, both of whom are the dead who are not reborn but adhere to human society and pester villagers with all manner of afflictions. Completing this chaotic society of fiends are several other idiosyncratic evils and a set of rarified evils whose presence is universal.[6]

The members of this malevolent group are of the same world as divinities and humans, but their exact whereabouts, numbers, and forms are less specifiable. They come in irregular groups—alone, pairs, threes, fours, sixes, nines, in hordes joined in all varieties of ad hoc arrangements. They are always there but in hidden or ambiguous places counter to the fixed sites of divinities who are associated with determinable spaces. *Nakhle mhang,* for instance, originated in India, traveled to Tibet, and now wanders, constantly threatening all places, never going and never staying. Like all harmful agents, Nakhle Mhang hangs about in intermediate voids. Lambus chant to one aspect of this evil, small mouth or *khai chung*, as follows:

> They say you come bashfully,
> They say you come dishonored,
> They say you come from hiding behind the door.
> They say you come from hiding in the nook of a bamboo divider.
> They say you come from the base of the house pillar.
> They say you come rumoring behind.
> They say you come rumoring in front.
>
> . . . . .
>
> Like the divided forehead of the deer,
> Like the forked tongue of the snake,
> Like the sliver under the fingernail,
> Changed like a greenfly [you] come,
> Changed like a butterfly [you] come.

Harmful agents hover around in midspace (*barkap*) and occupy heavens of confusion, gossip, licentious sex, closed mouths, open mouths, and the homeless.

Village shades and regional evil spirits are disjoined from human society through death but refuse to sever their attachments to humanity. They are, with one or two exceptions, those who have died premature or unusual deaths over the last several generations and thus cling to the world unable to achieve rebirth. Shades in Tamdungsa include a suicide, two homicides, three accidental deaths, several women who

[6]For the reader's ease, I use the glosses "shade" for shyingo and "evil spirit" or "evil" for mhang-mhung.

died in childbirth, people from distant villages who died while alone and wandering, and groups of dead witches (*bokshyi*) killed through sorcery. Shades also emerge when cremation is incomplete or when lamaic death rites fail to separate the shadow-soul of the deceased (*bla*) from human society. Also, those who are avaricious during life or disquiet about their worldly possessions at the time of death are likely to become shades. Witches who jealously crave the well-being of others likewise become shades when they die.

Shades roam the village and hang about in intermediate and undomesticated spaces. They lie in wait at crossroads, in open places, in stands of trees, in gullies and gashes in the surface of the earth, at the borders of the village, on cliffs, up in trees. Shades can come creeping up behind people or confront them boldly face to face. They prowl nocturnally, and Tamang (as much to embolden themselves as to scare the shades) shout and sing boisterously when they walk through the village at night. When Tamang return from outside the village, they construct symbolic barriers of stones and branches to keep shades and evil spirits from following them. In the same general category of village shades are the shades of neighboring Gurung, Newar, Bahun, and particularly the spirits of untouchable women who commonly attack Tamang children.

Once in the clutches of ghostly shades, people suffer from symptoms associated with the deaths of those who became shades. One lambu listed the following set of troublesome village shades:

"*Pitong khyuyu* (the old woman of Pitong). She hung to death in the Kharta site many generations ago. Another stays with her, Grandfather Balam. She died by hanging, and he cracked his head open on a rock. He causes headaches. They are joined together there in the Kharta grove.

"*Chhimi ḍuna*. This one causes the heart to sting. It can make you vomit. She died in childbirth and attacks women in childbirth. There are three of them; they all died in childbirth and were of the same clan. Anyone can expel them, but you must be careful. First, you only promise to feed them. If you expel them while the woman is giving birth, she will die. Later in the evening you give them cooked rice and an egg, then you cast the shades out.

"*Bashyai ble ki shyingo*. The whole body will ache. He was pulverized; he was murdered with large and heavy stones. After they killed him they threw him off a cliff. I was nine when they killed him. You need tobacco, some whiskey, and some fish. You call tobacco by its honorific name. You invoke the shade and tell him to go.

"*Ḍunḍe*. He was buried in a landslide. It makes your lower back and backbone ache in the extreme. You lean over like you were falling. This shade takes you along just like a landslide. It is no good. He was from the neighboring village and buried by a landslide. You must cut a chicken for him, cook up some rice, and give a flask of beer. You expel this shade in the evening.

"*Mlang guri*. He was a bombo and died in high pasture. He makes the heart sting, causes vomiting, and makes people rave; their bodies thrash about. The person gets very sick. He is not too much trouble; you just give him a cigarette and tell him to go.

"*Dar chhi*. This is the shade of Pemba [a local headman who was beaten to death in a dispute to the north of the village]. Your stomach gets huge and the breath becomes difficult. He died like that, they say. You give him an egg and whiskey: 'You were born in Tamdungsa. Your remains were brought from Kathmandu. Those who beat you were Lakpa, Ngyema, Mimar. After they beat you, you died. Release if you will, if you won't, I'll call [them].'

"*Mon nhurbu*. He died of a disease where none of the joints move. He was stiff and bent up. He could not move. He attacks humans and livestock. You just give him some rice and vegetables. You don't need any meat. He is easy to get rid of.

"*Ambla ble ki shyingo*. There are a whole bunch. They have joined together and adhered with Shyingmardung. They all died from disease. They were killed by the people of the village. Their names were written on paper, and the lama and bombo performed the exorcism where the paper is burned in the shooting flame of whiskey poured in hot oil. They were all witches, and now they are shades. They still cause harm and pain. First the wife died, then the two daughters, then the father died. This was thirty years ago. They were all relatives of villagers. You cut a chicken and give them some rice.

"*Karki teng ki shyingo*. They are a mother and a father. He was a wanderer, he came to the village up the hill and he died. He carried Shyihbda [that is, was a lambu] so when you expel him, you must also honor Shyihbda. You need a chicken and cooked rice. Shyihbda gets rice and incense. They cause serious disease to humans and animals. We do not know much about this shade. It is from another village, but those two houses up the hill throw it out once a month.

"*Serku wati shyingo*. This was about twenty years ago. The mother died of cholera, then the daughters, then the father and the son. They were witches. The daughters were very beautiful, but they were not allowed to go with the young men of the village. Their brother told them not to because other villagers called them witches. When they looked at anything, it would not give birth. If they watched a buffalo giving birth, the calf would die. I don't know what happened or what the villagers did but they all died. You give them a chicken and rice. They cause the stomach to hurt and the heart to sting. They make all the muscles ache [as in dehydration accompanying high and prolonged fevers]. Now there is only one witch in this village, an old woman Blacksmith. Witches are not given a chance in this village. We ruin them right away."

Thus shades, as in these examples, induce common ailments such as dysentery, headaches, backaches, heart burn, bellyache, distended stomachs, muscle pain, bone pain, chills, fevers, sore and irritated throats, conjunctivitis, general body aches, colds, loss of strength, flu, strained breathing, arthritis, and sometimes, severe and life-threatening troubles such as difficult childbirth.

Tamang, though, usually attribute the most serious afflictions to the fearsome regional evil spirits. Unlike shades (shyingo), which hide in the confines of the village, evil spirits (mhang-mhung) roam throughout the region. They swoop down from the high forests and soar up from the low valleys, causing severe sickness in humans and livestock and destroying the benefits of prosperity conferred by the divinities and Buddhas. Like shades, evil spirits all died painful and anomalous deaths: all alone, wandering, in the jaws of tigers, in a bed of stinging nettles, murdered, or from extreme terror.[7]

Lhai mhang is particularly frightening and comes in two aspects: one from the front and the other from the back. Villagers say that even mentioning this evil spirit will invite affliction, but one man related the following origins of the evil spirit when he was far from the village in Kathmandu. Everyday, two high-altitude herders set snares for game along a trail near their herding station, but someone always stole their catch. One day they hid and waited for the culprit, whom they caught. They then tied him to a tree and left. A year later when they returned to the same spot, they discovered a bleached white skeleton bound to the tree, which crumbled to a jumble of bones at the moment of their gaze. The two herders died instantaneously of fright. They became the aspect

[7]The evil spirits of the area where I worked were the following: *lhai mhang, thong mhang, pisku mhang, di mhang, tshota mhang, longai mhang, aktang mhang,* and, of course, *nakhle mhang*. Many are the spirits of deceased herder-hunter bombos and thus are close to mapon.

of the evil that comes from behind and brings violent chills and fevers, an aching and swelling stomach, swollen limbs, and icy cold extremities. The murdered man comes from the front and causes severe body pains particularly in the chest.

About ten evil spirits afflict Tamdungsa villagers and, like divinities and shades, reflect the diversity of social and geographic experience. Lhai Mhang, for instance, comes from the forested mountains above the village and is thus addressed in Tamang language and presented appropriate offerings. *Yambui mhang* or the Kathmandu evil, on the other hand, is exemplary of those that come from below and consists of seven virgin sisters who died of polio, vomiting, and dysentery and who came from a temple in the Kathmandu Valley. They now attack children in Tamang territory. Yambui Mhang wanders up from the Kathmandu Valley and is thus addressed in Nepali and given offerings appropriate to city dwellers. When this evil spirit is thrown out, lambus offer things pleasing to Newars and tell it to return to the south.

In addition to the shades and evil spirits, rarified evils—often also referred to as mhang if not by their names—are a constant presence, alighting anywhere to disable all and everyone. Nakhle Mhang—known to lamas as *mhiga ḍumdo*—is the most generalizable evil known to Tamang. It is, in large measure, prototypical of all evils, much as Shyihbda is of all divinities, and I will discuss it at length in the next chapter. Born in India, it travelled to Tibet and was expelled south into Tamang territory. Tamang are continuously compelled to appease it and send it on the trail back to its place of origin in India. Lamas cast out two other rarified evils who devitalize well-being and are found universally: a cannibal fiend with three heads and a lusting evil with a large red phallus. Tamang associate all three of these rarified evils with generic malaise rather than with specific ailments. Another prominent cosmic evil is *mhamho*, the mother agent and carrier of all manners of disease. According to Tamang lore, Mhamho used to catch the children of humans and feed them to her own children. A Buddhist hero (*guru rhimborochhe*) kidnapped and hid Mhamho's children and did not return them until she promised to cease to eat the children of humans and to consume only human pollutions: snot, spittle, dirty water, and garbage.

This accounting of classes of evils is not by any means complete, and to shades, evil spirits, and rarified evils we can add a host of other specific evils such as bombo-like spirits (mapon), who carry weapons and drums, have hair knots, wear old clothes, and with dogs sneak down from high secret places (beyhul) to eat nectar and to fish in the river valleys. Tamang can hear them drumming at night; sight of them means certain death, and even their scent can cause severe illness. Other evils are spirits of the evening, planets that have inauspicious influences, and all kinds of named evils: *masān, lut, du, shyingmon-brābon*, and others. All these evils contort the proper forms of sociality, an issue addressed in succeeding chapters.

Lu, Tsen, and Other Ambiguous Spirits

Several beings in the Tamang ritual field are accorded recognition like that accorded divinities, yet, they sting humans like harmful agents and thus retain an ambiguous position. Lamas and lambus regularly propitiate *lu*, beings who live in the earth and are associated with water; Tamang imagine them to be amphibian or reptilelike but humans cannot see them.[8] Lu lie in wait for humans in unclean places and plague them with sores, rashes, goiters, and sometimes stomachaches even though they have received offerings. As one specialist explained, "When it cannot get food, it stays where people defecate. You only find out that you have been bitten when sores appear. You do not know immediately. Lu do not know humans. When it gets nothing to eat it goes to where we defecate, where we urinate, and where we wash our hands. Not knowing us as those who have already given food, it bites. After it stings us like that, it knows it will get another offering. After it is fed, it goes to its own place to stay." Every house has a special receptacle to hold offerings to lu.

A horde of other spirits occupy intermediate positions in the cosmos and have a particular importance in shamanic ritual. Chief among these are tsen or midspace sprites who reside in high-altitude passes, promontories, cliffs, and peaks. Tsen, like lu, can be nonharmful or they can sting; humans "honor" tsen as they honor divinities rather than "throw out" tsen as they do harmful agents. Also important in the shamanic repertoire are *lenṭe* and *shyultu* or the spirits of deceased bombos, who attack like shades but only their own lineal descendents. If honored they become allies of bombos and accomplices in shamanic forays into hidden heavens. Bombos also invoke *phamo* (guardians), *lashye khaṇḍangmo* (female furies), *khyung* (a primordial, fierce bird), and other beings in their recitations, all of whom we will encounter in detail in the discussion of shamanic soundings.

[8]There are lu (called *jalgini, nāgini*) in the Kharta site, and each house has its attached lu.

The Buddhas

The Realms of the Buddhas

Overlooking this world of humans, divinities, and harmful agents are the Buddhas (sangkye), who occupy the highest and most honored positions in the Tamang pantheon. Although they reside in removed, otherworldly heavens, their worldly presence can be detected during rituals through shimmers visible on the dough forms that lamas mold for them to embody. Mythically they imposed order in the cosmos through oaths (*damla*), and from them power (*wang*), long life (*tshe*), and other immediate blessings ultimately issue. Buddhas do not, however, intrude into everyday life the way that divinities and harmful agents do, and their influence, although worldly, is both more universal and removed. Small temples (gombo) dedicated to them are found in many villages, usually sitting high on hills and promontories, where images of the Buddhas peer down on the village with its human, divine, and malevolent residents much as the Buddhas in their removed heavens survey the worlds below.

Primordial Buddhas brought original order to the cosmos through oaths as in the following version of creation, which lambus chant when they expel Nakhle Mhang: After rocks, earth, and grass took hold in water, a cosmic tree grew up. From the branches and flowers of this tree Buddhas emerged in the four directions.

The Buddha from within
Bound an earth oath to the earth
A rock oath to the rock
A water oath to the water.

After binding water,
Oaths to those who move and feel were bound.
The male and female of humankind were oathbound.
The females of humankind were oathbound
Within the mountain *lapsang karpo*.
They were oathbound to stay
In the *lo ḍemo* river.
The males of humankind were oathbound
Within the mountain *lari*, within the hill *ganrhejung*.
They were bound to stay in the hill *sati*.

A mouth-oath, a heart-mind oath
To exchange in marriage,
To exchange hearts and minds,
To exchange mouths,
Within the nine territories was clasped round.
In the year of the mouse,
When the oath to exchange in marriage,
To exchange heart-minds,

To exchange mouths was bound,
An oath to the four cornerstones [of houses] was bound.
After fixing the four cornerstones,
After house and fields were made,
Oaths to sons and daughters were bound.

The creation continues until grain and domesticated animals were given to the care of humans.

Sprouts rose up in the air.
Flowers' buds burst forth in profusion.
Grains by the thousand were placed.
Prosperity in grain, abundant wealth, resiliency
Like a rounded hill of blessings stayed.

Along with binding productive order into the cosmos, Buddhas and *guru rhimborochhe* (Tibetan *Gu ru Rin po che*) in particular brought formerly autonomous divinities and harmful agents under the sway of Buddhist order. One lama explained that since their conscription to Buddhist oaths, divinities are like ministers to a king bound to carry out the orders of the Buddhas.[9] Buddhas likewise entwined harmful agents in oaths, and thus these evils should be without influence.

This containment and suppression of divinities, harmful agents, and human society within Buddhist purview is reflected in *mhane* (small stupa) or Buddhist earthen-stone monuments, which are found throughout Tamang territory. Lamas have erected these monuments on peaks, promontories, passes, and village sites. They are often found in close proximity to, or on top of, the sites of local earth divinities, thereby stressing the preeminence of Buddhist order over autochthonous powers. Lamas construct these monuments according to the basic patterns of greater Buddhist formulations and thus infix an elaborate design onto the earth (see Snodgrass 1985). Attention to this design by Buddhologists and others, although revelatory of greater Hindu-Buddhist iconography, often neglects the most immediate and dominating feature of these works. For the Tamang or for that matter for any other passerby, these works proclaim the ascendancy of Buddhas and Bud-

[9]Dough images or tormo of tamed divinities and harmful agents are arranged on the sides of the central images of the Buddhas on lamaic altars. One local school of lamas places tormo of a fierce guardian (*gonpo*), a guardian *tsen*, a tiger devil (*ḍāmar*), *sintong*, six mountain divinities, and Shyihbda. All of these beings are under the oaths of the Buddhas and are arranged in positions secondary to the central images of Buddhas.

dhist dominion over the space they mark out. From the spires of these works and from alcoves in their sides the eyes of the primordial Buddhas stare out over the world of humans, divinities, and harmful agents, marking out earthly territory and the beings who inhabit it as ultimately within the confines of Buddhist legitimacy. This territory not coincidentally is coextensive with lands of the village. Villagers report that their ancestors erected the central village mhane to mark out their claims against those of other groups in the region.

Tamang Buddhas derive historically from Tibetan variants of Buddhism, and Tamang lamas possess texts written in Tibetan language. Yet lamas vary considerably in their ability to identify Buddhas according to textual formulations, and each has an idiosyncratic knowledge of Buddhist cosmology according to Tibetan (or for that matter Tibetological) standards. Lamas cannot "read" or translate the Tibetan language of their texts in ways familiar to us; for Tamang lamas and laity alike texts are the inscription of the words and oaths of the Buddhas, and although they are chanted in all lamaic ritual, they are not employed primarily as sources of knowledge about the cosmos or truth. Lamas acquire their knowledge from teachers, from their associates, and from their travels. Nonspecialists can make few if any specific iconographic identifications and for the most part speak only of the Buddhas (by various names) as a class of beings. In spite of such variations (and ignorance from the vantage of literate Buddhists and Buddhologists), lamas, lay singers (*shyepompo*), and specialists in chants (*gurpa*) share common lists of Buddhas, and through exegesis, rituals, and iconography, a regular place for the Buddhas in Tamang cosmology takes shape. Lamas construct altars housing dough images and display iconographic paintings of the Buddhas and other beings.

Tamang portray the Buddhas iconographically in a variety of poses: they appear in benign and meditative demeanors, in sexual union with consorts, or in fierce and terrific form. The terrific and the sexual, however, are controlled and channeled. Rampant, unrestrained sexuality is disruptive, and Tamang embody this form of sexuality in the rarified evil discussed above, which is the antithesis of the ordered and productive sexuality of the Buddhas. Likewise the fierce, which is present in the harmful agents and the divinities, is transformed to a new posture in the Buddhas. This fierceness is contained and becomes protective, adding a dimension of awful power to the reign of the Buddhas.

From the theoretically long lists of Buddhas—which appear in Tibetan renditions—local Tamang culture makes a selection. First, specialists recognize Buddhas in each of the five directions: north, south, east, west, and center.[10] Buddhas of each of the directions are known in several different manifestations or bodies. Tamang lamas focus on the western set of Buddhas: the celestial *hopame* or *nawathaya*, whose active or engageable form is *tsherpame* (see Tucci 1949:350); the bodhisattva or "would be Buddha" *chenreshih* (Snellgrove 1967:21); and the earthly or physical body Guru Rhimborochhe, the Tamang variant of the Sanskrit *padmasaṃbhava.* (Tamang also call him *guru pema.*) Tamang do not consciously link this western set; they treat each of its members individually. Their selection, however, probably relates to the fact that in Tibetan thought the western set is valued in the pursuit of immortality in life and in death and that Tamang lamas are above all performers of death rites. The western paradise is also the most fortunate domain for rebirth and is important in the *Tibetan Book of the Dead* (Evans-Wentz 1960; Rinpoche 1975). Tamang lamas do not offer these explanations, but their rituals are paratextual confirmations of these high-tradition formulations. In memorial death feasts, lamas pass the shadow-soul (*bla*) of the deceased to Guru Rhimborochhe, who passes it to Chenreshih, who acts as a guide and nurturing protector for the motherless soul. Chenreshih then passes it on to Hopame.

In Tibetan formulations, Hopame is "infinite light" and Nawathaya is "the Law, the absolute" (Tucci 1949:348), but Tamang lamas do no more than list their names and point out their images on iconographic paintings. Tsherpame or the active reflex of these Buddhas played an important part in Tamdungsa village life until recently and is still commonly invoked by lamas. Iconographically, he carries a "vessel of immortality" and in Tibetan schools was the means to "endless life": "The hope of the Tantric school to attain immortality through magic, alchemy or liturgy, contributed to his individuality and popularity with later Vajrayāna schools. The God of infinite life became the god of immortality; those initiated into his mysteries are rescued from death" (Tucci 1949:350). A golden image of Tsherpame graced the gombo of Tamdungsa until about twenty years ago when it was stolen. According to local lore, this image flew each spring to the plains of southern Nepal and returned with flowers and sweat on the brow. Every spring,

[10]Tamang list the five Buddhas of the directions from the center, through the north, south, east, and west as follows: *nhangba nhangjen, doyang dukpa, rhintsen jungla, dorje simpu, nawathaya/hopame*. For Tibetan equivalents see Waddell ([1895] 1972:349–53). The Tamang *dorje simpu* (Tibetan *rdorje-sems-dpa*) is the "adorned reflex" rather than "the celestial victor" of the eastern direction.

lamas paraded the image through the village, collecting grain for the benefit of the temple and communicating blessings of long life (tshe) to villagers. Chenreshih, in Tibetan renditions "the keen seeing lord, the great pitier and lord of mercy" (Waddell [1895] 1972:356), is known to Tamang in eleven-headed and thousand-armed forms—an all-embracing, all-seeing, and compassionate presence in human life. Lamas refer to him as mother (cf. Ortner 1978a:141–42; Paul 1982:132–50), and Chenreshih is focal in death rites. Finally, also emanating from the west, is the historic Guru Rhimborochhe, the most celebrated of the Buddhas, who in both Tibetan and Tamang forms embodies principles associated with the Buddhas in general. Around Guru Rhimborochhe resonate myths elaborating the meaning of the Buddhas in Tamang cosmology.

Multiform Guru Rhimborochhe and the Binding of Oaths

Guru Rhimborochhe, or Guru Rimpoche as he is known in Tibetan areas, is famous throughout the Buddhist Himalayas as the tantric adept who suppressed and subjugated territorial divinities and demons to Buddhist discipline. Although ancient Buddhas imposed orderly productivity in the cosmos, Guru Rhimborochhe represents the active power of oaths or damla in the order of the world for Tamang. Guru Rhimborochhe's central yet enigmatic place in Himalayan Buddhisms is recorded by many scholars, most recently by Paul, who has reassessed the legend of Padmasambhava in psychoanalytic terms; among Sherpas, he notes, "It is the duty of every member of the community to offer spiritual aid, support, and comfort to Guru Rimpoche, in his constant struggle to control the demons, through offerings and worship" (1982:152). Tamang lamas also accord considerable ritual attention to Guru Rhimborochhe; statues of him are central in Tamang gombo, and lamas prominently display his paintings on their altars along with his dough image. As one Tamang lama put it, "Guru Rhimborochhe is the least important of the Buddhas, but it was he whose oaths bound all the beings of the earth."

Local lore brings Guru Rhimborochhe into direct association with the region of Tamdungsa. He passed through the area on his way to Tibet from India, subduing a local mountain divinity, binding oaths, impressing his footprints in rocks, bending hills, and leaving hidden texts and ritual implements. In recent years, some regional lamas, under the tutelage of a Bhutanese teacher, have embellished these accounts. They claim that several rocks in the region, all in or near the sites of earth or mountain divinities, contain books with diamond and golden letters. Tamang lamas say that Guru Rhimborochhe now resides in a western heaven where he is taming cannibal fiends (*simbu*; Tibetan *srin-po*).

Not surprisingly, Guru Rimpoche or Guru Rhimborochhe, an ascetic adept, stands in the Buddhist pantheons of the Himalayas in much the same structural position as Shiva in the Hindu pantheon (see O'Flaherty 1973). Like multiform Shiva, Guru Rhimborochhe among other things oscillates from the ascetic to the erotic and from the tranquil to the fierce.[11] Snellgrove and Richardson have remarked on these apparently contradictory aspects condensed in one figure:

> Even in Tibetan Buddhism with its fantastic variety of theories and practices, *Padmasambhava* remains an unusual figure. He is the only main tantric divinity (and this is his chief function), who has the semblance of historical reality in a well-defined period. The other "historical" buddha is *Śākyamuni* himself, but he remains the recipient of simple prayers, whereas *Padmasambhava* in his divine manifestations is the centre of a number of tantric rituals. He appears as the "Gentle Master" (*Gu-ru Zhiba*), as the "Fierce Master" (*Gu-ru Drag-po*) when he is identified with the "Tiger God" (*sTag-lha*), which is a very early Tibetan divinity common to both Buddhists and *Bon-po*; he appears as the "Union of the Precious Ones" (*dKon-mchog spyi-'dus*) where he is manifest as the whole complex of divinities based on the set of Five Buddhas in their fierce and tranquil forms; he appears as the "Perfector of Thought" (*Thugs-sgrub*) in either a red or a blue manifestation with his entourage of attendant divine forms. (1968:171–72)

In Tamang iconographic renditions, which synchronize these contradictory forms, Guru Rhimborochhe is depicted according to standard Tibetan practice. In the central image, he carries a powerbolt (*dorje*) in his right hand and the vessel of immortality (*bumba*) in his left. The powerbolt for Tamang signifies the potency of the Buddhist word both in binding the world into order and in conveying absolute truth.[12] The

[11]Paul notes the following from one passage of the legend of Padmasambhava or Guru Rimpoche: "In this episode, Padma is presented as both ascetic hermit and erotic male; first he dismisses women with disgust; but he ends by falling in love and marrying the girl he loves, seizing her from a rival" (1982:168).

[12]Here I follow Snellgrove, who has given dorje the most comprehensive definition: "The term 'powerbolt' is my newly coined term for the Tibetan word *rDor-rje* (Sanskrit *vajra*), for which there exists no satisfactory translation in any European language. It is sometimes translated as 'thunderbolt' or 'diamond,' but both these translations are unsatisfactory, and

display of the powerbolt in lamaic lore is directly linked to the exposure of illusion and the revelation of the true nature of things (see chapter 8). The water vessel associates him with immortality. Flanking the focal image in paintings (*thangku*) and also his clay image in temples are two female figures whom Tamang—incorrectly from the vantage of formal Tibetan iconography—refer to as the wives of Guru Rhimborochhe. Villagers say that one wife was a Tibetan princess and one a Newar princess from Nepal.[13] In images peripheral to the central one, he appears seated with legs crossed, reflecting the principles of the meditative Buddhas, and in a terrific and destructive aspect linked by the Tamang to his suppressive powers. Tamang renditions of Guru Rhimborochhe suggest structured suspensions of a set of contrasts: male and female, ascetic and erotic, ferocious and tranquil, one and many. Guru Rhimborochhe, like Shiva, thus encompasses a full field of possibility out of which particular pantheonic manifestations appear as selections from the total symbolic field.[14]

Guru Rhimborochhe as a key tantric figure, then, stands in sharp contrast to the historic Buddha (Tamang *shyakya thupa*; Sanskrit *śākyamuni*) celebrated in Theravada, reformed Tibetan, and most Western formulations of Buddhism. Guru Rhimborochhe in contrast to the celibate historic Buddha marries and engages in sex and is in both meditative remove and terrifying worldly engagement. Where Shakyamuni reflects a unitary, renunciatory principle, Guru Rhim-

---

in any case the Tibetans usually employ different terms for these particular meanings. *rDorrje* is used in Tibetan in the sense of the ritual instrument which symbolizes divine power in its absolute indestructible form, and also in the sense of penis, specifically that of the yogin who unites ritually with his feminine partner. . . . But since the powerbolt alone represents divine power in its absolute indestructible form, it is identified in this kind of Buddhism with the supreme and absolute truth." (1967:33). The temptation in interpreting Guru Rhimborochhe or for that matter any of the symbology of tantric Buddhisms is to privilege the psychosexual as a rudimentary and unmediated reality. The powerbolt can literally signify penis in Tibetan traditions, but Tamang never made this equation. Although the sexual is obviously an important part of tantric imagery, it unfolds in a wider semantic field where sexual opposition and union convey more arbitrary cultural messages. It is as possible that the sexual became symbolic of the power of the dorje not the inverse; more likely the construction results from a dialectic.

[13]Tibetan history records that *Srong-brstan-sgam-po*, the first protector of Buddhism in Tibet, married one woman from China and one from Nepal. Tamang seem to have incorporated this event into the life history of Guru Rhimborochhe.

[14]This encompassing quality is not unique to Guru Rhimborochhe. A focal image in lamaic ritual is *shyihṭu* or the tranquil and the fierce represented by Tamang lamas as Buddhas in terrific aspect in the pose of sexual union (*yab-yub*) or as a tranquil blue Buddha with a white consort. Shyihtu is at once passive and fierce, meditative and active, one and many. Sherpa monasteries know *zhi-khro* as "the tranquil and fierce," encompassing forty-two tranquil divinities and four sets of fifty-eight wrathful divinities (Snellgrove 1957:229–32).

borochhe includes this principle and its opposite simultaneously. Although this symbolic tendency can be attributed to tantric formulations in general, the figure of Guru Rhimborochhe among Tamang takes on some highly localized features as well. Tamang do not view Guru Rhimborochhe only as a prototypical lama binding oaths and taming fiends; if one looks carefully at his iconographic representation, villagers say, one can detect a hair bundle (*rhalbo*), which is the mark of the bombo. Guru Rhimborochhe emerges as encompassing and hierarchically ascendant within the pantheon in much the same way that lamaic ritual, as we shall see, does in the ritual field.

Time and Ritual Life

Rituals can be understood as simultaneously activating these beings in Tamang imagination and responding to their existence. Rituals likewise create and respond to temporal schemes. Villagers propitiate divinities and protect themselves from the onslaughts of evils with calendrical regularity. Most life-cyclical rites also become attuned to the calendars. The prominent exceptions are incidental propitiations or exorcisms succeeding birth, death, or misfortune. Tamang refer to both the Hindu and the Tibetan calendars in their timing of ritual observances and synchronize these calculations to the oscillation of seasons. Rituals occur throughout the year; however, rhythmic alteration between a period of intensified ritual activity in a dry season and a period of relative quiescence during a wet monsoon season structure ritual life. The concatenation of Indic, Tibetan, and Tamang calendrical systems is organized into a synthetic temporal system that includes cosmic cycles, twelve-year cycles, years, two divisions to the year, months, periods of the waxing and waning moons, days and nights, and times of day.

The Twelve Years

On the grandest scale, Tamdungsa villagers invoke cosmic cycles drawn from Indic formulations. Lambus and bombos place themselves in the disintegrative age (*yuga*) of *kāli,* as in these two chants by a lambu and a bombo, respectively:

> In the disintegrative age of Kali,
> The curses of evil men may emerge,
> May they be diverted.
>
> Respectful greetings, Guardians!
> In the disintegrative age of Kali
> I have acquired a troublesome burden,
> I have acquired a distressful load.

Lamas, however, conceive the temporal position of humans in the cosmic cycles somewhat differently. This discrepancy reflects what has always been an articulatory distinction between cyclical Hindu notions of time and more linear Buddhist notions. One lama insisted, "People say that it is now the Kali age, but it's not; it's the pure and perfect age. At [a nearby confluence of rivers] the divinities have appeared; on [a nearby ridge] the golden book is coming out. Then after that one comes out [others] will come out. This is what it says in the Barju Lamtsen Book and it's turning out exactly right. Guru Pema (Rhimborochhe) bound everything to his oath." Villagers remain relatively unconcerned with cosmic fluxes or progressions, but they are attentive to the lower-level cycles of time that infix individuals and the course of their lives in cosmic mechanics.

Villagers locate events in the turn of twelve-year cycles derived from Tibetan calendrical formulations. They associate each year of these repeating cycles with an animal and count these cycles beginning with the year of the rat followed by years of the bull, tiger, goat, sky-dragon,

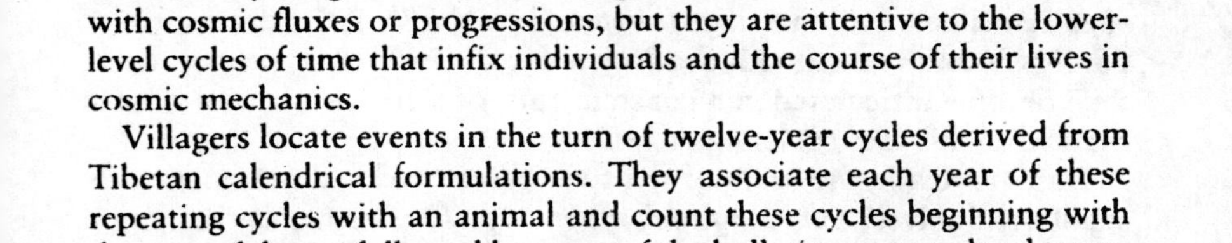

snake, horse, sheep, monkey, chicken, dog, and boar. All years have a potential for sympathetic influence. When bombos or lambus expel generalized evils, they protect their sponsors with invocations like this one: "May the inauspicious darting of the rat year be returned." Individuals are linked to particular years at birth. The animal year of birth provides the basis for the simple horoscopes that lamas derive from Tibetan manuals. Individuals reckon their ages and past events in terms of so many twelve-year cycles and of such and such an animal year. Moreover, passing through a twelve-year cycle marks the informal passage to adulthood. At roughly the age of twelve, a child develops a life-force (*so*), which renews in each succeeding twelve-year cycle. Further, Tamang do not perform full-scale mortuary rituals for a child who has not passed through a twelve-year cycle. The year of birth plays a final significance at the time of death, when the animal year of an individual's birth and that of the day of death determine the necessity of the performance of certain exorcistic rites and the prognosis of the deceased's horoscope.

Reference to these formal cycles situate individuals according to the regularized arrangements of years and astrological mechanics, but villagers also define the progression of life in life-cyclical rites beginning with purifications and naming at birth (*namchung*), continuing through the first rice feeding (*ken wāhpa*), tonsure for boys at age three, five, and/or nine (*chhewār*), which also has significance for sisters,[15] the giving of the first skirt to girls at age seven (*shyāma pimpa*), rites associated with marriage (*bhya* and *pe rhimba*), the death rites of parents,[16] and ending with death rites for the individual proper. Lives then become articulated in a constant turn of birth, death, and rebirth marked by distinct social passages.

Tamang divide the years of the twelve-year cycles into two ritually significant halves: *yharsung* and *mharsung*. The former is the period from the full moon of February-March (*phālgun*) to the full moon of August-September (*bhadāu*), and the latter is the period from the full moon of August-September to the full moon of February-March. Major divinities of the village are accorded recognition and a host of propitiations on the household level occur during both of these periods. Villagers recognize supporting divinities during both halves, and

[15]Chhewar articulates the tight ritual obligations of brother and sister and thus defines a boy's sisters in the social scheme of things at the same time that the rite focuses on the boy.

[16]This is particularly true at a father's death when it is most likely that an extended family will make a final division of property, if they have not already, and establish independent households.

some propitiate tsen during both halves although the propitiation is not necessary. Everyone protects against Nakhle Mhang, lu, and, if they have livestock, two other evils during both halves of the year. These formal calendrical divisions are linked with the fluctuations of the wet and dry seasons. Yharsung observances to Shyihbda, for instance, occur near the full moon of April-May and precede the rains. Mharsung observances fall in August-September and precede the harvest and dry season.

Tamang further separate the year into twelve lunar months. The months are named according to the Nepalese (*vikramāditya*) system, which is ritually structured by a four-month period of dissolution and regeneration (see Gaborieau 1982). This is also the official calendar of Nepal, and it is the most common referent for villagers. But the Tibetan calendar remains influential in the timing of various ritual events. In the past, villagers celebrated the Tibetan new year at the village gombo, and most major lamaic rites are timed according to the Tibetan calendar. Tamang refer to both calendars without apparent contradiction and recognize three new years: the Hindu, the Tibetan, and one they refer to as their own, which occur, respectively, at the beginning of April-May (*baisākh*), the new moon of February-March, and the full moon of January-February (*māgh*).

The lunar logic of the formal calendars gives significance to the new and full moon days, and villagers never perform heavy labor or any labor that disturbs the earth on these days. Moreover, villagers count the days of the month with reference to new and full moons; each day has an animal name drawn from the same series that mark the twelve-year cycles. The day after the new moon is the day of the tiger, and the days that follow are in the order of the years. Likewise the days after a full moon are counted from the monkey. Tamang also calculate the days of the month according to the Hindu calendar in which days succeeding the new and full moons receive ordinal names yielding two cycles of fifteen. Tamang name the seven days of the week with their common Nepalese names. Days may be auspicious or not for a variety of ritual and practical tasks. Exorcisms and propitiations are effective only on certain days of the month or week. Times of the day also have a significance in ordering the performance of all rituals. Practitioners calculate the position of the sun and the moon along with certain prominent planets before conducting exorcisms. Shades and evil spirits are both most dangerous and most accessible at night. Shamanic soundings always occur at night, whereas most sacrificial and lamaic rites with the exception of certain exorcisms and a rite performed in honor of the divinities (*satsi*) occur during the day or evening.

These temporal cycles are, in turn, adapted to the climatic fluctuations of the Himalayas. The continual movement from a dry winter season to a rainy monsoon patterns work and ritual life. The monsoon rains begin in force in May-June and increase in intensity and frequency through June-July, July-August, and August-September and then taper off into a dry season.[17] Intensive agricultural labor precedes these rains and continues through them well into the dry season when the main harvests occur. Plowing, fertilizing, preparing seed beds, planting, intercropping, weeding, and harvesting of maize, millet, rice, soy beans, mung beans, and other crops leave villagers scarce leisure from April-May through November-December. The dry season with intense sun and cooler temperatures, which begins in September-October, eventually allows villagers greater freedom after rice is harvested in November-December. They complete necessary but more incidental chores—repairing houses and fields, weaving, processing grain, collecting stores of firewood, making rope, traveling, and trading. Dry fields sit empty, yielding space for communal gatherings.

Moreover, the dry season means that stores of grain are high in direct contrast to the relatively lean months that precede the harvest. With as many as three-quarters of Tamdungsa villagers surviving on the margins of subsistence, the months from late February-March to July-August, when the first green ears of maize appear, are often severe. The dry season is the time for social rites and feasting. During this period, simple and elaborate obligations to feast increase; neighbors, affines, and friends from near and far drop by or are invited as guests. Trails that have been difficult to traverse become hard and dry; raging torrents turn to trickles. In these months, a typical household engages in as many as ten to fifteen memorial death feasts, five or more tonsure ceremonies, exchanges in association with marriage, pilgrimages, and festivals. All specialists are in high demand to complete recognitions of divinities and exorcisms of evils. The flux of wet and dry, labor and leisure, scarcity and abundance, social dispersion and reunion, and ritual quiescence and florescence pattern life significantly.

This alteration is formalized in the opposition of a dark month, when all rituals except cremations cease, and the period of the festival of *chhechu*, when all labor must cease. The former is the month of July-August at the height of the monsoon, when clouds enfold the village in a damp darkness and rains drench everything; the latter occurs in

[17]The months of the Vikramaditya calendar used in Nepal are lunar and do not directly correlate with the months of the Western calendar.

February-March in the midst of the cool, dry, season. One villager explained, "The divinities go into seclusion [during the dark month] and stay like that. They shut themselves in just as we close our doors at night and sleep. They perform austerities during this month." Demons, spirits, and shades roam unconstrained, and chaos is on the threshold of eruption. Immediatedly succeeding this cessation of ritual and dissolution of order are the regenerative sacrifices of lambus, the greetings of bombos to divinities, and the season of celebrations beginning with the all-Nepalese rites of *dasaĩ* and *tihār*, regional festivals, and soon followed by the round of social rites which regenerate relations in local society. *Chhechu* is a ten-day dance festival that occurs at the height of the dry season. This oscillation between two periods correlates with the formal calendrical logic revealed by Gaborieau (1982) for the Hindu calendar of Nepal.

A Permutable Pantheon

In summary, the cosmos extends from localized space to otherworldly heavens. The Buddhas and divinities run cosmographically in counterpoint to opposed harmful agents. Divinities inhabit worldly space from house and home to regional mountains, and Buddhas reside removed in celestial heavens. Harmful agents likewise range from local ghostly shades to universal evils like the cannibal fiends now being tamed by Guru Rhimborochhe. In contrast to Buddhas and divinities who are linked to specifiable sites, harmful agents steal about homeless and are inherently unstable. From another vantage the pantheon is structured according to relative benevolence and malevolence. The Buddhas are, in reference to humans at least, purely protective and never afflict them with hardship. Harmful agents on the other hand are purely afflictive and bring only misfortune and suffering. If properly respected, divinities protect; if forgotten or offended, they can afflict. Divinities, thus, retain an ambiguous nature. As a general principle the local and regional divinities and harmful agents have a more specific effect on human well-being than the more distant Buddhas, divinities, and rarified evils, who have more generalized effects. Village geography reflects this overarching cosmic scheme. The Buddhas housed in a gombo high on the hill look down on human and divine residences, whereas harmful agents roam in the margins of these fixed spaces.

One must be cautious, though, in reducing the pantheon to these terms even though an overview suggests this articulatory structure.

Each major class taken individually can include features of the total pantheon much as the Buddhas can contain ferocious and tranquil, celibate and erotic, and meditative and engaged features. Divinities, as we have seen, are inherently ambiguous and totalizing. Likewise, harmful agents begin to reflect the potential of the total pantheon. Some evil spirits have been historically upgraded to divinities, and others are formed like divinities into white-offerings/red-offerings, male/female, and protective/malevolent forms. The potentiality of each class, however, is never fulfilled, and the pantheon requires each class to be complete.

The cosmos, moreover, never resolves into a final totalizing image, for each practitioner approaches it from a distinct position, focuses on certain members of the pantheon, and establishes particular relations between humans and the extrahuman. Thus our overview remains artificial because, like the ritual field, there are only visions of the cosmos as created by different practitioners. Through the pantheon, then, we can introduce contrasts and relations among ritual domains, which we shall consider in succeeding chapters.

Major lamaic rituals, particularly memorial death feasts, feature the Buddhas in focal relief; even minor exorcistic rituals depend on the power and presence of the Buddhas, whose authority lamas incarnate. Villagers, in fact, honorifically refer to lamas during ritual performances as "sangkye" or Buddha. Central to lamaic altars and temples are images of Buddhas who preside over other secondary beings. Lambus, for their part, have special relations to Shyihbda and to Nakhle Mhang, and their rituals focus on either divinities or harmful agents who affect village life in an immediate way. Bombos have a special relation to distant mountain divinities and to beings associated with midspace between earth and sky. Their guardians are lente or shyultu—the spirits of deceased bombos who reside in secret heavens in the snowy reaches of the highest Himalayas; they also must honor tsen or midspace sprites. The different emphases of the practitioners are evident in differences in their altars, which recreate the worlds or places of the beings they encounter. Lamas' altars are raised high off the ground, bombos' off the ground but much lower, and lambus' are, with one exception, in or on the ground itself.[18]

These distinctions also figure in the chants that all practitioners recite when offering incense to Buddhas or divinities. Lamas first in-

[18]Lambus biannually perform a ritual called satsi, once in yharsung and once in mharsung. This rite requires a raised altar.

voke the celestial Buddhas and their western manifestations, proceed down through the high mountain divinities, and eventually arrive at the village and household divinities. Lambus work in the opposite direction, citing first the local divinities of village, neighborhood, and region and concluding their incantations with the names of the most distant, usually leaving out the Buddhas altogether. Bombos, like lambus, move from localized divinities to more distant ones; however, in contrast to lambus, they move more from high hill or mountain peaks whereas lambus stick more directly to earthly trails. As one lambu put it, "Bombos sing only the names of high hills and mountains, and lambus sing the names of all earthly places."

Although each practitioner ritually focuses on particular sets of beings and may refer to beings unrecognized by the others, it would also be a distortion to characterize sets of beings as exclusively lamaic, shamanic, or sacrificial. Lamas, lambus, bombos, and nonspecialists ultimately share a common cosmos and pantheon. Buddhas are not just lamaic; bombos and lambus invoke them and in fact derive some of their authority from them. Guru Rhimborochhe is not just the originator of powers exercised by contemporary lamas; bombos also ultimately trace their ritual authority to Guru Rhimborochhe, and for this reason bombos will not perform sacrifices with their own hands. Likewise lambus attribute some of their exorcistic practices directly to Guru Rhimborochhe; for some exorcisms, lambus are enjoined from killing sacrificial victims with their own hands. Likewise, Buddhist lamas ritually recognize divinities and harmful agents that are more properly the focus of sacrificial or shamanic ritual. There are not separate pantheons for each practitioner; rather, each specialist brings a special authority and attitude and has a selective vantage. I next turn to one such vantage, that of the lambu who sacrifices so that humans may prosper.

5 Sacrificial Ordination

> For if we know anything about sacrifice, it is this: every time the sacrifier sets in operation the sacrificial process, it is the satisfaction of his desire and the order of the world that are brought into play.
>
> Olivier Herrenschmidt,
> "Sacrifice: Symbolic or Effective"

In the origination account (*ṭhungrap*) that lambus must recite on the occasion of the ritual expulsion of Nakhle Mhang, the protoevil of Tamang imagination, two countervailing forces in the cosmos are starkly revealed. At Ui Same in Tibet, the first Buddhist gombo was being erected; all day long people built stone walls only to discover that at night the walls collapsed. This happened repeatedly, and they made no progress. The kings of all the directions then called on Guru Rhimborochhe to come and reveal the source of the degenerative forces that negated their every creative activity. He revealed that the destruction was the work of Nakhle Mhang. After proper offerings were placed and expulsive sacrifice conveyed,

> Longevity began.
> The gombo stayed.
> Gold stayed.
> Silver stayed.
> A rounded hill of blessings stayed.
> The good fortune of the earth stayed.

These counteractive forces, metaphorically condensed in the image of continual construction and collapse of walls, took form at the inception of the cosmos.

Before lambus narrate the incident, they recount the history of creation from a time when there was neither earth nor sky and proceed through the time of the formation of land in primordial water, the binding of oaths to men and women to exchange in marriage, the establishment of households and their fields, and the genesis of domestic prosperity. Well-being blossomed forth unhindered:

In the air sprouts rose up,
Flower buds burst forth in profusion,
Grains by the thousand were placed.
Prosperity of grain,
Abundance of wealth,
Strength of things stayed.
After strength of things stayed,
After foods of many kinds stayed,
Oaths to all [domestic] animals were bound.

At the very same time that human life-force (*so*) and long life (*tshe*) originated, the forces of degeneracy appeared to undermine and destroy:

From within India,
The four mhiga [Nakhle Mhang] originated.
The four mhiga came for all time to harm.
Came for all time.
At the time of eating and sleeping, they occurred.

Nakhle Mhang hampers and spoils human prosperity, as do all harmful agents. Lambus invoke Nakhle Mhang in the following terms:

They say you enter above the mothers of buffalo calves,
They say you enter above the mothers of cow calves,
They say you enter above mothers of goat kids,
They say you enter above the mothers of human children,
They say you enter the house and fields.
They say you enter the iron spike.
They say you enter abundant wealth.
They say you enter prosperity of grain.
They say you enter the strength of things.

Ritually Nakhle Mhang is a metaevil among the array of shades, evil spirits, and rarified evils who are constantly ready to afflict humans, their fields, their livestock, and their produce. Like all harmful agents Nakhle Mhang represents the forces of degeneracy that constantly threaten well-being; exorcism of Nakhle Mhang, as of all harmful agents, allows prosperity and good fortune to flourish.

Counter to these primordial forces of decimation are the divinities who, as we have seen, control the forces of natural productivity, social harmony, and the evils themselves. Although the Buddhas bound the potential for prosperity into this world through oaths, for all practical ritual purposes it is divinities like Shyihbda whom villagers call upon to procure well-being. To maintain conditions for the generation of prosperous essence in grain (*brui hong*), abundant essence of wealth (*nhorgi yang*), and resilient essence of things (*sehgi chut*) and to stem the forces of degeneration, humans must honor divinities at the same time that they throw out (*khlāpa*) evils in a continuous and repetitive round of sacrificial rituals.

Sacrifices assure regularized relations between humans and the divinities and harmful agents who inhabit and affect the immediate world in a direct way. Although lamas and bombos also recognize divinities and appease harmful agents and make offerings as an elementary part of their rituals, Tamang turn to their lambus—a sacrificial technician par excellence—for the regular and incidental sacrifices or offerings that propitiate divinities, expel harmful agents, and keep a tense balance in cosmic forces.

Sacrifice is a primary form of ritual action through much of Nepal, yet little attention has been devoted to it as a particular form of practice. The study of sacrifice has a long history in anthropological thought, and Valeri has reviewed four general theories: "1. Sacrifice is a gift to the gods and is part of a process of exchange between gods and humans. 2. Sacrifice is a communion between man and god through a meal. 3. Sacrifice is an efficacious representation. 4. Sacrifice is a cathartic act" (1985:62). My purposes here are less to elaborate extensively on these theories or to propose an alternate theory of sacrifice than to sketch the form and meaning of sacrifice as encompassed within Tamang culture, that is, in relation to the shamanic and the lamaic. The isolation of sacrifice outside specific social and cultural circumstances has been one of the weaknesses of general theorizing. This was true of Hubert and Mauss's (1964) comprehensive study (Valeri 1985:64)—the influence of which will be evident in the analysis here—and of Girard's (1972) attempt at a universal theory based on a psychologism. These totalizing theories also conceive of sacrifice as a unitary phenomenon. Herrenschmidt (1982a), though, has identified two distinct types of sacrifice, "Brahmanic and testamentary," which are distinguished by different relations between world order, divinities, and humanity. Moreover, all sacrificial rituals are shaped within particular cultures and social contexts.

Nevertheless, several of these approaches open Tamang sacrifice to interpretation, particularly those associated with exchange and efficacious representation. Exchange, though, emerges as a secondary aspect of sacrifice and is subsumed within the overarching end of sacrifice. Sacrificial exchanges are coercive and properly operate in the maintenance of measured relations with divine and malevolent agents and thus stability of natural and social domains. Sacrifice has more extensive formulative powers as well, taking the differentiations of world experience and arranging them into an order.

Sacrificers, Sponsors, and Their Obligations

Lambus are sacrificers who on behalf of intergraded sets of sponsors maintain an equilibrium with divine and malevolent agents through sacrifices or consecrated offerings.[1] Their power derives primarily from the act of sacrifice, which distinguishes their authority from that of lamas or bombos; lamas derive their power from the word and bombos from unique powers of sight. What makes a lambu in practice is the precise control over detailed ritual procedures and specialized invocations. Tamang even refer to household heads, village headmen, and knowledgeable laity as "lambu" when they occasionally sacrifice.[2] With few exceptions, any man can become a lambu as long as he knows the proper invocations and procedures, and lambus, in contrast to lamas and bombos, require no special initiations. One village lambu, however, has the special status of communal lambu (*kuingyam lambu*) and presides over recognitions of divinities on behalf of the whole village. This position passes hereditarily from father to son or to fraternal nephew. In Tamdungsa, there were seven men whom villagers referred to as "lambu" and who regularly practiced as sacrificers.

Lambus are distinguished from other practitioners in several ways. Although two lambus in the village were also bombos and another a sangtung, apparently merging the two ritual roles in one person, lambus remain clearly distinguished in Tamang thought. When a bombo practices as a lambu he is called "lambu" not "bombo." Most lambus

[1]This chapter succeeds the contributions of Höfer (1971a, 1981), who brought lambus and their rituals to our attention through the translation of their recitations. Here, though, I examine the recitations in light of their ritual function to create proper order and in light of their "magical power" (Tambiah 1968a). Höfer (1971a) has attempted to trace the etymology of lambu, but here I refer to the lambu as "sacrificer" because of what he does. Following Valeri, I consider all consecrated offerings—whether or not they include the killing of living things—under the rubric of sacrifice (1985:37–38). This may seem to pose problems for distinguishing between lambus and their sacrifices and bombos and lamas because the latter also make consecrated offerings, but as I will make clear the rituals of lamas and bombos are encompassed in different logics and in the case of the bombo toward a different end.

[2]Tamang employ the term "lambu" much as Nepali speakers use "pujāri"—as a general term for ritualist.

(including those who are bombos) declare that bombos are under an oath of the sangkye not to kill; one lambu explained that "bombos should not do slitting and cutting [of consecrated animals]. When they came to be bound by the oath of [the Buddha] Kalten Sangkye, they had to sit in austerity. . . . Whenever I tell this history, bombos say I tell it so that I get all the meat! A bombo's work is curing people." In soundings bombos respect this oath, and if sacrifices are required, as they usually are, bombos will not kill the animal themselves but call on an assistant (usually the mha or sister's husband of the sponsor) to perform this task. Lambus find themselves under similar restrictions when they expel Nakhle Mhang because the oaths that compel this evil spirit to depart originated with the Buddhas.

Several other distinctions separate lambus and bombos. Lambus shudder (*chhekpa*) in a minor way when they invoke Shyihbda and expel Nakhle Mhang: "While we chant, we become a bit scared and shake for strength. After we chant, we become cold. This after thinking of the divinities." Bombos on the other hand "shake hard" and ritually "carry" divinities and harmful agents on, and in, their bodies as a distinguishing feature of their rituals. Lambus, moreover, have no special costume or paraphernalia; as a Tamang saying goes, they have only their mouths. Finally, although some lambus claim to acquire their ritual inspiration in dreams, they depend in an elementary and more exclusive way on the memorization of techniques and recitations. Unlike lamas who derive authority from the Buddhas and bombos from ancestral spirits and midspace sprites, lambus rarely claim connections to special powers or beings.

As ritual technicians, they act on behalf of sponsors, who range from individuals to the village at large. They complete minor propitiations and expulsions for individuals necessitated by illnesses, misfortune, or desire. They perform incidental and calendrical sacrifices, representing residents of households, clusters of households adjacent to neighborhood divinities, and the village as a totality. They also convey offerings on behalf of the sponsoring clans at the time of all social rites. Prior to the formation of Nepal in its present form, it is likely that lambus conveyed sacrifices to regional sites on behalf of overlords. In this array of ritual acts, humanity fulfills its obligations to the divinities and harmful agents.

Sacrificial observations are as numerous as the divinities (and harmful agents) they oblige. A day rarely passes (except those on which rituals are proscribed) without lambus practicing. At the outset of the agricultural cycle, as close to the full moon of April-May as possible, lambus complete the half-year propitiations to the village divinities Shyihbda, Shyingmardung, and Kharta on behalf of the community. Usually on the same day, lambus make sacrifices to a regional goddess for each household. Along with these daytime offerings, the communal lambu performs *satsi* (nonsacrificial propitiation and invocation of divinities) at night. Thereby they assure the security of the earth. In May-June, when all village *busing* (clan sisters) who have married out of the village return to their natal homes, lambus sacrifice to Shyingmardung on their and their natal kins' behalf. During the full moon of August-September, lambus sacrifice chickens to Shyihbda and release chicks for Kharta, fulfilling the second half of the yearly (mharsung) obligations of each and every household. In September-October, villagers celebrate Dasain, with buffalo sacrifices to Durga. In March-April, every household must sacrifice a chicken to Bhimsen in celebration of small Dasain. In April-May, the yearly cycle starts over with attention once again to Shyihbda. All these sacrifices are either communal or are performed simultaneously by all households in the village; all respond to the turn of the calendars and some to the oscillation of the halves of the year.

There are innumerable other sacrificial obligations. All households must regularly sacrifice to neighborhood and directional divinities and make offerings to lu. Many Tamang also try to sacrifice to deities in neighboring villages. Household heads (acting as lambus) propitiate supporting gods of households twice annually. Finally to these attentions must be added the sacrificial obligations to all village divinities and several neighborhood divinities incumbent on the community before the performance of a ten-day Buddhist festival (*chhechu*), the idiosyncratic responsibilities of particular households and individuals, and incidental recognition of divinities at the time of illness or misfortune. Lambus also communicate offerings (nonsacrificial propitiations) to village divinities on the occasion of life-cyclical rites: births, tonsures, marriages, memorial death feasts, and any other occasion where humans feast or celebrate. In fact, at every meal, simple or elaborate, villagers allot token portions to divinities and harmful agents.

These propitiatory chores are supplemented by exorcistic responsibilities. Most are incidental because of the unpredictable and capricious manner in which evils assault. Lambus daily expel one or another shade that has grasped members of some household or their livestock. In addition to these continual incidental exorcisms, lambus have several calendrical expulsive responsibilities. All households exorcise Nakhle Mhang at roughly the same times that they propitiate

Shyihbda. They also do so communally at the division of meat in Dasain. Those households that maintain herding sheds and keep animals must annually appease two spirits who attack animals particularly.

Although lambus fulfill sacrificial obligations to a host of divinities and harmful agents, sacrificial obligations to Shyihbda—a prototypical divinity—and Nakhle Mhang—a prototypical evil—have a marked place in the ritual repertoire of lambus; both beings "perch" on lambus, and villagers usually define lambus with reference to their ritual attentions to these beings. Rites to both Shyihbda and Nakhle Mhang have a generalized effect even though they do not obviate the recognitions dedicated more exclusively to the hosts of divinities and harmful agents who inhabit the cosmos. Propitiations of Shyihbda include offerings and recognitions of all local and regional divinities. Along with the expulsion of Nakhle Mhang, lambus show the trail to an array of evils bringing every form of degeneracy. One lambu chants:

The fields and house
Of the master and mistress of this place,
Have been harmed
From the earth trail,
From the sky.

Even if it be the male shade,
Even if it be the female shade,
If it be the raw shade,
If it be the familiar,
If it be the headless shade,
Defeat and take away,
Return and take away!

. . . .

Harm has occurred while eating, while sleeping.
Large sores have occurred.
Pimples have occurred.
Bodies have withered.
Stupors have occurred.
Gossip from behind,
Bragging from the front,
Defeat all and take away,
Return and take away.

In the house and fields have entered
Male ghosts, female ghosts,

The returning *si*, the *du si*,
The 108 si,
The hiding si.
Defeat and take away all!
Return and take away!

The great horned owl inauspiciously hoots,
The dog howls,
The chicken sneaks off,
The bull snorts,
The inauspiciousness of each
Defeat and take away!

. . . . .

The *ha yebbi* evil will occur,
The *hu yebbi* evil will occur,
Return the eastern harm to the east,
The western harm to the west,
The southern harm to the south,
The northern harm to the north,
The central harm to the center.
Return the curses of lamas,
The curses of bombos,
The curses of sangtung.

Shyihbda appears at the head of general recognitions of divinities in all social rites, and Nakhle Mhang is expelled at all weddings, tonsure ceremonies, house constructions, and other propitious occasions. The close linkage of these two beings in Tamang symbology is evident in the expulsions of Nakhle Mhang. After calling Nakhle Mhang, lambus immediately implore Shyihbda to protect all that it destroys. Villagers address Shyihbda and Nakhle Mhang, as they do all beings, in a social idiom and imagine them sociomorphically.

Sacrifice and Exchange

Divinities and Harmful Agents in Social Construction

Tamang efforts to mete out portions to all, whether beggar, rich man, or king, are evident at every commensal occasion, whether feast or simple meal. Both the general egalitarian ethos of Tamang exchange and the hierarchies of village order are expressed through exchanges and have their correlates in the dealings with divine and malevolent beings. Divinities are like headmen or kings and harmful agents are like the lowly untouchables of village society in that the former are wanted but reluctant guests, the latter uninvited but persistent presences. In general, Tamang imagine divinities as though there is potentially an absence of relationship and evils as though there is an excess of relationship. Divinities must be brought from a remove into social engagement with humanity. The invocations to Shyihbda always repeat this refrain: "Remember [us] when [we] need remembrance. [Provide us] refuge when [we] need refuge." Divinities are always on the verge of retreating, forgetting humans, and thereby allowing events to unfold without constraint. No attempts to contact divinities during the "dark month" of their austere retreat will avail, and harmful agents wantonly disport. Even when not in retreat, divinities must be coaxed out of a primordial formlessness. Divine retreat and human neglect of divinities presage calamity; forces of degeneration reign out of control. Once brought into engagement with humans, divinities are inherently subject to human pleas and become protective benefactors; in this sense they are, to borrow Obeyesekere's description of Sinhalese gods, "just" (1966:6). In sacrificial formulations, divinities are made ascendant regents overseeing worldly domains and conferring order; they become included in a society coterminous with that of humanity.

Lambus must attempt to exile evils from an unrestrained attachment to humanity—an adherence that violates the form of measured conduct and rules of reciprocity essential to social order—to a sated distance. The regulation of speech, sex, and food are elemental in Tamang social life, and evils transgress all restraints. Violations of the harmful agents are parsimoniously condensed in the three rarified evils: the three-headed (tiger, boar, and bull) cannibal fiend (*krasompti mhang*), the evil with a huge phallus (called the "evil of the three old men" after the old men who carry it), and the four orphans (Nakhle Mhang). All constitute generalized social evils: cannibalism and gluttony over and against measured commensal order, irrepressible sexual desire over and against the tempered sexuality of marriage exchange, social indeterminacy and the incompleteness of exchange over and against patriclan order and total exchange. Nakhle Mhang comes in two sets of siblings; the elder two are called *khai ḍa* or the victorious-boisterous mouth and the younger two are called *khai chung* or small mouth. The former comes boldly, the latter timorously. Unrestrained by the etiquette of proper human relations, they gossip and rumor behind people's backs or blatantly confront them. All violate the values of order in the abstract. They undermine general well-being and do not cause the specifiable malaises of local harmful agents toward whom lambus usually direct their ritual attentions. Tamang expel these abstracted images in the communal rites of Chhechu, a time when all the Buddhas as well as the divinities receive human offerings and humans feast among themselves.

It is in a commensal idiom that Tamang most often discuss everyday harmful agents. One expert explained: "Shades fly around like flies or crows and cause trouble. A shade thinks it has no father, no mother. It has no food so it flies around. It gets into the insides of people and makes them sick. Then you must call a lambu or a bombo. Shades soon develop habits. If you feed them all the time, back and back they come, causing trouble and more trouble. They are like people who travel to faraway villages and search out distant relations and after that always lodge with these people again and again. Wherever a shade will get food, that is where it will go, that is where it enters. You must be careful [when you feed them because they may come back again and again]." Harmful agents get inside people and eat their flesh and undermine their generative essences. Thus evils not only take without giving, they consume the antithesis of human food, human flesh.

If divinities in their inclusion in the rounds of exchange are potentially satiable, harmful agents in their exclusion are perpetually unsated. Their excesses and transgressions originate for Tamang in a primeval insufficiency of exchange. Harmful agents grasp and sting because the distribution of just portions is never complete. Like Nakhle Mhang, they are left out of otherwise inclusive commensal exchanges, especially those of the all-inclusive memorial death feasts that define Tamang society. Lambus invoke Nakhle Mhang in these terms when they exorcise:

> After you died,
> They say you had no memorial death feast.
> When you lived,
> They say the portions were insufficient.

As the four orphans—motherless, fatherless, kinless, and homeless—Nakhle Mhang is by definition denied a place in a society based on clan affiliation. Shades adhere because they were prematurely wrenched from fortunes of the world and social embeddedness. They are lost and pitiable: "[They] do not go to the heavens of the divinities or Buddhas [nor are they reborn]. They live in heavens of gossip, in heavens of trouble and distress. They do not go away. They just wander about, homeless and hungry." Denied life, in death they emerge as unjust, amoral, and fearsome social presences, unbound to social convention and motivated by a ravenous attachment to the living. Harmful agents jealously adhere to humanity and ruin through their craving: "Envy is what happens when people have the feeling, 'Oh! What a beautiful meal! What a fine meal!' They want it themselves and think, 'Oh! If I could only have that too!'" This envy is not just a feeling; craving coheres to its object.

The society of harmful agents is thus the antithesis of the proper arrangement of human affairs. Divinities are ascendant patrons who can be swayed into profitable relations of reciprocal benefit; harmful agents originate in the primeval incompleteness of exchange and remain unfixed in the patterns of orderly interchange. In a general way Tamang evils conform to Kapferer's characterization of Sinhalese demons who "introduce an abnormal ordering of the world. . . . Demons order disorder" (1983:1). Violation though takes a specific form among Tamang, a form that responds to the logic of exchange as a contortion of the conditions of normal sociality. Tamang anxieties about enfolding the world in exchange become realized in the images of evil.

The evils of imagination who are outside exchange find human counterparts. Although Tamang try to be totally inclusive in their exchanges, they implicitly recognize that social closure through exchange is impossible. Neighbors and kin strive to provide for the impoverished and landless residents of the village. To deny a share is to violate an articulatory social norm and to incur the wrath of the excluded. Yet they are confronted by this reality in everyday village life, and not surprisingly it is those low castes who are excluded from exchanges that are the most likely targets for accusations of witchcraft. Villagers most often accuse lowly Blacksmiths of activities that undermine the well-being of households, livestock, and fields. Like the envy attributed to harmful agents, witches (*bokshyi*) ruin through their desirous glances. Other living evils actively contort the principles of social order: *mengko* poison others to acquire immortality, and rich people are often accused (along with impoverished bokshyi) of stabling familiars (*bir*) to plunder the wealth and well-being of others for their own enrichment. When these witches and poisoners die, they continue their violations as members of the hordes of shades who trouble villagers.

The Effects of Sacrifice

Sacrifice in its most explicit mode operates to infix divinities as the dominant force in the world and to banish harmful agents to the margins from which they originated. In the words of Hubert and Mauss, "Sacrifice shows itself in a dual light; it is a useful act and it is an obligation. Disinterestedness is mingled with self-interest. That is why it has so frequently been conceived of as a form of contract. Fundamentally there is perhaps no sacrifice that has not some contractual element" (1964:100). Sacrifices are obligations in the sense that divinities and harmful agents are facts of the world; their existence and power is unquestioned and to neglect or offend them is to terminate productive relations, causing their retreat (in the case of divinities) or their unbridled assault (in the case of harmful agents). The anxiety expressed and reexpressed in sacrificial invocations is that divine and malevolent agents will split from humans in a speechless anger.

Sacrifices are useful acts because they sway the world into a specific order. Through sacrificial gifts lambus effect a tenuous balance with divinities; their invocations make this abundantly clear. Not only are all sorts of offerings spread out in sacrifices, lambus list them over and over again. They invoke Shyihbda as follows:

Shyihbda great blank one,
Originating above Dobarlap,
Originating in Serong Chhok,
Staying in Kalleri Gombaro.
La Ngyingpo [male aspect],
Lai Mhiktung Rhemo [female aspect].

In the winter season,
In the summer season,
At the auspicious time,
An incense offering,
Delivered offerings,
Communally [we have] placed.

Within the soil of Tamdungsa,
Let the wetness of rain begin.
Shut down violent storms.
Send off evil men.
In the time of eating,
In the time of sleeping,

They will emerge;
Pain will emerge.
Send pain off.
Epidemics will emerge.
Send epidemics off.

Here is a golden throne for a divinity,
Partake of meat.
Offerings are placed.
The incense sequence begun.

Lambus likewise enumerate their offerings to Nakhle Mhang in the following terms:

On the golden earth,
On a golden basket,
Offerings of grain and other things are purely placed.
Four leaf plates are placed.
Pure beer residue is honorifically placed.
On a golden plate, rice and beer are placed.
On the beer flask, butter is affixed.
A golden cup, incense, milk, shyalchya,
Beer are all purely placed.

Honorific words, honorific gifts are purely placed.
A complete, beautiful chicken,
With undamaged beak, with undamaged nostrils,
With undamaged feathers, with undamaged feet,
A complete, undamaged chicken has been placed.
A golden basket with an iron stone is placed.

In a clear astrological configuration,
Overflowing offerings are placed.

Not all offerings to harmful agents, however, are conveyed so honorifically; many common shades and evil spirits receive their offerings with a harsh and colloquial "begone!"

Lambus proffer gifts to divinities as though they were royalty. The male and female aspects of Shyihbda, for instance, are earth king and earth queen, whom the lambu invites to sit on a golden throne. Lambus address divinities honorifically and tie string turbans (a sign of royalty) around their stone images. Flowers, cloth, and colored thread embellish their altars. Lambus remind divinities that they have bowed re-

Figure 6. A lambu sacrificing to Shyihbda

spectfully and offered "golden" rice and an array of other gifts (incenses, popped corn, milk [to the male aspect], egg, millet beer, liquor, money, and as the sacrifice proceeds, blood [to the female aspect], meat, and cooked rice), which they place on the altar (see Figure 6). The gifts awaken divinities to a remembrance of dependent humans and their need of refuge. Divinities, then, take form as the "superhuman" (cf. Gombrich 1971a:48) regents who return protection to humans for their gifts.

Lambus list the expectations of humans in the form of invocational pleas. Tamang depend on Shyihbda to suppress earth, rocks, and water; to contain landslides, mudslides, and earthquakes; to fend off the fury of violent rains, hail, and lightning bolts. They call on Shyihbda to defend humans and their livestock from lurking evils and to avert curses that strike while sleeping, eating, or moving. They ask Shyihbda to place steps on dangerous trails and to keep people from reeling at precipices. They invoke Shyihbda to banish epidemics, vomiting from above, dysentery from below, and all manners of pain and distress. They also ask Shyihbda to suppress human dissension, gossip, fighting, and boisterous bragging. Lambus call on Shyihbda to make feet like iron, backs like gold, and innards like copper and to watch over humans, their children, and their livestock.

Sacrifices to evils are substitutions for the objects of their ravenous consumption. Shades, the agents of everyday illness, cause pain by consuming parts of human bodies. When lambus expel specific shades and evil spirits they often chant the following refrain: "You do not have the habit of gnawing human flesh, of sucking human blood, of crunching human bone. Here, take this beautiful chicken." Offerings to shades and evil spirits range from the simple material of occasional sociality such as tobacco and everyday food to offerings of chickens and goats. These offerings drive and cajole evils away from the village. Lambus tell Nakhle Mhang:

> The mha (sister's husband) has apportioned and given meat;
> The daughter has apportioned and given beer.
> Be satisfied with the meat!
> Be satisfied with beer!
> In your own place above *yho*,
> Open your ears,
> Remember in your heart-mind.
> Do not separate [from us] in speechless anger.

Lambus coax Nakhle Mhang along a trail down and away from the house and village:

> Go and stay
> Where all kinds of people gather in bazaars.
> If they expel you from there,
> Where will you go?
> Where will you stay?
> The golden drying mats,
> The silver drying mats of Indian Kings is yours, they say.
> Go to your own place within India.
> Go and stay!
> Eat and go! Drink and go!
> Until you are satiated and can eat no more!

Lambus must at the same time communicate with them and sever relations with them. Not limited to imperatives in their attempt to banish evils, lambus trick and tease them away as well. They remind Lhai Mhang, for instance, that they are herders and that their sheep and goats are bleating all alone in their high-altitude herding station. Lambus used to carry the dough image of another evil to a crossroads, where a hidden accomplice would blast it with a shot from a village-crafted blunderbuss.

Thus, the overall purpose of propitiatory and exorcistic sacrifices is to form contracts of patronage with divinities and to appease and drive off evil spirits. Lambus show divinities the trails down into human affairs and show evils the trails down and away. Sites of divinities are permanent fixtures of village geography, and altars in houses are meant to attract divine presences. Forms of and offerings to evils are most commonly taken to crossroads, open places, and the borders of the village where they are pitched over precipices. The rice dough images of Buddhas and divinities are usually taken upstairs to the grain storage areas and after several days of accumulating good fortune for the house they are eaten; the black millet effigies of evils are left at the outskirts of domesticated spaces to be consumed by roving dogs. Exorcism in conjunction with propitiation keeps at bay an antithetical society, allowing harmonious orders to prevail.

The sociopolitical formations of sacrifice that position divinities in ascendance and exclude harmful agents extend into human domains. The village as a sociopolity also finds representation in sacrificial events. The communal lambu in calendrical recognitions to village divinities acts on behalf of the community as a totality under the authority of headmen. Headmen organize communal observances of village divinities, collecting equal contributions of grain from every village household for the purchase of sacrificial victims; they themselves supply all the other necessities. At the conclusion of sacrifice, headmen divide the meat into equal portions and distribute shares to each household. Höfer reports slightly different procedures in another Tamang village; in the sacrifices he observed, either the traditional headman performed the ritual (1981:36) or a lambu presided over the sacrifice on behalf of the headman who officiated at a communal feast (1971a). The all-Nepal rites of Dasain, which Tamang celebrate according to distinctively local customs, among other things also ritualize and legitimate the political orders (including divisive factions) of village life.[3] In

[3]Tamdungsa, of course, was not without its factions, and there was not always agreement about who was the final authority in village affairs. Sacrifices, particularly those of Dasain, are legitimating events, and often various headmen vie for ritual recognition.

the more strictly household recognitions of divinities or expulsions, lambus act on behalf of local "masters and mistresses" whose dominion is a specific house and fields, thereby extending the sociopolitical idiom from village to household. Lambus, largely because their authority is linked to village divinities, headmen, and household heads, rarely act outside an exclusively village context. Ritual declarations of more encompassing social fields occur primarily in lamaic ritual contexts.[4]

Throughout a calendrical cycle, then, lambus establish a continuity in human and divine society, bringing closure to their affairs in idioms of reciprocity and hierarchy; they simultaneously repress evils who embody violations of order. The generative processes of sacrifice, however, extend beyond the social in a more encompassing attention to representation.

Oration, Differentiation, and Creation in Sacrificial Performance

It is not only acts but words that make sacrifice effective. One lambu chants as follows:

> The right is mine,
> The left is yours,
> After ripping,
> After sewing,
> After there was a hole,
> After patching,
> Like a flower blossom,
> Round and round the heart,
> After a flower quickly adheres,
> Knowledge be erect, inner strength rise up.

[4]Although sacrifices to Shyihbda are now restricted to local geographic and political units, there is evidence that a regional cult—linked perhaps to Ghale principalities—existed in the eighteenth century. Western Tamang recognize a regionally prominent site, invoked as the "staying place" of Shyihbda, at which there is an annual festival. Many Tamang households go there to sacrifice individually every few years. Tamang, however, no longer control this site as they probably did in the eighteenth century. Since the early part of the nineteenth century, shortly after the Gorkhali kings consolidated Nepal, Gurung who migrated from the west of Nepal have apparently controlled this site. Gurung probably represented the authority of the early Gorkha state in many western Tamang regions, and their control of the Shyihbda site symbolically declared their political ascendancy in the state of Nepal. Now Tamang can only transmit offerings to the regional Shyihbda through the hands of a resident Gurung sacrificer. We know that control of earth divinities was closely associated with political authority in Gurung country (Pignède 1966:301–2).

. . . . . .

If the mouth oath does not stay,
If the heart-mind oath does not stay,
The ancient sin of nine chopped [killed] suns,
Of nine chopped moons, will adhere.
The sin of nine disintegrated gombo will adhere.
Of nine killed monks will adhere.
The sin of nine cut cows and bulls will adhere.
Sin will come.
Mouth oath do not waver.
Heart-mind oath do not waver.
If the mouth oath wavers, if the heart-mind oath wavers,
Sin will come.

So far, we have concentrated on the elementary manipulations of the lambus' sacrifices as a transposition of idioms of human sociality to extra-human realms. As essential as these ritual acts and gestures are invocations that are creative in their very utterance. This creativity works on two levels. First, the recitations and manipulations have what Tambiah has called a "magical power":

> Language is an artificial construct and its strength is that its form owes nothing to external reality: it thus enjoys the power to invoke images and comparisons, refer to time past and future and relate events which cannot be represented in action. Non-verbal action on the other hand excels in what words cannot easily do—it can codify analogically by imitating real events, reproduce technical acts and express multiple implications simultaneously. Words excel in expressive enlargement, physical actions in realistic presentation. (1968a:202)

Second, the words—again in combination with the gestures and manipulations—create an infrastructure of world differentiation; the differentiating functions of sacrifice are linked to the creative function and in performance oration becomes a form of manipulation.

In the first instance, Tamang sacrificial orations have a conjurative power and lambus always recite the origination accounts (*ṭhungrap-kerap*) of the beings they address, thereby actuating them and the forces they embody. The narrations also work homeopathically by metaphorically associating the specific context in which the lambu performs with primordial events. The origination account of Nakhle Mhang, which begins with creation, is not, then, simply the retelling of a history; the lambu uses oration to manipulate ritually the state of the house and fields of the sponsors in a recreation of primordial prosperity. He begins his origination account with the emergence of a cosmic tree from sterile nothingness and the appearance of the Buddhas, who bind productive order into the cosmos. The lambu then describes each step in the genesis of primeval human prosperity, a genesis he strives analogically to reproduce in the specific milieu in which he performs: men and women are created, they exchange in marriage, they establish houses and bear children, they sow grain and keep livestock; life-force flourishes and harvests are bountiful. At this moment, as we saw at the beginning of this chapter, degeneration in the form of Nakhle Mhang also appears on the scene to hamper and undermine this well-being.

This situation of households on the verge of prosperity but always threatened is exactly the worldly condition in which Tamang find themselves. Later on in the ṭhungrap, the lambu formally narrates the events at Ui Same, which conclude with the original expulsion of Nakhle Mhang by a primordial lambu. The evil was successively passed down from Ui Same gombo to other gombo, where different forms of sacrifice were performed until Nakhle Mhang eventually reached Tamang country. There, after several attempts, an ancestral lambu eventually satisfied the evil with a chicken. The evil then was expelled from some twenty-seven Tamang villages until it reached Tamdungsa, and then it was expelled toward India.[5]

These localized sacrifices, which are repeated hundreds of times a year in the village, then, are directly analogous to the original expulsion at a pass outside Ui Same; the lambu associates households of the village with the gombo of Ui Same, their fields with the universal and productive earth, their masters and mistresses with primordial humanity, and himself with the first lambu:

> Be happy with the beautiful body of a chicken!
> I, Dorje Lambu, reborn dharma, have not offered up.
> By the mouth oath of Guru Pema, it is offered up.
> By the heart-mind oath of Guru Pema, it is offered up.
> Be satisfied in your own place above *yho*.

The metaphoric linkage empowers and supplements the essential transfers of sacrifice.

[5]For more comprehensive descriptions of the expulsion of Nakhle Mhange see Holmberg (1980:239–276) and Höfer (1981:42–99).

To characterize these ritual recitations only in terms of their analogic powers and practical ends, however, overlooks an essential property of oration. All orations include long enumerations that also have a creative function. The opening lines of all propitiatory invocations include the listing of types of incense that are conveyed in the five directions. These are regularly succeeded by catalogues of types of land, pollutions, evils, curses, diseases, hardships, body parts, house parts, divinities, and place names. These listings (several examples of which appear above) reveal a drive toward completeness and inclusiveness in an inventory of worldly experience.

These listings are central in orations known as *rhikap*, which structure two main portions of all sacrifices: the *sangrap* and *chhoppa* sequences of divine propitiations (and major exorcisms that include divine recognitions). In sangrap, lambus fumigate the world with incense; in chhoppa, they convey offerings to the divinities. As incense smoke rises and offerings are handed up, the lambu chants the names of places while he "carries" his oration over the trails of the earth. Lambus carry their chants universally from the marked spaces and divine sites of the village to the north, south, east, and west. They cover the immediate earth as they know it. In invocations to Shyihbda, one lambu situated the village in reference to some one hundred named places. In the expulsion of Nakhle Mhang, another lambu recited over eight hundred place names. He began—as all lambus do—with the spot where he sat, his clothes, and the array of offerings before him. Next he proceeded from the divinities of hearth, home, clan, neighborhood, and village to the places of the earth as he knew them—from the northern plains of India to the sacred sites of the Tibetan plateau and from the western to the eastern reaches of Nepal. The rhikap or place sequences recited during the expulsion of Nakhle Mhang eventually arrive at the primeval grounds of Ui Same where Nakhle Mhang first adhered and where it was first expelled to wander perpetually.

Although these invocations ritually infix households and village within a geographic order, thereby supplementing the ordering functions of sacrifice, they—along with all the other listings in sacrificial rituals—make differentiations. These differentiations are primary creative acts in and of themselves. The obsession to enumerate reveals more about the motivations of sacrifice than do the contents of the enumerations. As Lévi-Strauss concludes in reference to the manipulations and words of American Indians, "Ritual makes constant use of two procedures: parcelling out and repetition," a process he describes as a "maniacal urge to discover the smallest constituent units of lived experience by fragmentation and to multiply them by repetition" in order to guarantee "against any kind of break or interruption that might jeopardize the continuance of lived experience" (1981:672, 674). Parceling out and repetition and the urge to represent the range of experiences in the world characterize both the sacrificial repertoire as a totality and the orations and manipulations of particular sacrifices. As we have seen, Tamang are incessantly inclusive in their incorporation of divinities who inhabit their world, and villagers are obliged cyclically and repetitively to recognize all of them and their malevolent counterparts; their recognitions are accompanied by an anxiety about their potential incompleteness. The extensive representations embedded in the repertoire are complemented by an intensive ordering readily apparent in the enumerations of specific sacrifices such as the place sequences and others described above.

Sacrificial ritual, though, cannot be reduced to the mechanics of differentiation alone; the process of differentiation is contained within the overall function of sacrificial ritual. In the same sense that sacrifice as exchange contains the divine and the malevolent in social order, differentiations of sacrifice formulate world experience in a particular grid, arbitrary though it may be. The sacrifices to Shyihbda and Shyingmardung, which are focal in the village repertoire, encode an arrangement of oppositions in village experience in a convergence of anxiety about well-being and world order: Nepali/Tamang, female/male, social/natural, red (blood)/white, up/down, affliction/protection (see chapter 4).

In this pursuit, Tamang sacrifices are not predominantly events of cathartic transformation (Girard 1972) but technical acts. Sacrifice for Tamang is not usually an intense experience in the same sense that it is among groups like the Nuer (Evans-Pritchard 1956:197–285). Sacrifice is, with some exceptions, experientially a matter of fact. Only one sacrificial event—small Dasain, which occurs in the spring—yields a fairly large flow of blood and includes the milling about of many villagers, but this is not the norm.[6] These sacrifices to a manifestation

[6]Unlike Sherpas, who are repulsed by the sight of blood and can become physically ill in the vicinity of butchered animals, Tamang take the slaughter of animals much more in stride. If we make sacrifice a religious experience among Tamang because animals are killed, should we label butchering a religious experience and those who simply butcher animals ritual specialists? Tamang often joke that they sacrifice when they get hungry for meat. Although I do not want to equate butchering and sacrifice of animals, we do not want to privilege the experience of killing and blood in our interpretation either. For killing and the flow of a

of the goddess Kali, like Dasain sacrifices in greater Nepal, may highlight blood offerings, but this is not true of all sacrifices.

Lambus' sacrifices are routine and far from dramatic. The usual course of sacrifices is as follows: The lambu (in a pure state if it is a divine sacrifice) constructs an altar and consecrates it. Throughout he acts alone most often. Offerings are arranged in precise order. The lambu recites in front of the altar. The recitations include sangraprhikap (incense and place sequences) and thungrap (origination accounts). After these consecrations, the offerings are presented (chhoppa-rhikap). Offerings may or may not include the killing of a victim. Then the lambu passes bits of the offerings to those who are present. The meat of the sacrificial victim is usually cooked and consumed in the home of the sponsors after sacrifice. Although the recitations may be elaborate and the offerings numerous, these acts are sacrifice for Tamang.

The gatherings for these events are usually very small and often include just the sacrificer and maybe a helper from the sponsor's home. The lambu is a technician, and people rarely pay much attention to the style of his manipulations. The words and acts are seen as sufficient in and of themselves. Communal sacrifices to Shyihbda among western Tamang are a case in point. Very few people attend these sacrifices even though all residents of a village are in a sense sponsors. In fact, Höfer reports that in Kallaveri village "the members of the community do not have the right to attend the ceremony, and their participation is indirect" [my translation] (1971a:148). At the regional site of Shyihbda, only the Gurung sacrificer who presides over the central cult attends. In Tamdungsa, although attendance was not restricted, usually only a few children would accompany the lambus during propitiations. Household exorcisms are similarly undramatic; householders provide the lambus' necessities and fulfill the necessary gestures. The central sacrifice is done outside the house with no witnesses. These manipulations confirm that sacrifice is as much exchange as expiation. Tamang sacrifices, then, sometimes include themes of expiation and displacement of violence; however, they do not independently determine their form. Sacrifice as a type of ritual in the context of the total

---

victim's blood to become the basis for an explanation of sacrifice, there must be evidence of the importance of these events in the experience of the sponsors. One would not want to argue that expiation is absent in the Tamang case but only that it does not predominate. Revulsion to killing animals and blood is mediated in specific cultural milieus in specific ways.

field of rituals among Tamang is an efficacious exchange and orders the cosmos.

In a similar vein, the recitations of lambus rarely gain an attentive audience; the mechanical enumerations and the formulaic invocations are far from engrossing. Most recitations unfold in the hubbub of everyday life. Moreover, lambus chant for the most part in a formalized and archaic form of Tamang. Although all Tamang know the general meaning of the recitations and manipulations, few, including the lambus themselves, can give confident word-for-word translations of the recitations. As Höfer correctly notes, "What [counts] for them [the specialists] from the very beginning of their training is performing—and not exegesis" (1981:38). This stress on proper performance leads us away from a view of the orations exclusively focusing on their contents—although these are revealing. The orations acquire their power in proper performance; the archaism of the language enhances the power of the words precisely because they are not ordinary language. They are special words used for special purposes. Here then the obscurity of the language must be interpreted not in reference to its putative ancientness but to its sacred distance from ordinary speech, something akin to a mantra or magical incantation. It is quite probable that if the Tamang did not have an obscure or archaic ritual language, they would invent one. The archaism of the language is, on this level, its message and relates directly to the confidence the Tamang have in the creative power of the word.

Tamang sacrifice then emerges less as experience than as technique; the lambu is a technician in the mechanics of cosmic order. Above all else, the success of sacrifice depends on proper and standardized performance, and routinization is a marked feature of the lambu's rituals. A fixation on performatory technique is evident in the rituals from the arrangement of the altar through the timing of sequences to the proper recitation. Any man can become a lambu as long as he has confident control of standardized manipulations and invocations. One lambu explained, "He listens to others; he does not believe in gurus. The lambu learns that certain sections of the chant are associated with such and such acts." Invocations, in large measure, are powerful by the very fact of their proper recitation, and Tamang attribute disasters, misfortunes, and troubles of all sorts to the slight errors lambus make or to improper procedures. A rumor kept spreading through Tamdungsa that a new communal lambu was required because the present one, owing to the absence of all his teeth, was polluting the altar with spittle during recitations.

This obsession with orderly procedure points to a summary of the logic of sacrificial ritual. As Herrenschmidt has put it: "We are thus dealing with a ritualistic system, in the strong sense of the term, that is, with a formalism: the rite is effective if it is carried out correctly, since, in its very carrying out, the order of the world is reproduced and maintained. The right order of sacrifice is, and assures, the right order of the world" (1982a:26). Apprehension about order envelops the sacrificial process and generates an interminable repertoire, which works to infix cosmic differentiation, ordination, and human well-being against their antitheses.

From the Acts of Lambus to the Words of Lamas

Lamaic and sacrificial rituals replicate each other in several domains and converge in contrast to shamanic soundings. On the surface, lamaic and sacrificial rituals could not be more opposed if sacrifice is defined as bloody offerings, an approach that obscures a primary motivation to sacrifice among Tamang. Buddhist doctrine emphasizes *ahiṃsā* or nonviolence toward living creatures as a central tenet, and sacrifice often includes the slaughter of animal victims. Just as early Buddhism in India opposed a dominant sacrificial orthodoxy through the assertion of nonviolence, Buddhism in Tibet competed with, and eventually superseded, an elaborate ritual structure (not unlike Vedic ritual formulations in ancient India) replete with "manuals for ceremonies and liturgies used by various kinds of sacrificial priests" (Tucci 1980:231). In many respects, the history of Buddhism in Tibet was a conflict of Buddhism with a Bon religion that was less a shamanic cult than a sacrificial cult.

Whereas values of nonviolence eventually came to reign in the Buddhist socioreligious orders of Tibet, sacrificial killing remains an essential element of Tamang ritual life. Many Tamang lamas (but not all) are no less explicit than their prestigious counterparts in the monasteries of Tibet about the evils of ritual killing and point to killing as an example of the worst sorts of demerit that one can accumulate. At the same time, though, they support offerings of animals to divinities and harmful agents and avail themselves of the services of lambus with the same regularity as other villagers. Moreover, as in Tibet, lamas sacrifice dough images and effigies of various sorts in a substitution for blood sacrifice. Among Tamang, the ascendance of lamaism over sacrifice represents less a supersession of Buddhism over sacrifice than a replacement of one form of sacrifice for another.

Lambus and lamas can and do replace each other for all sorts of rituals. With the exception of death rites, which are the sole prerogative of lamas, either lamas or lambus can preside over life-cyclical rituals. Likewise the rites of Dasain, although now featuring lambus as ritualists, allowed lamas a prominent position in the past. Lamas also propitiate divinities and exorcise evils, although they do so without killing. The rituals of the lamas and the lambus then are not as divergent as they might appear on the surface. Both can be viewed as "sacrificial," but only if we view sacrifice as more than simply consecrated offerings of the bloody type and direct our attention to the ends of sacrifice.

Here Herrenschmidt's distinction between "Brahmanical" and "testamentary" sacrifice can clarify key distinctions. In this typology of sacrifice, the lambu's rituals are of the Brahmanical type in that they depend on acts: "Man becomes the master of the universe (which he maintains through the repetition of the rite) and of the divinities (whom he feeds through the rite)" (1982a:30). In lambus' sacrifices, divinities, cosmos, and humanity take intergraded order through the performance of the ritual. The event is creative in and of itself. Lamaic ritual proceeds from a different authority. Lamas work from the primeval word, and in Herrenschmidt's typology their rites are "testamentary" sacrifices. Lamas reactivate the Buddhas' oaths that bind the cosmos and its beings into an order. In testamentary sacrifices "there is no order except through the divine word" (1982a:31). The divinities and harmful agents upon whom the lambu focuses are controlled and tied up in the oaths of Buddhas; divinities are ministers to kings (Buddhas) and have no independent power or reality. In lamaic ritual, the beings are controlled not directly through acts (including words) but through the mediation of the Buddhas. Of course, the rituals of lambus are not purely "Brahmanical," including as they do "oaths"; nor are the rituals of lamas completely "testamentary," with their sacrificial acts. Yet the distinction is useful in pointing out the similarity of their ends: world order.

This shift in conceptualization of order from sacrificial to lamaic transforms ritual authority and action but not the ends of ritual, which are the realizations and impositions of order; both ritual systems assure continuity of the cosmos. The divergences of lamaic and sacrificial rituals (in the sense of the lambu) occur on other levels. Buddhist ritual, as we shall see, introduces ethical values for action in the context of reflections on death and thus complements the worldly sacrifices of lambus. Shamanic ritual erupts in the margins of the orders generated in both lamaic and sacrificial rituals.

6 Shamanic Soundings

In the midst of the sun rays,
A costumed bombo I am not.
In the midst of the moon rays,
I have dressed.
When all breathing, moving beings sleep,
When the sun sleeps,
I dress [as a] bombo.
Come take my bombo's body.
Come take a golden horse.
Come take a silver horse.
By the sky trail let's fly.

A Bombo's chant

Shamans must be dialecticians, agile and capable of maintaining exactly the right relation between the opposites they bridge.

Barbara Myerhoff, "Shamanic Equilibrium: Balance and Mediation in Known and Unknown Worlds."

Bombos cure, go mad, and shake. They shoulder divinities and spirits, carry them off, toss them about in the air as one would bounce a small child. They invite harmful agents to consume their flesh. They go into the divine and achieve dreamlike revelatory states, journey to hidden hills to clarify the condition of life-forces (*so*), search out lost shadow-souls (*bla*) from the margins of order, divine sources of distress, and foretell the future. They honor hosts of divinities and spirits and cast out hordes of afflicting evils, thus supplementing lambus and lamas in their efforts. They especially unveil the faces of the divine and suspend the demonic in all its fury. When bombos perform, villagers say they "sound their drums [*rhappa*]," and here I call their ritual performances "soundings." Soundings and comparable practices found throughout the Himalayas generally fall under the anthropological rubrics of "shamanism" and "spirit possession."[1] Tamang bombos

[1]Our purpose here is not to reassess the history and study of shamanism or spirit possession, the bibliographies of which are extensive. A constructive review of shamanism, following the precedent set by Lévi-Strauss in his review of totemism (1963a), however, is much

conform in large measure to most of the classic definitions of shaman; however, I use this term with caution for the form of Tamang shamanic practices is unintelligible outside the specifically Tamang ritual field. More generally, shamanism (or better, shamanisms) cannot be approached as an isolate.

The Shamanic Illusion

Shaman derives from a term the Tungus of Central Asia use to refer to one of several ritual practitioners in their society (Shirokogoroff 1935). Although scholars like Hulkrantz (1978) have called for an ethnographically specific application of shamanism, anthropologists, historians of religion, and psychologists have come to apply the term generally and incorporate disparate practices from all over the world into an isolable object of study. Shamanism retains a resiliency in contemporary studies, something that has not been the case with animism, animatism, totemism, ancestor worship, and other "categories" in the anthropology of religion characterized as "insipid" by Geertz (1973:122). Several general explanatory approaches to shamanism(s) are articulated in anthropology. Some reconstruct shamanism as a primeval religious phenomenon associated with hunters and gatherers; an old anthropological saw even goes that the first profession was that of shaman. These approaches invoke historical processes to account for ritual systems in which shamanism is but one strand among many; primeval shamanism was historically supplemented by other forms of ritual practice. Similar to these evolutionary approaches are those that locate the origins of shamanism not in the bedrock of human history but in the substrata of the human mind.[2] Shamanism, in these approaches, is an "altered state of consciousness" associated with trance experiences variously attributed to "spirit possession," "soul journey," "magical flight," and the like, some of which are linked in certain parts of the world and in certain historical periods with the ingestion of hallucinogens. Eliade (1972), working less from the idioms of psychobiological science than from those of the history of religious experi-

needed. For one of the clearer delineations of the issues at play in the study of shamanism see Hamayon (1982). For extensive bibliographies consult Eliade (1972), Hultkrantz (1978), Lewis (1971), Peters and Price-Williams (1980), Lambek (1981), and Noll (1988).

[2]Evolutionary and psychobiological approaches have been combined recently in the study of rock art. See Lewis-Williams (1986).

ence, approaches shamanism as an "archaic technique of ecstasy" whereby humans communed with a supreme deity. One of the more common approaches to shamanism has been the psychotherapeutic, which relegates the shamanic to the "medical" in our terminology. Shamanic rituals from this vantage become psychodramas in which "patient," "curer," and "community" come to terms with psychic and social tensions; it has also been suggested that shamanic curing can effect physiological transformations (Lévi-Strauss 1967b:6). Closely related to these therapeutic approaches are sociotherapeutic explanations associated with Lewis (1971), who makes the important but often neglected observation that shamanism and spirit possession must be considered in relation to other ritual practices.

Although a rich ethnographic literature is subsumed under the term *shamanism,* shamanism remains intractable as an object of general study, in part because disparate practices have been disassociated from larger cultural contexts and linked to universal motivations. These generalizing explanatory strategies above all relegate shamanism to domains other than the cultural; they work from what Geertz (1973:37) has called "stratigraphic" conceptions of humanity in which symbologies reflect and take shape according to universal organic, psychic, or social—and, we could add, historical—forces. Eliade's explanation depends on the historical conjecture that early religions posited a supreme being, and "ecstasy" was a method of making contact with the divine (Eliade 1972; see Reinhard 1976). In reference to organic arguments, Lambek, in a vein similar to the one developed here, demonstrates that although trance experiences are reported nearly universally (Bourguignon 1967, 1973), they have no culturally unmediated reality: "The symbolic structure is necessary to form and generate the behavior in the first place" (Lambek 1981:6). A parallel critique can be made of clinical models that attribute the form of shamanic symbologies to projections or manipulations of psychomental processes. Although personal experience is an inescapable dimension of possession or trance (Obeyesekere 1981), therapeutically oriented studies proceed as though experiential states are transparently accessible and readily translatable into the language of clinical psychopathology.[3] The most radical application of Western modes has been "introspective" (Peters 1981) and suggests that the experiences of the ethnographer constitute evidence for the study of experience in other cultures.[4] Imputations of experience outside extrospective appreciation

[3]See Noll (1985) for a discussion of shamanism and schizophrenia.

[4]Assessments of "person," "mind," and "self" cross-culturally (Carrithers, Collins, and Lukes 1985; Shweder and Levine 1984; Marsella, Devos, and Hsu 1985; Daniel 1984),

of the problematics of translation are tenuous. They originate in a medicalized worldview that seeks to demonstrate generic forms of mental life. As Bateson argues, "Emotional significance can only be ascribed after the culture as a whole has been examined" (1958:33).

Sociological approaches depend on a conception of religion that presupposes a tight referential linkage between social structure and ritual symbology. For instance, Lewis (1967, 1971) explains the involvement of women in what he calls "peripheral" possession cults as responses to the sexual, social, and political subjugation of women by men in jural and domestic relations. The universal application of this explanation is highly mechanistic. In most societies, practical power rests with men, a dominance that is legitimated in formal ideologies and central religious cults. Women, who are secondary in these orders, resort to "peripheral" cults of possession that allow them a modicum of power; these practices operate as female auxiliaries, recompensing the dispossessed (1971:32). In such an approach to religion, ritual has no meaning except in its functional purpose and responds to conditions created by a social infrastructure. Although social structure and ritual have intrinsic relations, ritual practices and symbologies are more than veiled social and domestic politics, direct templates of social order and contradiction. They are meaningful in the sense that religions are "systems of meaning" that respond to suffering, among other things (Geertz 1973:100). Soundings are irreducible to clinical therapy, social mechanics, or altered states of consciousness.

The Tamang shamanic is inherently related to lamaic and sacrificial ritual strands of an encompassing field. It is best conceived in its own terms, which appear more accessible in an anthropology of religion than in other approaches (cf. Csordas 1985). From this vantage, the reconstruction of shamanism as an isolate appears as an anthropological illusion. This illusion is historically comparable to totemism, the reality of which lies as much in anthropological conceptualizing as in ethnographic reality (Lévi-Strauss 1963a). Although the reconstruction presented here addresses the social and experiential dimensions of Tamang bombos and their soundings, it stresses the cultural premises behind social order and experience. I focus attention on an account of a

---

however, open up problems in the study of experience, the full implications of which are just beginning to be explored. Lienhardt's study of Dinka experience raised these issues ethnographically some years ago: "The Dinka have no conception which at all closely corresponds to our popular modern conception of the 'mind', as mediating and, as it were, storing up the experiences of the self. There is for them no such interior entity to appear, on reflection, to stand between the experiencing self at any given moment and what is or has been an exterior influence upon the self" (1961:149).

being known as *tsen* (midspace sprites), whose presence in Tamang households motivates the performance of what is a metasounding in the Tamang shamanic repertoire. Moreover, the origination account of tsen that is chanted in this sounding focuses on the paradoxes of cross-cousin marriage, the ambiguities of women in Tamang social imagination, and the enigmas of experience. This mythic account, then, points to reassessments of emotional correlates of soundings, although experience is not the primary concern of this book, which is to locate the shamanic in the ritual field.

Two Forms of Mediation and the Shamanic Vocation

Bombos are special mediators and are clearly distinguished from lambus and lamas. Moreover, they acquire their vocation in a manner less routinized than those of other practitioners. Bombos bring divinities and spirits directly into contact with humans by carrying the beings on their bodies and traveling into their domains during soundings. These mediations are evident in the process of becoming a bombo, which begins in learning to control seizures brought on by one type of midspace being and in establishing a relation with another.

Tempering Seizure

When bombos die, they do not become reborn as most humans do. Bombos who cause hardship to others during their lives become shades; bombos who die violent or inauspicious deaths can become evil spirits; most, however, become *lenṭe* or ancestral spirits of bombos. Lente inhabit secret heavens in the snowy reaches of the high Himalayas. Like shades, lente retain an attachment to the world of the living. Whereas most shades attack almost anyone, lente, with some exceptions, afflict only their direct descendants in either the patriline (*gyut*) or the matriline (*shyang*).[5] Again, in contrast to afflictions by shades, which are cured through sacrificial exorcism, assaults by lente can only be remedied by adopting the shamanic vocation. Lente most often grasp male offspring and most bombos are men; however, lente also seize women and women do become bombos. One woman in Tam-

[5]When these ancestral spirits of deceased bombos attack in the matriline they are sometimes referred to as *shyultu*. This term is used primarily in a derogatory fashion when bombos want to belittle the spirits of a rival.

dungsa was called "woman bombo." Although never formally initiated, she was proud to display her *rhalbo* or mats of hair peculiar to bombos and to recount the story of her lente and how they came to attach themselves to her.[6] In a neighboring village, a fully initiated woman bombo had recently died. Further, the whole shamanic complex is closely linked to women in Tamang society and to femaleness in Tamang imagination.

Assaults by lente are followed by unusual behavior. Seizure often occurs suddenly, as it did toward the end of my stay in Tamdungsa, when a young man ate coals and danced with a red-hot fire-grate over his head while a bombo was sounding. Villagers excitedly reported that the young man had flown from one sacred grove to another in the village. More prolonged sufferings accompany these dramatic outbursts. Those grasped by lente report fits of uncontrollable shuddering, long periods of dissociation, and severe illnesses. One bombo recalled dying and his kin preparing a cremation shroud. His breath returned and he eventually recovered after months of extreme bouts of violent shaking. The only ritual means of alleviating these prolonged assaults is to become a bombo and to honor lente regularly.[7]

At a minimum it takes several years to become a bombo, and for the bombos of Tamdungsa it took decades. In the interim many of those afflicted by lente practice as *sangtung*. They are said to shake "hard" under the effects of lente and to be out of control. Bombos eventually establish mastery over seizure brought on by lente and all other beings of the shamanic cosmos. Lente are converted to allies; they are ambiguously referred to along with other beings as *phamo* or guardians. In all soundings, bombos call on their own lente, any other lente to whom

[6]Kathryn March, who collected this woman's life history, reported to me that they were first attached to her husband, but he wanted to carry corpses in memorial death feasts—something bombos are precluded from doing. He thus passed the responsibility for appeasing them to his adoptive father [the mother's brother of his wife?], who practiced as a bombo; when he died the lente apparently adhered to her husband again and eventually to her son. Finally, they adhered to her when her son died.

[7]Accompanying the extreme suffering of individuals are general uncertainty and distress on the part of immediate kin and the community at large, making these afflictions the subject of active discussion and intense suggestive pressure. The young man who ate coals and "flew" during my residence would sit in silence, staring blankly for long periods as in a daze and would also wander off. Bombos were called upon to reveal the source of his distress, which turned out to be lente. The revealing bombo predicted the young man would die unless he responded to the assault with a pledge to become a bombo. By the time I left the village a few months later, the young man—still far from equilibrium—had made such a promise and had begun to wear necklaces especially associated with bombo; he turned up regularly at soundings and began assisting bombos in their ritual performances, activities associated with the adoption of the vocation.

they can trace a relation, and the lente of their *guru* or teachers. To learn the proper procedures for invocation of these guardians and all the other techniques and recitations associated with soundings requires association with, and the assistance, of a guru or preceptor.[8] A guru must be someone other than one's father. Gurus instruct apprentices in ritual techniques and recitations. Although bombos are formally initiated, training is ad hoc and highly variable. Many prospective bombos have practiced as lambus or sangtung for years and know many patterns of invocation and elementary ritual procedures. Further, most people who become bombos have frequented soundings for years and have thereby learned many techniques.[9] Although bombos can acquire a tremendous amount of knowledge in this way, there are several specific procedures, recitations of origination accounts (histories of beings, practices, etc.; myths), drum cadences, secret mantras or incantations, and ritual sequences that they must learn from an accomplished bombo. Bombos pride themselves on their store of ritual knowledge and their control over long recitations; competitions and challenges in such knowledge among bombos are common on pilgrimages. After they master ritual lore, gurus formally initiate them in performances of soundings called *lasol.* During the first performance of a lasol, the guru gives the student a drum and performs the ritual of grasping the drum. After performing lasol for three consecutive years in conjunction with the guru, a bombo can begin sounding independently.

Although bombos have formal affiliations in lineages called *bon* and commit procedures and recitations to memory, they rarely boast about their bon or their training; many, in fact, claim they are self-generated, notwithstanding their formal affiliations, and complain that their gurus never really taught them anything of import.[10] They stress their individuality and their unique internal qualities, in particular the well-

[8]Bombos convey honorific gifts of cloth, money, grain, and flasks of liquor to their gurus.

[9]Regular attendance even contributes to the tendency toward adopting the vocation; as one bombo noted, going to soundings can incline one toward eventual seizure: "[I] used to go where the bombos and lamas were sounding their drums, where they were chanting. I ate the things there; I would shake."

[10]The guru also reveals a particular affiliation or bon for the bombo during the first lasol. Bombos are always of a particular line or bon. According to origination accounts, five (sometimes six) primordial bombos emerged after the five primordial Buddhas in the five (sometimes six) directions—east, west, north, south, center, (midspace). Each bon is identified with one of the primordial bombos. The lists of bon vary from bombo to bombo, yet a common listing is as follows: *shyelkar* bon to the east, *balden* bon to the west, *sonom* bon to the south, *yurung* bon to the north, *doshyel* bon to the center, *dol* bon in midspace (*barkap*). The bon of the new bombo is revealed by the preceptor, who while listing the catalogue of bon during the first lasol, shakes when alighting on the name of the appropriate bon. Attacks by certain lente apparently require affiliation with a particular bon. The ancient bombo

ing up of a physical energy from their innards that causes words to flow from their mouths. Bombos often invoke sensations in their viscera even when they are describing revelatory visions. They claim to be less dependent than lambus and lamas on the formalities of training and the necessity of texts and proper procedures. According to bombos, both lambus and lamas need only to memorize the formal ritual recipes and set incantations of their disciplines in order to practice. Both concentrate on the application of texts, the former on oral texts and the latter on printed texts, and on precise ritual procedures. As one bombo told me:

> The bombo does not stay in seclusion [learning] like the lama. Bombos learn little by little. The bombo speaks from the stomach. You cannot [like lamas] say exactly what the guru says. You must learn how to say things for yourself. . . .
>
> Lamas read from books, bombos must speak from their mouths. All comes from the innards. It is not poured from a flask or dumped from a basket [the way lamas and lambus practice]. If you have no consciousness you cannot do it.

Bombos also recount that in the ancient past two brothers, one a lama and one a bombo, had books. The bombo threw his in the fire and ate the ashes.

Bombos may downplay their formal association with mentors and an authoritative textual corpus; however, the preceptor charges the student's internal energy and makes it evident. In addition to bestowing a drum, assigning a bon or lineage, and completing the sequences of a lasol three times over, preceptors convey *wang* or power, which issues in a lineal relation from the lente through the guru to the bombo. Active control of, and inducement of, seizure by divine and malevolent beings depend on the generation of an internal strength that rises up in bombos, allowing them to shoulder divinities and harmful agents without harm. This internal power (*shyerap*) is activated in part by the

---

associated with one's bon and the lente are closely related but not the same because lente can be of different bon than the bombo. Bombo, though, invoke their lente at the same time that they announce their bon. During soundings, bombos, accompanied by their lente, travel to the hidden heavens (*beyhul*) of their bon and from there they reveal. When asked what a beyhul was one bombo replied: "It is the place of your own lineal bon. Some go to midspace, some to the north, some to the south, west, and east. You go to your own place. These are called beyhul. . . . [There] you reveal and tell [what you see]." Bon thus refers to a lineage associated with a primordial bombo who in turn is associated with the hidden heavens. In formal recitations, each bon is announced in association with different types of altar, water vessels, and disciplines; in practice, however, soundings vary little from bombo to bombo. and when they do, variation is a function of their training with a particular guru rather than their official bon.

ingestion of wang, allowing bombos to shake in counterbalance to the forces of external agents. They must shoulder these beings and toss them about during soundings. One bombo explained it this way:

> If an evil comes, it can make you shudder (*chhekpa)*; if a divinity comes, it can make you shudder. Shyerap (internal energy) comes from wang (external power); wang comes from shyerap. If you have no wang, shyerap cannot come. If no wang comes, if no shyerap comes, you do not shake much. If you do not have wang, you become very tired. If you have no wang, those beings come and really shake you; if you have wang, you cast them off easily. They can grab you tightly and completely. If you have wang, when you are grasped the forces are made equal and you make them meet; the forces are equal, they do not overcome you. You shake them along evenly and slowly. If you do not have wang and shyerap those things can tie you up like a rope.

During soundings, gurus call down wang from high mountain lakes and from the ancient bon; this wang accumulates on the guru's drum and/or in his water vessel and is fed to the apprentice, who upon ingestion shudders and shakes, generating internal strength. A guru feeds wang to apprentices during the first three performances of lasol; later, bombos invoke wang or power for themselves and ingest it.

Ritual knowledge and internal energy, then, combine, allowing bombos to carry all manner of divine and demonic beings. The passage to the position of bombo is, above all else, marked by a transition from a state of extreme subjection by uncontrollable forces to mastery of lente and, by extension, mastery of the divinities and harmful agents who inhabit the cosmos. As Höfer aptly observes, possessions occur only in soundings and bombos alone shoulder divinities and harmful agents:

> I have stated that possession is not a "dramatic" event in the rituals of the Tamang shaman in Central Nepal. If it [possession] occurs, as it has to at every seance, the Tamang shaman is not a passive vessel of the possessing agent. A state of possession is rather controlled than simply "endured" by him. A second characteristic of possession among the Tamang is that it never befalls laity. As a matter of fact, laity is excluded from every kind of ecstatic communication, be it by possession or by other ritual techniques. (1974:159)

Afflictions by lente are the most uncontrolled seizures in Tamang life, and the edifice of Tamang practice is to temper these seizures and contain them by orienting the afflicted toward the shamanic vocation.[11] Thereafter, possession becomes an essential feature of all soundings. Tamang speak of seizures using three transitive verbs—*tsungpa, shyappa,* and *ngyeppa*. These terms are used for everyday afflictions by shades, evil spirits, and divinities as well as severe attacks by lente. Although bombos speak of being seized, once they master lente, they invite possession, beckoning divinities and harmful agents to soundings. These beings alight on bombos and bombos carry (*nāpa*) them, playfully bounce them in the air like little children (*tengba*), or shoulder them (*khurpa*) like a sack of grain. Bombos invite harmful agents to enter their bodies and consume them. Evidence of this contact is shuddering (*chhekpa*).

To both practitioners and nonpractitioners, the bombo becomes the meeting point of human and divine or malevolent beings and a master of those encounters. In this general sense, the bombo becomes a mediator by placing opposed worlds in direct and contained juxtaposition. In the process bombos reveal the nature of divine and malevolent beings in a new light from lambus. Bombos also mediate in another sense—divinities and harmful agents not only come to them but bombos travel to the realms of these beings to reveal them. This form of mediation is announced in the link of bombos with midspace sprites.

Tsen, Mediation, and Revelatory Vision

All bombos must honor sprites known as tsen, relations with whom, along with relations with lente, are essentials of shamanic practice. Among Tamang specialists, only bombos ritually attend tsen; lamas and lambus claim ignorance of the ways of tsen and usually treat them as secondary evils. Bombos have practical dominion over tsen in the Tamang ritual system. As one bombo explained: "If lente and tsen-men seize someone, it is all right for them to become a bombo. If it is only tsen that causes one to shake, the innards will not open up. If tsen-men and lente strike at once, then as you honor the tsen, the lente emerge opening the innards [words come forth]." Tsen do not strike bombos as lente do; rather, bombos must activate relations with tsen and honor a personal tsen. The close association of bombos to tsen revolves around their mediatory positions. Tsen inhabit midspace between earth and sky and delight in the nectar of flowers that flourish in high-

[11] Lay are grasped by all kinds of ghosts and spirits, but possessions are indicated by illnesses quite different from possession by lente. Villagers reported that at one wedding, several people were "grasped" by a neglected divinity and shook like bombos. This was the only instance of lay possession spoken of in Tamdungsa.

altitude passes and in the pastures and forests of mountain peaks. The bombo, like tsen, travels between the human and divine and in going to the divine is able to unveil, open up, and reveal. Tsen are related by analogy to the special powers of sight attributed to bombos. According to the origination account of tsen (which I consider in greater detail in conclusion), humans and tsen intermarried in the ancient past but after an offense to a tsen wife, the tsen separated from her husband, a human, and disappeared into divine domains out of human sight. During soundings, bombos reveal those hidden heavens.

Tsen are attached not only to bombos but to women, a relation marked in the association of women with flowers, to which tsen are intensely attached. The most fashionable women's earrings and nose ornaments resemble flowers; women adorn their hair with flowers and appreciate gifts of floral patterned cloth. Tamang also imagine that the life-forces of children reside in flowers, which are thus likened to wombs. As Höfer notes, "flower" is a euphemism for vagina among some Tamang (1974:178).

Beyond these associative links, there is an essential ritual one. Tsen become attached to households through women who in their movement from natal to marital homes bring tsen with them. As I noted in chapter 3, when a woman marries, she receives, depending on the economic situation of her natal home, variable amounts of movable wealth: gold, silver, and bronze jewelry, money, cloth, bronze plates and bowls, copper water jugs, and livestock. A tsen attached to her natal home will travel with the gold, silver, fine cloth, and even the bronze plates she takes with her to her husband's home. Usually, this tsen is one that originally came from her mother's home at the time of her mother's marriage. Thus, tsen are passed from mothers to daughters, tracing a matrilineal relation directly counter to the formal order of social organization. Tsen can attach themselves to women in two other ways: if a woman adorns her hair with a flower in which a tsen has alighted, she must thereafter ritually honor that tsen; second, if a bombo inadvertently applies the blessing of tsen to a woman not previously associated with one, she must honor it.

Once attached through a woman to a particular household, tsen affect general domestic well-being. To keep tsen in a nonharmful stance, householders must observe food restrictions (no consumption of wild boar or stinging nettles) and must regularly sponsor shamanic soundings to honor tsen. If tsen are well pleased, they bring general blessings of prosperity, wealth, strength, and offspring into a household. If they are neglected they can "sting." Specifically, tsen can cause infertility and menstrual difficulties in women (by licking up their menstrual flow as they lap up the nectar of flowers) and blindness in men. To avoid obligations to tsen, women will sometimes refuse to take valuable jewelry from their natal homes. Soundings in reference to tsen occupy a special place in the shamanic repertoire.

The Bombo's Repertoire

Powers of mediation are marked by the relation of bombos to lente and tsen, the former delineating the capacity to carry extrahumans and the latter to attain revelatory visions. Both forms are essential to shamanic practice and mark it in contradistinction to lamaic and sacrificial rituals. These latter ritual domains construct the divine and malevolent in accessible and resolved imagery and at a controlled distance. Although much of the shamanic repertoire includes propitiation and exorcism and supplements the ritual efforts of other practitioners, these services do not define or limit the communications of soundings.

Schematically the bombo's repertoire includes three types of sounding— calendrical soundings, incidental soundings, and pilgrimages— all of which ensue from their mediatory powers. There are four calendrical soundings that must be performed on a regular schedule. Bombos must perform *lai shyal phepa* or the unveiling of the faces of divinities at the end of the "dark month" and their own lasol every year or once every three years to propitiate their lente and tsen.[12] Lasol, although uniquely performed for bombos, is almost identical to *mālo lhoba,* a third calendrical sounding. Malo lhoba is the only calendrical sounding conducted in lay households and usually is performed only by those households with attached tsen, who require, like lente, annual or triannual recognition in the yharsung phase of the year. Villagers report that some people who do not have tsen attached to their houses also perform malo lhoba but without the specialized remembrance of tsen. The only difference between lasol and malo lhoba is that lasol includes an elaborate recognition and offering to lente. In addition to this sounding, some of the more rigorous households add another known as *tsenṭol,* which propitiates the tsen for the mharsung phase of the year.

[12]This sounding also serves as a communal recognition of the bombo; villagers proffer whiskey, grain, and money to the bombo, who returns blessings of long life. Moreover, lamas erect prayer flags in support of bombos, which fly in direct association with the life-force trees erected by the bombos themselves.

Tamang call bombos to conduct incidental soundings primarily for the retrieval of lost shadow-souls or the revival of life-force, both of which lead to generalized states of morbidity. Tamang also call bombos when they cannot get a successful diagnosis or treatment of a continuing ailment. In addition to these three primary curative services, bombos list a variety of other specialized soundings.[13]

The retrieval of lost shadow-souls, the revival of life-force, and divination all depend on the bombo's unique powers of sight. Humans have nine bla or shadow-souls, all but one of which can roam away from the body and become lost. Bla are also lost in instances of fright; for example, when lightning bolts flash, when thunder crashes, when feet trip on precipitous trails, when one encounters fighting dogs or bulls, or when one happens upon horrible demons or spirits in the forest, at crossroads, in high pastures, or at night in the village. When children show obvious fright, parents call out "come shadow-soul, come" to avoid loss of their shadow-souls. Once separated from the body, bla take refuge in a variety of intermediate places or are captured by harmful agents. Shadow-soul loss leads to a generally weakened state; one becomes open to the attack of a variety of malevolent forces. If one has been sick and uneasy for long periods of time and the ministrations of lamas and the endeavors of lambus have been to no avail, bombos call back the shadow-souls from wherever they may be lost or have taken refuge. Tamang believe that wandering shadow-souls dream our dreams, and thus Tamang are always careful to call out the names of people before waking them; otherwise, the roaming shadow-souls will not return to the body.

So or life-force, on the other hand, dies with the body. An individual develops a life-force at about age twelve, and it grows up through the torso like a tree. On a heavenly hill, which only bombos can reveal, there is a *so dungma* or life-force tree that is directly linked to the condition of the life-force in the body. When these heavenly trees are damaged—when the branches break, when the trunk rots, or when the tree bends over—the damage reflects the condition of the internal life-force. During soundings bombos reveal the condition of so dungma and erect tree saplings outside the house, resuscitating the weakened life-force (See Figure 7). Children have no proper so or so dungma.

[13]If a mother is unusually anxious about the health of an unborn child or a sickly child, bombos can pledge these children to the care of divinities. If one is attacked by the caretakers of trees, stones, and water (*shyingmon-brābon-chhubon*), who look like miniature bombos (they have tails that come up between their legs with which they beat drums), or by *māpon* or forest bombos, one also requires the services of bombos. Some bombos also stop the attacks of *bir* or familiars reputedly kept by some well-off households.

Figure 7. A bombo erecting a life-force sapling

Children's life-force is in the care of "motherers" (*kale ama*) who construct the human body as wasps construct mudhives. The life-forces of children play in all kinds of flowers and Tamang speak of a child's *so mhendo* or life-force flower. When children are ill, bombos "open up" or "clarify" their so mhendo.

Just as the retrieval of shadow-souls and the revival of life-force depend on unique powers of sight, revelation depends on these powers. In the middle of soundings, bombos "go into the divine" and make the sources of distress apparent. There they have dreamlike visions. Upon descending from the heavens, they interpret these enigmatic signs for whoever has requested revelation.

Pilgrimages, the third remaining type of sounding, are manifestly revelatory journeys and are homologous to the revelations that occur in soundings. A bombo undertakes these journeys to high mountains or low valleys at the request of groups of villagers who present the bombo with gifts of cloth. Upon arriving at the divine sites at the end of a pilgrimage, bombos launch themselves into divine heavens which they reveal for all who ask. Dancing from house to house upon their return, they repeat their prophesies for all villagers. Pilgrimages are often associated with large regional festivals, and masses of people along with scores of bombos gather for revelries.

A Metasounding

A prevailing strategy in the explanation of ritual events like Tamang soundings is to demonstrate that specific rituals provide remedial effects for individuals, whether sponsors or specialists, and for the community at large. For instance, case histories are often recounted in light of how specific rituals organize and channel experiential states in the symbolic logic of a particular culture.[14] Tamang do speak of bombos as those who "cure" or "repair" (*kyompa*) those afflicted in unusual ways, and the performance of incidental soundings is motivated by malaise; but our concern here is to show how the effects of soundings are contained in an overarching discourse about affliction more religious than therapeutic. I proceed, then, not from a specifically therapeutic sounding but from malo lhoba, which is motivated by the

[14]The penetrating recountings of personal, social, and cultural symbols in the works of Turner (1967:359–93), Crapanzano (1980), Lambek (1981), and Obeyesekere (1981)—to mention but a few—are obvious examples.

attachment of tsen to women's property and thereby specific households, not by an incident of malaise.

The sounding that honors tsen, although not performed as a cure, hierarchically subsumes curative services in a portrayal of divine and demonic forces. Both malo lhoba and lasol are totalizing soundings. As we have seen, lasol is at once an initiatory undertaking, a training session, and a ritual obligation; it exhibits every major procedure a bombo needs to know in order to perform most other soundings. Not only do lasol and malo lhoba subsume the curative services of incidental soundings, curative soundings always hark back to malo lhoba and have the same set of events. They differ only in the relative emphasis given particular sequences. For example, when someone asks a bombo to retrieve a lost shadow-soul, the bombo goes through the sequences of a malo lhoba, emphasizing and elaborating the soul-calling sequence. All soundings, then, have an identical structure. Malo lhoba also incorporates the primary sequences of other calendrical soundings. In this sounding, as in all soundings, bombos "unveil the faces of the divinities" and go into the divine, the key sequences of lai shyal phepa and pilgrimages, respectively. Malo lhoba, then, like lasol, can be conceived as a metaritual to which other soundings are logically interconnected and from which we can situate the shamanic in relation to sacrificial and lamaic ritual forms and communications. Before turning to these relations, though, the sequences of these typical soundings need to be outlined.

The Process and Structure of a Sounding

Every Tamang household maintains a continuing relation with a particular bombo who fulfills ritual requirements whether calendrical or incidental and who acts as a consultant in times of difficulty or distress, diagnosing and recommending courses of action.[15] If a sounding is necessary, sponsors must formally summon their attending bombo with gifts of grain, whiskey, and token coins, conveyed most often by the mha (sister's husband of the male head of the household), who also acts as the bombo's assistant during the sounding. On their way to the house, the mha sounds the bombo's drum, announcing the imminent performance. Performances proper do not get under way

[15]Bombos (and other knowledgeable folk) divine by taking pulses, reading rice grains, examining the innards of sacrificial animals, or, in special circumstance, revealing hidden heavens, a service that in itself requires a sounding.

until after nightfall, usually a few hours before midnight, and continue on into daylight the following morning. Some Tamang say divinities and harmful agents live in an inverse world and are only accessible at night. Others say they are too busy to be contacted during the day. Harmful agents in particular are thought to be most active in the dead of night, roaming the village paths, fields, and groves.

People begin to gather at the sponsor's house while bombos prepare themselves, and they come and go through the night. Whether performed at a bombo's house as in lasol or in villagers' houses as in malo lhoba, soundings attract spectators. Not only do members of a household usually attend, but many people from the immediate neighborhood and often from the better part of the village crowd into the hearth room of the sponsor's house and spill out onto the veranda and courtyard, especially if a famous or particularly skilled bombo is sounding. Incidental curative soundings, although less open events, usually include at least close kin and neighbors. Whether or not soundings are well attended, everyone in the village knows when one is underway from the beats of the drum resonating through the still night air. Village chatter soon communicates to everyone who is sounding, why they are sounding, and, later, what the results of the sounding are.

After sponsors feed the bombo, bombo and mha make preparations for the sounding, beginning with the construction of an altar near the hearth. The altar is a raised platform supported by small saplings on which colorful cloth is draped, forming a three-sided enclosure. Flowers adorn the enclosure and the rafters directly above the altar. The altar bridges earth and heavens and is the conduit whereby divinities and spirits descend into ritual presence and bombos ascend into revelatory realms. If the altar is oriented toward the heavens, the door is oriented down and away and is the direction in which bombos exorcise harmful agents.

The altar is also a microcosm, and the bombo arranges a ring of *tormo* or dough images of various divinities and harmful agents in the enclosure.[16] Along with these tormo are vessels of water and milk

[16]Bombos in Tamdungsa rarely know more than the names of these tormo and follow the practices of their gurus by rote. Tormo are for the most part the forms or bodies of the divinities. One bombo molded this set for a lasol: *ḍamar* or tiger devil, several mountain divinities, Shyihbda, *lai mhiktung*, the four directions, the pillars of the earth, a bull, the sun-moon, a cock, the principle of opposites (*yab teng yub*), tsen-men and their children, a Tibetan wife (of Guru Rhimborochhe), a Newar wife (of Guru Rhimborochhe), a triangular image called *chholo*, a tormo representing the twelve years and called "nine lives and ninefold prosperity," and two tormo formed like a bombo. Bombos gave highly variable explanations for these images, which form a ring in front of the bombo with Damar in the center. The two images of bombos face the other images just as the presiding bombo encounters the divinities of the cosmos.

representing the high-altitude lakes, the beak of a great hornbill, which stands for the mythic and Garuda-like bird known as *khyung,* and various ritual implements used during the performance such as a trumpet made from the thighbone of a tiger and the horn of a plains antelope. In the center of this microcosm is the *tsheṇe* or the seat of the divinities.[17] It is the locus of power and is highly charged when activated by divine presence. Bombos carry tshene on their pilgrimages in order to attract divinities and to accumulate their aura.

The bombo orients ritual attention to the altar: the bombo sits in front of it, beckons divinities to descend into it, directs invocations toward it, and dances in front of it. The bombo makes excursions toward the door and outside for the most part to expel harmful agents. Below the altar on a raised board are the flasks of whiskey and beer, bowls of rice, and burning incense that the bombo requires during the performance. For soundings all bombos don a special habit, which includes a pleated skirt, usually of white cloth, and a colorful camise. They wrap strands of bells in a crosshatch across their torsos along with strings of *ruddrāche* beads made from the dried fruits of Elaeocarpus. Most bombos also wear necklaces of lamaic prayer beads and attach protective amulets around their waists. Others have special necklaces and talismans of various sorts. All bombos also unfurl their rhalbo or matted strands of hair on the back of their heads so that it hangs down their backs. They never cut this hair, and male bombos usually keep it coiled up under hats or turbans.

The majority of malo lhoba or tsen soundings have nine distinct, often lengthy, sequences, most with a professed purpose:

1. An overture that includes an invitation to spirit allies and divinities, an incense-offering (*sangrap*) and place-listing (*rhikap*) that consecrate the altar and cosmos; and a concluding "unveiling" of divine faces, marked by the lighting of a butter lamp.
2. A request for wang or power.
3. An exorcism of a horde of evils and their minions.
4. An honoring of tsen.

[17]The tshene is a specially arranged basket filled with grain to which bombos add yeast, dried fish, and black and white quartz rocks. Bordering the rear edge and stuck into the grain are tail feathers of the high-altitude impeyan pheasant and the lowland peafowl, along with porcupine quills. In the midst of the quills and feathers are an iron trident and an implement called a *darlung,* which is a stick with small streamers of cloth and acts as an antenna attracting the aura of the divinities who come to sit in the tshene. The tshene accumulates and radiates the power and protective beneficence of divinities. It is also a *ne* or place of the divinities. When bombos reveal the faces of the divine they light a butter lamp in the altar. It is a microcosm of the heavens.

5. The revelation of the abodes of the divinities or "going into the divinities" (*lari ngyipa*) and the calling of shadow-souls.
6. Divine work (*la get*) where the bombo is possessed by an array of beings.
7. The expulsion of *mhamho* or the consumer of human pollutions; a purification of the householders.
8. The resuscitation of life-force.
9. The invocation of long life, power, and well-being for the householders.

Soundings like the metasounding outlined above are long and multifaceted performances. The purpose here is less to unravel or to attempt to explicate each of the sequences in detail (see Holmberg 1980:297–321) than to isolate some of the outstanding features of the sounding as a genre. The salient features here are that the bombo brings human, divine, and malevolent into direct contact. In the process, the orders defined by sacrifice are revealed as tenuous.

Shamanic Suspensions

The shamanic defies attempts to contain it analytically. Bombos often laugh at direct questions about their practice or revert to their measured chants. They evade positive declarations and acquire their authority from an elusiveness. Although often deadly serious, some joke that their soundings are deceptions. This tricksterish quality will return us ultimately to the relation of tsen to the shamanic, but first we must review the mediatory displays of bombos, their shoulderings of divinities, spirits, and harmful agents, and their revelatory flights. These practices suspend in ritual space enigmatic beings and open up their hidden realms. These mediations, as we have seen, define bombos as practitioners and are the ritual prerogative of bombos.

Divine and malevolent agents descend on bombos and make themselves evident during soundings in at least four ways. Bombos shoulder beings collectively referred to as phamo or guardians; they shoulder divinities and spirits; they induce beings to enter their bodies and act like those beings; and they shoulder harmful agents. The invocation of phamo is essential to a successful sounding, and phamo have a special role as allies to bombos.[18] Invoked at the inception of all soundings and periodically throughout the sounding, they accompany bombos in their ecstatic flights and in their encounters with all kinds of beings. Under the rubric of phamo, who are invoked by name, are usually the

[18]*Phamo* also can mean "mother."

bombo's personal lente (ancestral spirits), the lente of the bombo's guru, ancient bombos, the supporting divinity of the household where bombos sound, and, depending on the idiosyncratic practices of individual bombos, various other spirits. Both in the ritual chants and in shamanic exegesis these phamo are said to be carried on the shoulders (khurpa) and tossed about in the air with the hands (tengba).

For instance, at the conclusion to a sequence, one bombo chants out to his phamo:

> I, self-generated Shyelkar Bon, toss up.
> I carry off.
> . . . . .
> On the right [shoulder] carried off,
> On the left [shoulder] carried off,
> We, an ancient Bon, have bounced you about.
> Respectful greetings, Guardians.

Carrying also implies an identity or merging of bombo and phamo, at least when one bombo calls his lente:

> Watch out for both the good and the bad.
> If harm comes from the front, watch over me.
>
> You and I in one trail,
> You and I eating from one dish,
> You and I drinking from one bowl,
> You and I sitting on one seat,
> To reveal the hidden heavens,
> Let's go everywhere.

The reference to eating from one plate implies an intimacy witnessed socially for the most part only among intimates. Bombos are usually highly particular about their commensal purity. Closely related to phamo are other beings invoked by the bombo for special ritual purposes. One bombo, for instance, calls on *khaṇḍangmo* or furies who "come down grasping" and lead the bombo to the gates of the revelation. Another bombo, for the same purpose, calls down his phamo, whom he accompanies to the gates of the heavens:[19]

[19]Here the symbology of the chants remains obscure because the bombo may "ride" the horses he invokes up into the otherworlds rather than shoulder the phamo. In the same invocation, the bombo refers to his own body becoming that of a white horse. Moreover, many bombos use ritual implements depicting carved horses with bombos riding on their backs.

Come and make steps for me of an ancient lineage.
Make water flow easily Shyelkar goddesses.
Come down in the form of a white horse to me of an ancient lineage.
Come down in the form of a red horse.
Come down contentiously with an iron sword.
Come down contentiously with a copper sword.
Come down [as] a white horse in a circling wind.

Along with these allies, a host of other beings come into attendance at soundings.

Some bombos use the term *phamo* to refer generically to all the divinities they invoke or represent in their altars. In general divinities are constructed as allies; however, their assistance is less specifically conceived, and they do not appear to ride with bombos throughout their ritual chores. Divinities take up residence in the altar after being invited. When bombos burn incense at the start of a sounding and recite the names of divinities in a rhikap or place sequence, they shudder upon the naming of divinities. Bombos explain this experience in two ways. First, they shudder at the thought of divinities when they recite their names. Second, divinities literally arrive at the sounding and upon arrival pulse through their bodies; bombos then shoulder or carry the divinities momentarily. In most colloquial contexts, shuddering is taken as evidence that divinities have alighted on the backs of bombos. These encounters are brief and occur repeatedly in a sounding. Many lengthy passages in soundings oscillate between recitation of divine names in cadenced chants and rhythmic shuddering at the thought or presence of the beings named. The shaking of their bodies rings the bells wrapped around their torsos and rattles their drums. This shuddering, jingling, and rattling are the only evidence of the presence of divinities, who despite the fact that bombos "unveil" their faces, never make themselves known through speech, activity, or sight. Identical to these divine manifestations through the bodies of bombos are the arrival of tsen, who when named similarly cause bombo's bodies to quiver.

Related to these forms of shouldering divine agents are the dramatic displays in the "divinity work" sequence. Bombos briefly act out characterizations of a set of comical and sometimes fearsome beings. A similar display occurs in the exorcistic sequence when bombos become the mythic bird khyung who battles with *si*, a kind of ghostly spirit. The bombo calls khyung into his body and dances fiercely about the room with the skull of a dog in his mouth, biting the evil spirits as the evil spirits bite humans. Bombos also dance like tsen when they honor them. These displays are brief. Bombos shake these beings on and off quickly, and this form of possession supplements, as we shall see, the general pattern of possession during soundings.

The embodiment of harmful agents works out in a similar idiom but with a slightly different twist. When divinities arrive at a sounding, they are invited respectfully into the altar. Harmful agents are not invited to the sounding until the exorcistic sequence and then not into the altar but to the side; they are eventually shown the way out the door. Dealing with the demonic involves a measure of trickery and deception along with power. Many bombos begin by enticing harmful agents from the sponsors' bodies into their own:

From the flesh,
From the blood,
From the bone,
[Go!]
Eat my flesh,
Drink my blood,
Eat my bone.
Chew my flesh,
Suck my blood.

Once harmful agents are in their bodies, bombos coax them into the bodies of sacrificial substitutes, thereby releasing humans from their afflictive grasp. If the sounding does not have a specific curative end, as in malo lhoba, then bombos need not shoulder the harmful agents directly in their bodies. They exchange a sacrificial victim directly for the bodies of the sponsors. Bombos do, however, carry all the invited harmful agents in their bodies when they arrive for their feast. These possessions, like those of divinities, are brief; bombos contain them momentarily within their bodies "shaking them along evenly and slowly."

Bombos also "clarify" (*salpa*) and "reveal" or "unveil" (*phepa*) intractable worlds hidden from human sight. Although bombos can achieve visionary states at several times in a sounding, revelation is concentrated in the sequence of "going into the divinities." After attaining visionary consciousness, bombos make clear the condition of their sponsors' shadow-souls and life-forces and see signs indicating the causes of human misfortune and the course of future events in people's lives.

Although bombos do not speak of flying or "soul journey," they are clearly associated with the imagery of flight, and their orations at the time of revelation directly map an ascendance through space. Bombos list the high hills and peaks, moving up through the Himalayas until they reach the gates of the heavens outside Ui Same as though they were making such a journey. Furthermore, an implicit association between revelatory visions and dream images relates bombos and their perceptual powers to bla or shadow-souls, which as we have seen are thought to leave the body during sleep to dream our dreams. Bombos leave the social body and envision divinatory images in the same way that shadow-souls experience human dreams.

The pursuit of clarifying visions, takes bombos into *ne* or demonic and divine domains. These ne, although mentioned separately, are apparently attained simultaneously when the bombo crosses through locked gates: "The beyhul [secret places] and the places of the divinities are the same. There are beyhul in all the directions and the nine territories. They are all in one place. The place where you arrive is the same. We go with the lente." The ne listed by bombos are numerous and include foremost the domains of the divinities named by the bombo before launching into revelatory consciousness, beyhul or secret places, and an array of hellish places and marginal spaces. The latter are particularly important in clarifying the condition of human shadow-souls and calling them back. Bombos while in these domains attain a visionary state. Lost shadow-souls can lodge in a multitude of intermediate and undetermined places or be captured by all manner of harmful agents. Bombos locate lost shadow-souls by "taking" their chants and their searches to places beyond human sight, usually inaccessible, ill defined, and frightening. One bombo listed the following places where souls get stuck:

In a heaven of the homeless,
In a heaven of confusion,
In a heaven of distress,
In a heaven of rumorous gossip,
In a heaven of cannibals,
In a heaven of closed mouths,
In a heaven of licentious sex.

Above a great rock,
Above a great tree,
Above a great cliff,
Above a great rent in the earth,
Above a crevasse,
In a low flying cloud,

In a circling wind,
In a great thunderbolt,
In a great lightning flash,
In the midsky,
In the puddles of a marsh.

In the place of the living,
In the place of the dead,
In the hand of an evil lama,
In the curse of an evil bombo.
With the Newar shades,
With the Gurung shades,
With the headless shades,
With the bir,
With Shyingmon-brabon [and attached shades]
With Kharta [and attached shades].

In a bullfighting place,
In the place of spinning and fighting dogs,
In the place of stealing off chickens.

In a banana grove,
In the high pastures.

Once launched through the gates and sitting withdrawn, silent and with eyes closed, meditating, visions of these realms appear to bombos sometimes in sudden bursts of light. One bombo described his visions thus:

> I go see whatever there is. When Khandangmo [female furies] come down you do not see with your eyes. You shiver. It comes down grasping. After bringing Khandangmo to mind, she goes in front of us. Just as someone in the village goes ahead on the trail, Khandangmo leads. When you reach there, it is like a flash of daylight. It is very bright just like sunshine or lightning. Then it becomes black like day. It can be back and forth like that. Then you sit there and meditate.

Another described his visions as faint images that appear like objects in a dimly lit room. Yet another stressed the visceral accompaniments to visionary states which he described as a quickening of the innards. From these visions, bombos report to sponsors and spectators.

The fearless and bold mastery of bombos in containing otherworldly beings and in crossing into divine and demonic realms have ameliorative effects, either protecting sponsors or curing them. Divinities are honored, powers invoked, evils exorcised, tsen appeased, conditions clarified and shadow-souls called back, spirits shouldered, pollutions carried off, life-forces revitalized, and blessings invoked. The symbolic manipulations of each individual sequence work toward protecting, energizing, and revitalizing the sponsors and their houses and fields; householders sponsor soundings for these restorative effects. Bombos "cure" (kyompa) those who are afflicted in an extreme way. At the inception of a revelatory sequence, one bombo, for instance, chants that the sponsor is under assault from all manner of harmful agents and in a state of fearful helplessness. He declares that she is frozen in fear (*thom-thom*), stumbling about in a dark haze (*rhi-rhi*), and vigorously shaken; "her body is helpless; her heart-mind is riven with anxiety." The revelatory sequence is performed to bring order to these inchoate states.

Similarly, bombos may effect both specific ritual ends and general dramatic catharses for sponsors, spectators, and themselves by embodying divine and malevolent agents. All these manifestations of guardians, spirits, divinities, and harmful agents through the vehicle of bombos during soundings are organized within the general logic of "shouldering" (khurpa) and "tossing" (tengba) in which the bombo remains the master. Höfer has aptly explicated the meaning of khurpa as connoting "riding pick-a-back," and Tamang in Tamdungsa use the term *khurpa* to describe the activity of carrying a burden on the shoulders and *tengba* to connote "'tossing' with one's hands," as one playfully tosses up a small child in the air (1981:73). Bombos thus are simultaneously shouldering burdens when beings ride their backs and dominating those beings when they jauntily manipulate them with their hands. The ambiguity in the use of the two terms is conveyed in the double implications of shamanic shaking or shuddering, which simultaneously indicates the presence of embodied beings and the power and internal energy of the bombo in controlling possession. These displays of shamanic control over beings always on the verge of overcoming humans and shocking them into uncontrollable anxiety and suffering, on one level, diminish those beings in human consciousness and transitively relieve humans from their torment.

This tense encounter of shamanic power with other worldly beings, though, carries meanings irreducible to these therapeutic idioms. In fact, nothing specific is at stake in a performance of the metasounding outlined above; there are not necessarily any lost shadow-souls to be called, life-forces to be revitalized, or intractable uncertainties to be clarified—the special curative services of bombos. Furthermore, even these curative services offered by bombos in incidental soundings are general in nature; sponsors never call bombos to sound for common ailments but only in the case of prolonged or intractable malaise. Most everyday ailments, in fact, are the ritual province of lambus and lamas—and more recently doctors, pharmaceutical compounders, and the like—who provide immediate remedies for aches, fevers, gastrointestinal complaints, colds, flus, weaknesses, infections, and rashes through sacrificial offerings, textual recitations, or medicines. Even serious illnesses that have a clear set of symptoms and etiology are more often than not the purview of lambus and lamas. Bombos are curers of a special type; they deal with the preconditions that allow particular forms of affliction to occur and with the meaning of affliction in general. They ultimately expose alien and unintelligible beings and realms. Bombos are not only figures of mastery, they are instruments through which enigmas resound.

Soundings have only an arbitrary closure. This is evident in several aspects of soundings but particularly in the portrayal of divine and demonic beings and domains. Possessions proceed continuously during a sounding, not simply as the accretion of singular possessions. Hundreds of divinities pulse through bombos' torsos; hordes of harmful agents sting and gnaw at their innards; scores of tsen quicken their flesh. Most of these divinities, harmful agents, spirits, and their minions are not those who intrude into everyday life or around whom are woven the symbolic templates of an etiology. They are on the whole vaguely known and obscure and are never cited as the direct agents of specific afflictions and misfortunes as are village shades, regional spirits, and temperamental divinities whom lambus regularly deflect and appease through sacrifice. Attention rarely focuses on a solitary divine or demonic being, but on agents, an effusion of cosmic classes. Moreover, divinities are heard, as we have seen, only in the clanging of bells and the rattling of drums. In "divine work," bombos display a type of possession closer to speech when they enact the monkey god, a dumb herder, a beggar, a horrible spirit, an antelope, or a powerful ancestral shaman. This sequence, however, has no purposive gloss, and all the beings enacted are dumb and, like all beings shouldered by bombos, obscure.

These irruptions then do not admit clear and directly accessible images of the divine and the malevolent that would allow a sounding to proceed psychodramatically in the clinical sense of such therapeutic processes. To begin with, only bombos shoulder beings, and although divinities and harmful agents arrive at soundings, no direct discourse between them and humans unfolds; thus there is no opportunity for an indirect communication among participants through the voices of spirits like that which Lambek (1981) has demonstrated for possession in Mayotte. Nor do patient and curer talk back and forth while possessed, as they do in Sri Lanka (Obeyesekere 1977). Furthermore, the engagements of sponsors and spectators during soundings are not intense. They are not riveted to the performance as participants; they come and go, eat and drink, chat, doze, and so forth while bombos sound. Sponsors and spectators are brought indirectly into contact with the spirit world, usually to convey an offering, accept blessings, and be purified. In fact, rapt engagement marked by sitting too near a bombo or overattendance at soundings are a sure course to uncontrolled possession that would impel one to become a bombo. Even bombos retain their distance and are not overtaken by the beings they shoulder. There is a tense separation of bombos and divine or demonic agents. Bombos also chant in archaic Tamang, a language few can fully understand, and these chants are usually drowned out by the incessant drumming and cacophony accompanying a sounding. Although sponsors and spectators come to witness shamanic encounters and have a general idea of the progression of a sounding, they are rarely acquainted with the details of shamanic recitations or ritual acts. Participants are most engaged when they whistle through blades of grass the eerie tune pleasing to tsen or when the bombo is in the ecstatic interludes of the performance.

Just as divine and demonic beings remain distant and lack resolution during soundings, so do the revelations bombos make when they go into divinities. Their visions as experience remain obscure even to themselves. As one bombo remarked, "Does it happen or not? I don't know. I don't see with my own eyes." The relation of bombos to sponsors and village spectators, as I noted, is analogous to the relation of shadow-souls to the body. According to the same logic whereby shadow-souls experience human dreams when they wander from the body during sleep, bombos attain visions for the social body when they launch themselves through gates of revelation (often in search of shadow-souls).

The visions of divine, demonic, and marginal spaces, like dreams, are known only in retelling and formalized cultural appropriation. Many bombos work from codes to interpret these images. For one bombo, visions of cows or white goats imply that someone is being troubled by lu, quartz signifies a curse, a snake emerging from someone's house means shadow-soul loss, and so forth. These codes are often the same that bombos use to decipher dreams. After returning from visionary consciousness, bombos do not literally recite what they have seen. Visions, again like dreams, cannot be re-presented. Not only are the visions opaque, the secondary recounting leaves room for ambiguity. The recitations are always told in the obscure languages of archaic Tamang or in Nepali and never in colloquial Tamang, adding distance and mystery to these oracular events. The bombo, moreover, usually does not declare exact causes of hardship or the course of futures but several possibilities. In one revelation, for instance, a bombo informed one person that a fight would occur in his household within a month, that the household would experience starvation, that someone would be sick, that relations with their supporting divinity were broken, that there was no prosperity in sight for the household, that relations with several divinities and spirits were not good, that a witch's familiar was at play in their well-being, and that the household had three enemies. The potential sources of hardship for this household were legion, and revelations like these are less final determinations than the basis for secondary and continuing digression about affliction. Bombos do not determine courses for ritual action during revelation but set the stage for such discussions. When confronted with many possible ritual cures for their sufferings, most villagers choose to sponsor rites in reference to them all. Significantly, it is never the bombo who effects the cures implied in most revelations; it is always the lambu or the lama who puts things in order by propitiating neglected divinities, banishing evil agents, or binding divinities and harmful agents to oaths. Thus, revelations are as much evidence of the intractability of divine and demonic activity as ordering declarations.

When bombos shoulder divine and demonic beings and disclose recondite worlds, they not only provide remedies, they communicate something essential about these beings and realms and reflexively subsume afflictive experience in a system of meaning. Bombos bring alien beings and obscure worlds into an immediate juxtaposition with humanity. In soundings, bombos simultaneously demonstrate the reality of an alter world of divinities and harmful agents and the elusiveness of these beings and realms that lie beyond direct apprehension. Bombos "unveil" (phepa) divine faces, yet paradoxically, the divinities remain beyond human perception. They see but their visions are fleeting. Thus although soundings clearly have boundaries and a ritualized closure—figured in the bombo's mastery of possession—large portions of a sounding are suspensions that lack narrative closure (cf. Siegel 1978).

The objectives of the sequences of soundings—honoring divinities, invoking power, driving off evils, honoring tsen, revealing the heavens, divine working, ridding pollutions, reviving life-force, and calling down blessings—can, then, also be conceived as glosses much as just-so titles on myths disguise a less-resolved reality.

The Anomalies of Order and Suffering: Tsen and the Shamanic

The shamanic, then, retains an intractability that supersedes the resolutions suggested by the glosses on the individual sequences. This feature of shamanic ritual communication is most apparent, however, from a vantage outside soundings as discrete events, a vantage that places shamanic ritual in complement to the sacrificial and the lamaic. These relations are exposed in the beings called tsen, who have special analogical associations with bombos and women and whose attachment to households motivates a metasounding in the bombo's repertoire. Tsen reveal a problematic fundamental to the Tamang ritual field.

Bombos are theoretically restricted from simple propitiatory and exorcistic sacrifice. Even when someone practices as both a lambu and a bombo—which several do—villagers are quite explicit about the distinction in roles. When a bombo practices as a sacrificer, he is never called bombo, and when a lambu sounds he is never called lambu, only bombo. For bombos to practice as sacrificers blinds them to revelatory sight. This is particularly true, as one bombo explained, if bombos expel Nakhle Mhang, a defining ritual of lambus:

> Usually it must be the lambu who throws out Nakhle Mhang. Bombos cannot. When I used to be a lambu, I threw out Nakhle Mhang, but when I became a bombo and quit, everyone [insisted that] I come throw it out. If a bombo throws out Nakhle Mhang, then the "closed eye revelation" cannot be seen. Nakhle Mhang [exorcism] blocks the vision just as the sorting basket [on which lambus carry offerings when they throw out the mhang] blocks his sight of the trail. The expulsion of Nakhle Mhang is the work of the lambu. So is the expulsion of other evils and shades. The evil spirits do not obey the bombo, only the lambu.

This basic incongruity between lambus and bombos—and, as we shall see, lamas—reflects the fact that lambus expel, displace, banish, and remove evil agents from human contact and sight; they keep divinities at an honorific remove. Bombos, on the other hand, bring the divine and malevolent forces directly into human sight.

The alienation of human from divine is recorded in the origination account of tsen. This account, which bombos must recite during propitiations of tsen, focuses in large measure on sight, linking the divine sight of tsen to the revelatory sight of bombos. According to this account, tsen and humans had not separated at the time of origination; they lived in a common world and married each other. Gesere Tsen emerges from a flower of a cosmic tree. His daughter, Tingtsa Rani, marries a human referred to as *mhā* or sister's husband. One day, Tingtsa Rani's brother, called *shyangpo* or wife's brother, goes hunting with mha. A noted bombo related this colloquial version of the origination of tsen:

> After Gesere Tsen's daughter married, her brother [shyangpo] called out, "Oh mha [sister's husband]! We must go hunting." Shyangpo and his dog went up a hill to flush down game while mha stayed behind in the cleft of a cliff ready to catch any game that came down. A tiny bird flew by and he stuffed it into his shirt. When shyangpo and his dog came running down, mha said, "No game has come." But shyangpo's dog was running and barking around mha so he said, "Nothing came! Something must have come." Mha quickly pulled out the tiny bird and said, "Here it is." They divided the meat, and shyangpo said, "One hindquarter must be given to my sister." He gave that quarter to mha to take to her. They then gathered up the meat, which was so heavy that they hung it on a pole and carried it between their shoulders.
>
> Mha arrived at home and said to his wife [Tingtsa Rani], who was weaving, "Here! This gift has been sent from your father's home." He tossed down the quarter of the bird onto the thigh of his wife. It broke her leg completely. Gesere Tsen got angry and said that his daughter could not stay with mha. So the tsen went up a hill where they made a barrier of stones and branches and called back to mha, "Can you see or not?" Mha responded, "Only faintly." They went to another hill and asked again, "Can you see or not?" "Not well," he responded. This day and the next, from hill to hill they went away, asking at each hill whether mha could see them or not. After crossing nine hills, they made another barrier and called out yet again, "Can you see or not?" Mha said, "I cannot see a thing."
>
> Tsen then said, "You go to the lineage of humans; we will go to the lineage of divinities. We will eat the nectar of rhododendron flowers, we will reside in these flowers. We will also help humans. If you present the proper offerings, we will assure prosperity, abundant wealth, and strength. You will have many offspring."

Through analogies with vision Tamang articulate the differences between humans and divinities, the separation of humans and divinities, and the unique ritual functions of bombos. The human husband captures a bird, miniscule to him but of large proportions to his divine hunting partner; the bird, in fact, becomes gigantic, and they must carry it slung on a pole between their shoulders. When the human husband arrives at home and delivers the portion of meat due a sister from her natal home, he offhandedly tosses it down to her because to him it is but a feather. From her perspective, however, it is so heavy that it breaks her leg upon impact, forcing the separation of humans and tsen. Divine tsen and human husband see this differently, and the offense to Tingtsa Rani irrevocably separates them. Tsen travel away, upward and across hills, erecting barriers that incrementally dim the husband's sight until he, like all humans, becomes blind to the divine. Tsen like all divinities are beyond human sight, comprehension, and control; not only can humans not see divinities, they cannot predict their interpretation of human reality or their behavior. Bombos recover sight of the divinities and harmful agents. Their bodies are the meeting place of the human and an enigmatic divine and a terrific malevolence; they travel between heavens and earth; they clarify, unveil divine faces, open up hidden heavens, and dwell in cosmic uncertainties. Although bombos expose the divine, it is an alien and enigmatic domain, real but beyond direct apprehension.

The shamanic sounds in counterpoint to both lamaic and sacrificial ritual, both of which blind humanity to divine and malevolent uncertainty or domesticate divinities and harmful agents. Sacrificial ritual works to banish the innumerable evils of the intermediate spaces of the cosmos. Lambus familiarize divinities with offerings of fine food, cloth, and honorific language, coercing them into measured relationship with humans. Lambus liken divinities to earthly royalty. The divine is humanized and its alien nature displaced; harmful agents are chased off and satiated. Above all, sacrificial ritual maintains harmonious order. Bombos are restricted from expelling Nakhle Mhang, the emblematic evil, because it would blind them to their special vision.

A Buddhist parallel to shamanic tsen announces a comparable ritual movement. In the same cycle of origination accounts in which the tsen events unfold and through which they articulate their history, humans marry other beings that occupy an intermediate place in Tamang imagination: *lu* or earth-water sprites, who, like tsen, are invoked as divinities and when neglected cause festering sores, rashes, and skin ailments.[20] The offspring of humans and lu in the myth are like lizards and toads, reptilian humanoids. In this case, humans and not lu decide that marriage is unacceptable and effect the separation. Upon the emergence of monstrous progeny, lamas etch sacred Buddhist words into rocks and intone the lu text, adjuring lu and containing its harmful influences. Since this separation, as one lama put it, "humans can no longer see lu." Whenever lamas ritually encounter divinities or harmful agents, they conscript them to the text and, like lambus, put them out of sight. As the same lama explained, since those times, bombos have gone the way of tsen and lamas the way of lu.

If sacrificial and Buddhist rituals deny divine enigmas, these enigmas are regularly confirmed empirically. Lamaic and sacrificial ritual attentions should protect and remedy; nevertheless bad weather, poor crops, disease, pain, and social dissension persist. Humans slight temperamental divinities in unknown ways, absentmindedly defiling them, forgetting proper offerings, and failing in their ritual efforts. Here the problem of theodicy is not resolved, at least in the immediate sense, through karma, where suffering is attributed to prior births (Obeyesekere 1968), as in Buddhism, but through a specific demonology. Harmful agents remain unbound and continually return human offerings with more pain and suffering; they attack out of nowhere at night, they attack on lonely trails in the early morning mists or late at night, they attach themselves to travellers, they sneak up from behind, they attack boldly from the front. They remain outside direct human perception, and bombos must reveal their nature. The images they reveal, however, lack the resolution of lamaic and sacrificial construction; the shamanic images of the divine remain, as the divine itself, intractable. The lamaic and sacrificial cannot ritually account for alienation and suffering, and thus they leave room in the ritual repertoire for soundings. In fact, the contradictions inherent in sacrificial and lamaic assertions of cosmic order can be said to motivate the shamanic.

The apparent incompleteness of the sacrificial and lamaic also plays out in the explicitly social themes of the tsen account, which provides a direct linkage between the shamanic and social paradox in the same way that the lamaic and sacrificial are linked to the genesis of social form. The tsen account emerges from the inherent ruptures of cross-

[20]See chapter 3. In fleeing from Tibet in one version of Tamang history, the clan of Dong Chhempo first tried marrying tsen, then lu, and finally incestuously.

cousin marriage, which is at the foundation of Tamang culture and society and places suffering, women, and the shamanic in a metaphoric association with ambiguity and irresolution. Before I elaborate on these relations, a more complete account of lamas in Tamang society and their most important rituals, memorial death feasts, is required.

7 An Amonastic Buddhism

Everything is male and female. It is like earth and sky. If there were only celibate nuns and monks, humans would diminish and die out. All living breathing things must exchange in marriage.

A Tamang lama

Among the Tibetans, grapholatry is more real than idolatry.

Robert Ekvall, *Religious Observances in Tibet*

Buddhism commonly conjures images of monasticism, celibacy, renunciation, universalism, ethical precepts, an otherworldly orientation, close relations to the evolvement of large-scale sociopolitical organizations, and a disjunction between lay and monastic communities.[1] Although Tamang know of monks and nuns in other societies, they have no monasteries or celibate monks and nuns as do Thai, Sherpa, Tibetans, and Sri Lankans.[2] Furthermore, neither local lamas nor villagers have any direct links to monastic communities.[3] Lamas as well as other Buddhist practitioners engage themselves in everyday life like all other Tamang. Although villagers speak of demerit (*pāp/dikpa*), rationalized formulations of karma and universal ethical values for action are seldom articulated outside explicitly ritual contexts. Tamang associate Buddhism with death and otherworldly concerns; however, they ritually pursue immortality and recognize lamas as sangkye or Buddhas because of potential worldly benefits.

On the surface, Tamang practice does not conform to orthopraxic

[1]These issues are in large measure the central ones in the anthropology of Buddhist systems. Much of the sociological discussion emerges from Weber's classic account of Hindu-Buddhist religious systems in *The Religions of India* (1958), synopsized and rephrased comparatively in Pardue (1971). Obeyesekere (1963, 1968, 1981), Kirsch (1967, 1972), and Keyes and Daniel (1983) all elaborate on Weberian themes. For alternate perspectives see Tambiah (1970, 1976, 1984), Gombrich (1971a), Spiro (1970), and Paul (1982).

[2]We could add contemporary Newar Theravada Buddhists (Gellner 1986), yet, for the most part, Newar pursue a Buddhism without monks (Allen 1973).

[3]In many regards, they become like the Sherpa village lamas who perform a host of worldly rituals; the primary difference is that where Sherpa are tightly enmeshed in relations with monastic communities and respect renunciatory ideals, Tamang are independent.

models; however, values prevalent in all Buddhist societies find expression in Tamang symbology. Tamang lamaic institutions have thrived in relative autonomy and have evolved an independent cultural form tied largely to the constraints of a clan-based society and to an imagination more mythic than rationalized. Tamang culture subjects the values of greater Buddhist ideology to a regime distinct from more reformist evolvements among populations like the Sherpa of Solu Khumbu.

The localization of Buddhist thought replicates not only processes found throughout the Buddhist world (where Buddhism is always of a unique sort—Thai, Sri Lankan, Burmese, Newar, Japanese, Chinese, Tibetan, Sherpa, and so forth) but also the particularities of Tamang history in Nepal as one of isolation from Tibet and enclosure in a feudal state (see chapter 2). The formation of the state and particularly the imposition of Rana order intensified a process of social and cultural introversion. As their sociopolitical ties to the north weakened, lamas and village gombos were no longer at the frontier of a Tibetan religious polity, which they replicated on a local scale. As they were denied full participation in the encompassing Rana sociopolity, patterns emerged according to local social conditions in which lamas became further enmeshed with insulated sets of villages linked through marriage exchanges. They were disjoined from religious centers. This did not mean that Tamang lamas were out of touch with, and uninspired by, other forms but that they became independent of any superseding institutional constraints. Moreover, the surplus necessary to support a community of monks was appropriated by the state.

Connections north, especially to Kyirong, continued until 1959, when the Chinese established direct administration in Tibet. Before 1959, the lamas associated with the local gombo had resided in a monastic institution in Kyirong for periods of up to a year. Lamas from Kyirong would also be invited to Tamdungsa to initiate local lamas and to perform rituals, usually death feasts or exorcisms for prominent village families. The local gombo reputedly had a seal of authority from Kyirong. Increasing communications with eastern Tamang and the emergence of local *lopan* or masters in recent decades have reinforced the diffraction of lamaic institutions and Buddhist ethos into an autonomous Tamang form. Not only did this involutionary process embed Buddhism in Tamang culture, but Tamang lamas and lamaic rituals acquired a form untempered by the rationalizing and universalizing orientations of greater monastic Buddhism in state societies. This pattern is beginning to reverse itself among contemporary Tamang in an environment of social change and of greater contacts with

Figure 8. Tamang raised altar for the festival of Chhechu. Lamas sit opposite the altar, dancers revolve around it, and spectators watch.

other Buddhist populations in Nepal, including more rationalized Sherpa of the Helambu region, Theravada Buddhists in a nearby Newar town, and Tibetans and Sherpa in the Kathmandu Valley.

The adaptation of Buddhist forms in a local style is nowhere more obvious than in the physical structures of lamaic rituals. Most villages have one or more small gombos usually built and cared for by schools of lamas and their village patrons. These gombos usually house clay images of Guru Rhimborochhe, the hero of local legend, flanked heterodoxically by his two wives. These gombos, though, rarely become the locus for important lamaic rituals, all of which take place at temporary altars erected in fields in the village. There lamas construct raised platforms enclosed on three sides, which house iconographic paintings (*thangku*), dough images, offerings, and ritual implements (see Figures 8 and 9). These platforms are held up by four freshly cut saplings lodged in the earth from which stream pieces of cloth. The activities of major lamaic celebrations revolve around these raised platforms,

Figure 9. Tormo and paintings on a raised altar

whose saplings connect earth and heavens. These altars are vivid images of amonasticism and the involution of Buddhist ideology into the regularities of local society.

Tamang villages may not have permanent renunciatory institutions; however, around these temporary altars, villagers perform rituals comparable to those of monastically oriented state societies. In Tamdungsa, villagers, for instance, sponsor a local lamaic pageant known as *chhechu,* which defines local lamaic culture and society in much the same way as pageants like the Mani Rimdu of Sherpa do at monasteries in greater Tibetan society (Fürer-Haimendorf 1964:210–24; Jerstad 1969; Nebesky-Wojkowitz 1976; Paul 1979, 1982).[4] In Tamdungsa, Chhechu, which consists of some fifteen dances performed over a period of about ten days, requires extensive support from the village community. In principle, villagers perform Chhechu for three

[4]Similar dance dramas are performed in the region and toward the Tibetan border. In many villages, these dance dramas are known as *mhane shyapa.*

consecutive years and then sponsor a villagewide feast for the next three. This schedule, though, appears to be abandoned regularly. Among other things, Chhechu symbolically recognizes the structure of authority in the village and marks out the village in regional Tamang society. Recent bickering among political factions has undermined the consensus required to complete the event successfully.

The period of Chhechu is marked by formal prohibitions, which define it as a special time. Villagers may work only at absolutely essential chores, such as providing livestock with fodder. Moreover, villagers cannot groom themselves, bathe, wash clothes, pick lice, distill whiskey, plaster houses, play cards, or the like. The festival also defines the village as a bounded and contained community. For the final three days of the event no one who has entered the village can leave, and no grain or money may be exchanged outside the bounds of the village. Chhechu is the major dance drama of its type in the local area, and at its climax close to a thousand people from Tamdungsa and neighboring villages attend.

The fifteen dances are performed around a raised altar in the center of the village. One performance of Chhechu included the participation of some sixteen lamas from Tamdungsa and neighboring villages as well as two *gurpa* from a higher village. Lamas and gurpa perform several of the dances and chant from their books daily to procure power, blessings, and well-being. Village men and boys perform all but the lamaic dances. The dances and the accompanying songs of the *shyepompo* (lead singers) articulate themes varying from the establishment of Buddhist dominion, to battles between kings and marriage exchange, to obscene folly and carnivallike reversals. Several dances are explicitly exorcistic, ridding the village of primary evils; others are connected with the invocation of well-being. Most villagers say the performance yields benefits: the protection of the village from evils, the accumulation of power and well-being, a sense of social renewal, and entertainment. The festival is also the occasion for visits of affines from neighboring villages, and all villagers entertain guests in their houses. It is a time of feasting.

Chhechu is a long and intricate pageant, and only the main features of the event can be outlined here. It symbolically encapsulates lamaic culture and society on the local level. The sociorituai order of the event is announced in the distribution of the dough images (*tormo*) of Buddhas and divinities at the conclusion of the performance. The headman (or headmen if there is a conflict), the lead singers, the specialists in invocations of power (gurpa), the woman who manages the distribution of food and drink, the man who cooks the food, the lama who is attached to the local temple, the oldest men of the main clans in the village, the village lambu, the accountant, and the lamas all receive special tormo or parts of tormo. Others receive tormo or pieces thereof according to their contributions. Prior to these distributions, which occur at the conclusion of the performance, lamas mete out power blessings beginning with headmen of the village then to everyone in attendance. The evolvement of these unique structures and practices is also evident in the training of lamas and in mortuary rites. Through an examination of these practices the place of the lamaic in the overall ritual field will become more obvious. It will also allow comparison of Tamang practices with those of other Buddhists.

Lamaic Retreats and Lamas in Local Society

Tamang lamas, the primary Buddhist specialists, are married householders who farm like their kinsfolk, although, if possible, they avoid plowing. Even the most reformed of Tamdungsa lamas, those who are altering customary practices in light of contacts with reformed Buddhists from other parts of Nepal, remain very much a part of regular village activity, with wives, children, houses, fields, and the everyday engagements of worldly life. They don their red clothes and turbans and display their banner paintings and ritual implements on ritual occasions. Villagers usually show them deference by according lamas seats of honor, by addressing them in honorific speech, and by serving them food according to the etiquette of respect, which includes a small table for the placement of their food and drink.

Any man can become a lama provided that he has resources to pay a lopan or master and to acquire essential paraphernalia. Several forces converge in orienting an individual toward lamaic training. Some lamas cite pan-Buddhist justifications, invoking suffering and a desire to quell suffering as primary motivations. Heredity may also be a factor in the selection of lamas. The gombo lamas of Tamdungsa were proud to claim descent from lamas back to time immemorial and referred to themselves as "ancient lamas" as opposed to the new lamas, whom they called "hunter lamas." But even lamas who acquired their status partially because of hereditary processes also claim experiential motivation and follow the same course of initiation and training as other lamas. Hunter lamas also "find" that they had ancestors who were lamas, and they train their sons in Tibetan script and drawing.

Lopan or masters, though, can never be their fathers. Pursuit of prestige and power can also direct some to undergo training. Above all, to become a lama requires a specialized relation to texts and the acquisition of ritual skills, both of which lamas acquire in retreats along with their formal initiation.

Lamas do not take vows of long-term renunciation or attend monasteries for training in Buddhist meditation. Nevertheless they attend initiatory retreats that reflect monastic ideals. To become a lama one must usually attend several retreats (*tshamri ṭipa*), the first of which constitutes an initiation. Usually several prospective lamas jointly invite a lopan to conduct a retreat in the forests or high promontories above villages. There, in forests or pastures, they erect temporary dwellings in which they reside for anywhere from several weeks to several months. Lopan can be regionally noted experts but sometimes come from more distant places, such as the Kathmandu Valley, Bhutan, or Tibet. During retreats, the lopan allows no contact between novices and other villagers. This initial seclusion is called *wang tsham* or power retreat.[5] One lama reported that his lopan performed mock rites of death, removing the tuft of hair at the back of the head and removing accumulated demerit. In this initial retreat, the lopan also regularly feeds power balls (*wang roro*) to the initiates, who for their part must continually prostrate themselves in front of the lopan and an altar.

These retreats include intense training in elementary techniques of lamaic ritual. Novices are drilled in the pronunciation of Tibetan letters, learn to repeat elementary texts, memorize the meaning of ritual symbols painted on iconographic cards and scroll paintings, absorb mantras or formulaic incantations, learn to construct simple altars and to mould dough images of the Buddhist pantheon, and acquire experience in simple ritual procedures. Upon leaving initiatory retreats, novice lamas continue to study on their own and in association with other lamas in their home villages. Above all, they refine their abilities through practical experience and join accomplished lamas in rituals, at first beating drums, clanging cymbals, running errands, performing menial ritual tasks, and serving the superior lamas. Later they move upward in the hierarchy to more respected positions and tasks.

In addition to this initiatory retreat, lamas attend other seclusions throughout their lives in which they acquire specialized ritual authority

[5]My information on these retreats is sketchy and was gleaned from conversations with several lamas. I never attended a retreat.

and mastery over new texts. Retreats are not simply training sessions; they symbolically condense renunciation, celibacy, and removal in specifically Tamang idiom. They do not, like monastic residences, set up the differentiation between a permanent monastic community and a lay community, an opposition that is fundamental to other Buddhist societies. Retreats are intermediate between the initiatory rites of tribal societies and monasticism in state societies. For Tamang, temporary retreats are simultaneously the context for acquiring arcane powers—usually employed for beneficial ends but conceivably for malevolent ends—and for conveying ritual and moral authority to lamas.

Although lamas have no formal grades, a lama achieves status in the community of lamas over time and according to the number of lamas who count him as a lopan or superior. Lamas also accumulate texts, banner paintings, woodblocks, and ritual implements, all of which contribute to their position within the community of lamas as does seniority. This paraphernalia can be considerable, and in addition to texts and banner paintings includes conches, *dorje* (powerbolts), bells, *phurba* (ritual daggers), cymbals, drums, water vessels, thighbone trumpets, dancing garb and headdresses, masks, and butter lamps. Finally, the erection of a gombo with images of the Buddhas adds considerably to a lama's prestige and depends on receiving substantial gifts from a wide community and patronage from local political leaders.

Adherence to a particular lopan means membership in a particular lamaic school. In Tamdungsa and the immediate vicinity, two schools of lamas practiced and a third was active in the region. The ancient lamas of Tamdungsa were of a school referred to by other villagers as *nakpadoser;* hunter lamas were called *karmapa.* A reformist school, whose members called themselves *ḍukpa,* was also active in the region. Although these schools replicate sect differentiations in Tibet, they do not define themselves through doctrinal debates but in ritual rivalries. Lamas of different schools often practice together at memorial death feasts and other large Buddhist rites. On these occasions they contend over ritual procedure, choice of dough images or banner paintings, and seating precedence. These arguments, though, as we shall see, can gloss a more substantive division relating to the reformist tendencies of some Tamang lamas.

Divisions between lamas and schools of lamas, although defined by adherence to lopans, also relate to rivalries of local political factions. Through clan association and affinal relations, lamas have specific social identities and obligations. They own, inherit, exchange, and dispute over property; they marry, divorce, and procreate like other villagers. Thus located in an active social system, lamas are channeled to particular masters and schools and become linked into local polity with special allies. Likewise, the choice of any lama by any household for any rite also depends on these convergent considerations. To a considerable degree, lamas and headmen mutually legitimate each other in the village, and lamas legitimate the village and its headmen vis-à-vis other villages and greater Nepalese society. Local lamaic rituals, particularly Chhechu and the memorial death feasts, glorify village headmen, clan segments, and households. In the past, lamas presided at the national political rites of Dasain. This is no longer the case in Tamdungsa; headmen receive symbolic legitimation from village lambus in conformity with the sacrificial character of the rite throughout Nepal.

The Letter, Oaths, and Lamaic Authority

Because lamas derive their ritual authority from special links to the printed word, they distinguish themselves from bombos by their possession of texts. Retreats establish this link. Lamas learn the pronunciation of the Tibetan syllabary and the proper cadence of chanting. In many of the texts lamas master there are blank or missing sections. After a lama acquires control of the overall pattern of chanting a text, the lopan either inscribes missing or secret passages in the text using red ink or the student commits the missing passage to memory. Lopan also teach students secret mantras without which the texts would be ineffective. These missing words and secret phrases operate as keys, unlocking the inherent powers of the words that originated with the Buddhas. Lamas, as I remarked, claim that bombos once had texts but they threw them in the fire and ate the ashes; they hint that bombos lie and deceive because they have no texts. According to lamas, texts when properly invoked and chanted are incontrovertibly powerful and truthful. Bombos mock lamaic adherence to the rote lessons of their lopan and claim they have unique, self-generated powers.

Lamaic texts and printed formulas are in the Tibetan script and, with the exception of mantras (Tamang *ngālung*) which have no direct translation, in the Tibetan language. Lamas in the vicinity of Tamdungsa cannot translate these texts even in an elementary way. For lamas and laity alike, written words are not vehicles for communicating doctrinal abstractions or means to meditative truths. Tamang chant texts and apply letters because of their inherent power. Tamang extend the power of mantras or magical incantations found elsewhere in Hindu and Buddhist worlds to the whole textual corpus. The meaning of texts is not associated directly with contents that are "read," and lamas concentrate on learning a paralanguage associated with texts: proper pronunciation, cadence, gestures, secret passages, and ritual acts associated with particular moments in the recitation of a text; texts and their associated paralanguage are ritually effective in and of themselves. Tamang value texts metaphorically (Derrida 1976; Burke 1961); these metaphoric meanings are the message for Tamang as they are, at least in part, for other Buddhists.[6]

Tamang imagine texts to be the words of primordial Buddhas who brought order to the cosmos by binding oaths. Tamang origination accounts regularly repeat the refrain, "the Buddhas [*sangkye*] bound an oath" (see chapter 4). Contemporary lamas likewise bind oaths, and they are linked theoretically to these original Buddhas through a series of lopan or masters who date back to time immemorial. Guru Rhimborochhe embodies the essential characteristics of the Buddhas for Tamang and is important to an understanding of lamaic ritual. He bound the divinities and their awful power to Buddhist law and made them protectors of Buddhist truth; he banished and tied up all kinds of evil in entwining formulas. Contemporary lamas repeat these oaths. In the structure of the cosmos, contemporary lamas are the earthbound manifestations of primordial Buddhas who now reside in heavens at various stages of remove. A direct linkage between lamas and Buddhas is announced in death rites when lamas hand over the soul of the deceased to the Buddhas.

Like the Buddhas of myth, lamas reimpose the order of the Word in the world. All lamaic rituals, whether death rites or simple protections and propitiations, include the chanting of texts and often the fixing or literal application of letters imprinted from woodblocks. They etch Tibetan letters and mantras into rocks, they empower printed talismans to keep harm at bay, they attach wood-block prints with powerful mantras and symbols to the doors and windows of houses to protect them from the onslaught of evil forces, they dispense ingestible printed medicines, they recite binding texts to contain water sprites and earth divinities, they chant exorcistic texts to fend off asocial fiends, and they chant to acquire blessings. Above all, lamas are the directors

[6]My concern here is not with the important technological and sociopolitical correlates of writing (cf. Goody 1968) but with sacred writing. In contemporary Nepal, Nepali is the language of the state, and facility with the written word has important consequences (Caplan 1970).

of memorial death feasts, where textual authority allows them to erase demerit, to bind the shadow-soul to karmic process, and to pass the shadow-soul over to the Buddhas (see Figure 10).

This relation to texts and their authority has innumerable correlates in other Buddhist societies, particularly in greater Tibetan Buddhist society. For instance, Ekvall notes the following Tibetan beliefs and practices:

> By a strange working of the law of association, the written or printed letters themselves on any paper, even when the meaning is unknown, are also sometimes called *CHos* [religion; law] by the illiterate and accorded worshipful care and treatment by all. A devout Tibetan scholar will reverently touch his head with a Tibetan book, even when he knows it is secular in subject matter, because the letters in themselves retain something of religion. (1964:105)

Ekvall also reports that Tibetan monks "print pages of charms and formulas on the surface of water" (1964:114), thereby infixing the word and letting it ripple into the world. Even casual travelers cannot miss the ubiquitous prayer flags that broadcast printed formulas in the breeze, engraved rock outcroppings, walls of carved stones, hand-turned and water-run prayer wheels, and the reverence for books in both homes and monasteries. Pignède remarks that the Gurung likewise value the letter:

> Gurungs have a great deal of respect for that which is written. We have seen the importance given to the fact that the books of the pucu and the klihbri had been burned. On the other hand, the lama and the brahman read their prayers and consult written horoscopes decorated with illuminations. Many Gurungs have horoscopes made for them by Brahmans and, even though they often cannot understand them, they are proud to unroll the scroll of paper covered with letters, numbers, and multicolored figures [my translation]. (1966:389)

Similar observations have been made throughout Nepal (cf. Caplan 1970:69), and Tambiah (1968b) has demonstrated the importance of texts in Thai Buddhist ritual.

In this metaphoric value of writing, lamaic expression takes form not as doctrinal abstraction through reading and meditation but as ritual action directed toward immortality (*tshe*) (like other tantrisms) and well-being, *brui hong* or the prosperous essence of grain, *nhorgi yang* or the abundant essence of wealth, and *sehgi chut* or the resilient

Figure 10. Lamas chanting at a death feast

essence of things. This is more apparent in Tamang appropriations of the focal sexual symbology of tantric Buddhist systems. In philosophical elaboration, the dichotomies of male and female and their union are linked to distinctions between *saṃsāra/nirvāṇa,* compassion/wisdom, subject/object, consonants/vowels, all of which are seen as an "essential unity of an apparent duality" (Snellgrove 1957:83). One Tamang lama, however, explained the meaning of *yab teng yub* or the sexual union of male and female in these terms: "Mother keeps waiting in the house and father brings things. If the father comes and asks where the money is, the mother should show it. Therefore, the father should leave money with his wife. The man will finish it off quickly going hither and yon. He will take it and throw it away. If small amounts are built up slowly with the wife that is nhorgi yang (abundant wealth). Buddhas [too] must be like husband and wife." Similarly, Tamang lamas bring a more immediate interpretation to bear on a being they refer to as *shyihṭu,* who is iconographically represented by Tamang as a blue Buddha in sexual union with a white consort or alternatively as a set of terrific manifestations of Buddhas in sexual union with consorts.

According to Tibetan formulations, *zhi-khro* (*zhito*) are the "tranquil and the fierce" and include forty-two tranquil divinities and four sets of fifty-eight wrathful divinities (Snellgrove 1957:229–32). In Sherpa monasteries zhito is the object of meditative discipline and a psychological science:

> The whole ritual, which is based upon these schemes, resolves itself into a process of self-identification with this cosmic body. The bewildering variety of divine forms are evoked from the universal void, recognized for what they are, namely the mental product of the practiser, and then returned to their original state, bearing away with them all the mental construction of which they are the symbol and of which phenomenal existence consists. The ritual is nothing more than an exteriorized version of the monk's normal meditation. Its whole effect depends upon knowing the construction of the scheme and concentrating upon the process of its emanation and its dissolution. (Snellgrove 1957:234)

Tamang lama and laity are neither monks nor meditators in this sense, and they approach Shyihtu solely for the benefits of power and long life. For them, Shyihtu is the reservoir of *wang* or potency, the power of life itself, and the tormo of Shyihtu (along with that of *wangpo nengpa*) occupies a central position in the requests of one leading school of lamas for power (wang) and long life (tshe) during memorial death feasts or other large-scale lamaic rites. Lamas distribute long life and power in the form of water and dough power-balls, respectively. Good fortune issues, according to one lama, "rising from the earth like mist, falling like snow, descending like rain," enfolding homes and fields.

In an absence of monastic discipline, meditation, and interiorized reading, the "mysticism" and "innerworldly" ascetisms associated with such disciplines (Weber 1947:324–25, 1963:166–83) are unelaborated in local lamaic culture.[7] When Tamang lamas chant texts, they bind oaths. Lamas do not act ascetically in the world to attain experiential states or salvation. They perform ritual services.

The Lamaic Ritual Repertoire

After seclusions and the accumulation of practical experience, lamas can authoritatively preside over several rituals from individual household rites to lamaic pageants. In practice, lamas complete only a select number of rites. Lamas themselves employ lambus for sacrifices and bombos for soundings, and they allow blood sacrifice in the domains of their own rites. Villagers remain convinced of the effects of sacrifice over the binding efforts of lamas. Sacrifices replace the food (human bodies) harmful agents consume. Lambus (and bombos secondarily) exchange blood for blood, bone for bone, and meat for meat. Lamas personally under strictures of the value of *ahimsā* or nonviolence, cannot, in villagers' eyes, complete such exchanges effectively. Though some lamas claim to have the ritual techniques to recall lost shadow-souls and can divine, they have yet to obviate the performance of soundings.

Lamas regularly preside over Chhechu; they bind newly constructed houses against the onslaught of harmful agents, propitiate clan divinities when requested to do so, erect prayer flags (*lungdar*), and practice preventive medicine by dispensing amulets infused with the power to ward off evils. They also dispense printed medicines, which are swallowed like pills. Lamas were recognized by Tamdungsa Tamang as having a special dominion over *lu* even though householders or lambus can also conduct the rites, especially when someone suffers

[7]This nonliteracy is beginning to change as some lamas are able to translate minimally some of their texts after having trained with a Bhutanese lama who fled to the Tamang region when the Chinese took over Tibet.

from rashes and sores. The lu book of the lamas is thought to have special effectiveness. Lamas are also called to perform life-cyclical rituals, particularly those associated with birth—*namchung* or purificatory rites conducted nine days after birth. Again, other practitioners can perform these rituals, which are by no means the sole prerogative of lamas. In addition to this regular repertoire, there are several rituals associated with the village gombo and *mhane* or Buddhist monument (stupa). New year's rites (*lhosar*), sequences of Chhechu, and portions of Dasain have been associated with the gombo in the past and may be revived in the future. In conjunction with the performances of Chhechu, lamas usually reconsecrate the village mhane and regularly do the same with the numerous other mhane in the village. Lamas are also incidentally invited by some households for the exorcism of a trinity of generalized evils. Lamas can, moreover, perform rituals to encourage rain and to avert disastrous weather, although they have not been engaged for such services in decades.

Important as these rites may be, lamas are defined by their performance of death feasts (*gral*). Gral are socially encompassing and can involve from several hundred to a thousand people either directly or by implication. Most Tamang households during 1975–77 engaged in some ten to fifteen memorial death feasts in one role or another. They are performed in the dry season after the harvests of maize, millet, and rice.[8] In light of the focality of death rites, one could almost say that Tamang live for death rites, that their productive activity during the monsoon is as much to support the memorial death feasting as the inverse.

Moreover, the memorial death feast is the predominant Buddhist ritual among Tamang, especially since Chhechu has been performed only erratically in recent decades. Ritual action during death feasts includes more than narrow attention to the welfare of the deceased and the regeneration of a society of exchange rent by a death; the death feast marks the ascendancy of Buddhist dominion and lamaic authority. During these feasts, lamas always perform dances with no direct relation to the deceased. One school of lamas always dances the history of the assassination of Gyalbo Lungdar (Lang Darma), the anti-Buddhist king of Tibet (see chapter 3), by Dong Chhempo, their ancestor.

[8]The oscillation from intense labor during the monsoon and the months immediately preceding and succeeding it to a period of more occasional labor and leisure is beginning to change as villagers grow more winter crops and engage in supplementary economic activities.

Memorial Death Feasting

Almost every observer of Tibeto-Burman-speaking peoples in the Himalayas has noted that death rites occupy a predominant place in their ritual repertoires and are rites of social affirmation. The first systematic ethnographic accounts of Sherpa (Fürer-Haimendorf 1964) and Gurung (Pignède 1966) peoples, for instance, record the focality of death rites.[9] The importance of death as the context of social elaboration contrasts vividly with the emphasis on marriage in Hindu societies, including the Bahun among whom Tamang reside; as Dumont remarks, "Marriage dominates the Hindu's social life and plays a large part in his religion" (1970b:109).[10] Tamang ritually underplay marriage rites in their preference for elopements. The ritual ascendance of death as a frame for social creation even begins with marriage, where the minimal exchanges of marriage announce death and mortuary obligations. A bride's hoe and sickle will prepare her cremation site, and her brass bowl will hold the water with which she will wash her dead parents' and siblings' faces. She passes a bowl to her own daughters at their marriage so that they too will wash the faces of dead parents and siblings. Moreover, in memorial death feasts courtship play abounds and capture-elopement, the favorite form of marriage, is a common occurrence at death celebrations.

Tamang mortuary practices reflect several structures and processes identified in the works of Bachofen (1967), Frazer (1963), Hertz (1960), and van Gennep (1960)—interpretations elaborated upon in more recent studies (Bloch and Parry 1982; Huntington and Metcalfe 1979)—notably the inherently social character of the rites, the symbolic value of the intermediate state, and the prominence of imagery of regeneration. Mortuary rites, more than any other lamaic event, synthesize an ideal social order (and secondarily, its tensions) based on encompassing principles of opposition and exchange. My purpose here is less to confirm these features of death rites through Tamang ethnography than to elucidate lamaic order in Tamang society.

Death and death rites not only occupy a focal place in Tibeto-Burman religions and societies as events of social affirmation, they are the

[9]In accord with a general regeneration of anthropological interest in death, a recent issue of the Himalayan journal *Kailash* (Vol. 9, No. 4, 1982) initiates an ethnographic and textual discussion of death in a range of Himalayan cultures—Ladakhi, Tibetan, Thakali, Magar, and Gurung.

[10]This is not to say that death is not social for Hindus (Parry 1982) but that, as social rites, those surrounding death create the whole through absences as opposed to marriage, which articulates the social totality.

frame for elaborating Buddhist ideology. Elementary Buddhist themes of suffering and desire, karma and the calculus of merit/demerit, and the division between this world and another world take concrete form in reference to death, whether one looks to the meditations of monks or to the rituals of villagers. Keyes notes that death rituals are one of "two core rituals upon which the religion [Buddhism] is predicated. The first ritual—or more properly set of rituals—is that in which suffering in its most profound form, that is death, is subjected to Buddhist interpretation and juxtaposed with a course of action that moves people away from the abyss of meaninglessness to which ultimate suffering carries one" (1983:273). Death plays a role in the very procedures for becoming a monk in Theravada Buddhist societies, where monks are thought to be dead to the world, and becoming a lama in Tamang society, where gurus sometimes perform mock death rites on novices who are then reborn in a new status. Lamas and death are inherently linked in Tamang imagination, and lamas are defined as the "deliverers of the dead." Mortuary rituals are the only essential Buddhist rites for Tamang villagers and, given their prominence, are the primary vehicle whereby Buddhist ideology takes accessible form. Particularly apparent are the inherent powers of the letter and texts in defining order.

Although Tamang death rites with their revelries and heterodoxies appear to defy textual reconstructions of Buddhist thought, close examination reveals that Tamang ritual renditions of death rites conform to Tibetan and pan-Buddhist doctrine. The rituals thus can be conceived as paratexts that use a medium distinct from reading to etch out an order.

Life, Death, and Lamas

For Tamang, humans have bodies (*lhi*) composed of organs and consisting of bones, flesh, blood, breath, and internal warmth; they also have "heart-minds" or *sem,* which are the seat of consciousness and—along with heart (*ting*) and stomach (*pho*)—emotion. The relation of lhi to sem or body to consciousness is analogous to that of *so* to *bla* through which Tamang formulate ideas of life and death.[11] Life-

[11]For a review of Tibetan ideas of sem see in particular Tucci (1980); for reviews of Tibetan bla and *srog* see Tucci (1980:190–99) and Stein (1972:223–29). Tamang do not elaborate, however, on a psychology of consciousness (Tucci 1980:107–8). For *sae* among Gurung see McHugh (1984).

force is intrinsically linked to the body; it grows through the body like a tree, and when the life-force expires so does the body. One lama explained that when a corpse is burned, the bone and flesh return to soil, the blood to water, the breath to wind, and the warmth to fire. With the annihilation of body and life-force, there is nothing left but the bla or shadow-souls, which, unlike the life-force, perdure beyond the death of the body. Although Tamang attribute nine shadow-souls to every body, lamas conjoin these nine into one at the time of death, and it is on this unitary shadow-soul that they focus ritual attention.

Tamang associate shadow-souls with consciousness and emotion. After death, bla retain a consciousness like that of a living person (as we have seen, bla experience dreams); villagers attribute various propensities to these bodiless shadow-souls. In the time between death and the conclusion of the memorial death feasts months later, shadow-souls long for human contact and experience loneliness, jealousy, hunger, and confusion as they wander about pitifully like shades—homeless, motherless, and kinless. Lamas sever the attachment of shadow-souls to the world of the living in the concluding mortuary rites and send them along the trail to rebirth.

Although Tamang notions of karma (the effect of actions on rebirth) deviate somewhat from doctrinal formulations, they nevertheless are integral to their conceptions of death. Tamang rarely speak of karma per se but refer to demerit or sin using the terms *pāp, dikpa, nyheba,* and occasionally a particular form of demerit associated with killing, *lhayo.* Demerit/sin accumulates from killing animals, lying, cheating, gossiping, fighting, jealousy, licentiousness, hurting or harming the well-being of others through poisoning, jealousy, sorcery, theft, and the like. To avoid dikpa/pap one must show respect for lamas and fulfill ritual obligations. Tamdungsa Tamang do not formalize the positive notion of merit as directly as they do demerit; like other Tibetan Buddhists, however, they do recognize the importance of "good works" (cf. Tucci 1980:46). The same logic that allows demerit/sin to add up allows good acts to counter them: remembering the Buddhas, feeding lamas, giving alms to lamas on their annual rounds, contributing to the maintenance and construction of Buddhist monuments and gombo, acting with charity and fairness, going on pilgrimages to Buddhist sites, lighting butter lamps, and reciting texts. Overall, though, Tamang confine their discourse on karma to mortuary rites. Tamang, contrary to Sherpa or other more reformed Buddhists, do not convert their acceptance of karma into an ideology of ethical precepts for action. In the ritual contexts of mortuary rites, lamas erase the demerit inescapably accumulated during life.[12]

According to the amount of demerit/sin accumulated during life, a shadow-soul can be reborn in one of a number of forms and in a number of places. One can be reborn as a divinity in the heavens of the Buddhas—particularly prized is the paradisiacal realm of the west—or in a hellish place of cannibal demons or in other unsavory domains, such as realms of the homeless, of craving, of closed mouths, of licentious sex, or of bickering and confusion. Most Tamang, though, hold that humans are reborn in human or animal forms and most, including women, would prefer to be reborn in a richer version of themselves. In certain circumstances, shadow-souls are not reborn and become shades. This can happen on the occasion of anomalous deaths or when death rites are performed incorrectly. Becoming a shade is equivalent to being reborn in a hellish place from whence the shadow-soul in craving attachment to the world of the living afflicts the living with myriad forms of morbidity.

Without the ritual efforts of lamas, a proper rebirth is impossible; the shadow-soul becomes a shade or evil spirit. The term *gral* is cognate with the Tibetan *sgrol-ba* (Höfer 1969:27), which means "to rescue, deliver, save; . . . to lead, transport, carry, to cross, . . . to remove" (Jäschke [1881] 1972:122–23); all of these meanings convey aspects of lamaic ritual intentions. Lamas rescue the shadow-soul from demerit and a potentially horrible and hellish rebirth; they deliver or transport it into the care and power of the Buddhas—particularly the mothering Chenreshih; and they permanently separate the shadow-soul from relations with the living. They also lead or direct the shadow-souls to proper rebirths through the ritual display of trailblazing iconographic cards. They recite a text that, like the *Tibetan Book of the Dead* (Evans-Wentz 1960), instructs the shadow-soul on the way to rebirth.

Thus lamas are masters of death and ritually concentrate on the shadow-soul after death in contrast to bombos who revive the living and call back the shadow-souls to living bodies. Although lamas erect prayer flags (lungdar) that they call *so shying* or life-force poles, bombos are the specialists in life-force revival. Lamas erect *darju* or a

[12]Tamang, like other Buddhists (see Paul 1979), see the activities of everyday life as inherently accumulative of pap/dikpa. Lamas, for instance, regret that they must farm (and try to hire others to plow their lands); moreover, they sponsor sacrifices that are implicitly sinful.

form of prayer flag, though, at the time of death. Lamas make this prayer flag from a tree sapling that, as in *so dungma*, has been stripped of branches except for a cluster at the top. Unlike bombos, however, lamas attach banners of cloth stamped with blessings and luck prints. When these banners wave in the breeze they enhance the karmic condition of the shadow-soul. As one lama put it, "It is by the threads of that cloth that a shadow-soul can make its way to the paradises of the Buddhas," to a form of immortality.

Social Death

Individuals are more than body, heart-mind, life-force, and shadow-soul; they are social beings bound in a circle of kin. The reality of individuals is intrinsically subsumed in the social categories of clans. Mortuary rites deal with the dead in their social reality and as members of patriclans that stand in relation to others according to a calculus of exchange. Mortuary feasts conclude the social relations between the living and the dead and at the same time recreate the elementary structure of the society of the living, a society temporarily threatened in the breach of death. They conclude with the conveyance of blessings of long life and good fortune for the living.

No memorial death feast is identical to another. Depending on the social, economic, and political position of the deceased and the sponsors, it may be large or small, simple or elaborate. A mortuary feast for a poor man with no significant property to bequeath, no sons or other heirs, and no married daughters may be very short—only a day long—and include only residents of the village. The death of a prominent headman with married sons and daughters and many wives may be a huge gathering, bringing hundreds of people from outside the village. Ten or fifteen lamas may take three or four days to complete it.

All mortuary rites have jural overtones. Those who sponsor memorial death feasts acquire the legal rights over property—land in particular. Gral, thus, can be the occasion for disputes between potential heirs. Complicated inheritance problems usually arise when a man dies without sons or brothers and the property has to be passed from one segment of a patriclan to another. In such instances, the memorial death feast becomes the frame for constructing a case. Property issues can also arise when women die even though land passes from fathers to sons or close male agnates. A woman who survives her husband maintains ownership over a share of property equal to that of the sons or brothers of her husband until she in her turn dies. Then the property passes to her sons or husband's brothers. If a woman precedes her husband in death or dies outside an active marriage, property rights do not become an issue.

Before turning to an outline of the process and structure of mortuary practices, it is first necessary to delineate the key categories of kin activated for any memorial death feast.

The circle of kin and the village community. Death generates obligations on the part of every household in the village, and everyone in some fifteen neighboring villages who can trace an active trail of relationship. Every household in the village participates in cremations, preliminary mortuary rites during an intervening period, and memorial death feasts; those from other villages attend only the memorial death feast proper, except for principal affines, who are required at all phases. Every household contributes grain and money for the performance.[13]

Sponsors and those who carry grief. Sons or the structural equivalent (usually those who stand to inherit) arrange for the performance of "right side up" feasts in which children mourn parents (in the case of an unmarried woman, parents or brothers have this obligation). Parents sponsor "upside down" feasts in which they mourn the death of unmarried sons or daughters who have no offspring of their own. Parents simply bury or "throw out" children under twelve without ritual. Close male agnates make larger contributions than do other kin to the sponsors and are generally considered part of the sponsoring segment of memorial death feasts.[14]

Sponsors as well as other significant kin also formally carry grief (*du*). The parents, wife, children, and brothers, if they stand to inherit, carry grief when men die; husbands and children carry grief when women die. When a mature girl or woman dies unmarried, a mock marriage is arranged and a man is appointed as a husband to carry grief, allowing the system of formal obligations and gifts to unfold. A man does not require a mock union if he dies unmarried because significant kin are marked by a previous record of exchange; this is not true for a woman, who requires a husband to carry grief for her.

[13]Every household in the circle of kin of the deceased contribute four *mana* (about six cups) of unhusked rice, four of unhusked millet, and half a rupee to the sponsors toward the performance. People are obliged to give to the sponsors as much as they received from the sponsors when they themselves sponsored a gral.

[14]Households whose heads stand in close agnatic relation to those of the sponsors contribute greater amounts (usually a *pāthi* or about a gallon) of husked rice, four mana of unhusked grain, and half a rupee.

Moreover, parents carry grief for unmarried women, whereas they do not for married women. Grief is symbolically announced by several practices. Men have their heads shaved and women unbraid their hair and wail bitterly; these acts are repeated at particular moments throughout the mortuary cycle. Men should not wear blessings of red powder on the forehead (*ṭikā*), smoke if their father has died, or drink milk if their mother has died. Women should not wear ribbons in their hair. People carrying grief should wear old clothes, avoid putting flowers in their hair, and refrain from singing cheerful songs. During the days of the memorial death feasts proper, they must not eat peppers, salt, milk, or meat. Some claim that these restrictions should be followed from the time of death; however, it appears that this is a new innovation and only the more rigorous follow it.

Ashyang-shyangpo. Special obligations devolve on the ashyang-shyangpo or the mother's brothers–wife's brothers of the sponsors. These wife-givers expel (*khlāpa*) the grief of the sponsors and others who carry grief. When sons or daughters mourn parents, their ashyang or mother's brothers expel their grief. When a husband mourns a wife, it is his shyangpo or wife's brother who expels it. When a wife grieves a husband, it is her own brothers (his shyangpo) who expel it. When parents carry grief for a son or an unmarried daughter, their mother's brothers expel it. If a father dies, his sons, all of whom carry grief, must have in attendance not only representatives of their own mother's brothers but of their father's mother's brothers as well. The former are called the "young" ashyang and the latter the "old" (*khekpa*) ashyang. Young ashyang give cloth to all offspring of the deceased and to his wife; old ashyang give only to the eldest son of the deceased.

Mhā. Two categories of mha or sister's husband also have special roles. The mha and classificatory mha of the sponsors contract special service obligations at the time of death as does a mha known as the "grasping mha," who in the case of a deceased man, is (depending on availability) his daughter's husband, his sister's husband, his father's sister's husband, or his father's father's sister's husband (in order of preference). In the case of a woman, the mha is the same as for a man but calculated from the perspective of the woman's husband rather than the woman herself.

Clanswomen and wives. Daughters, sisters, clan sisters (*busing* of men; *ananenchon* of women), and, in the case of men, wives also have special obligations to mourn their dead parents, siblings, and spouses and to provide services and goods. Moreover, the clan sisters of daughters, sisters, mothers-in-law in the case of women, and mothers and wives in the case of men also make special exchanges among them-

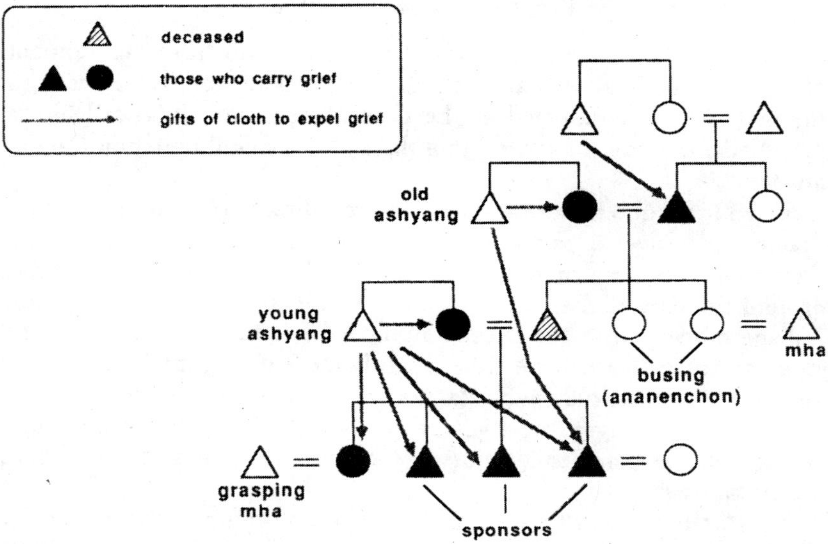

Figure 11. Exchanges and elementary structure of the memorial death feast for a dead male

selves, declaring solidarity as women of the same clan (ananenchon).[15] Daughters or sisters clean the faces of the dead.

Most of these social categories are marked by a principal representative but include parties of people who are classificatorily linked to the principals. Obligations reflect relations of patriclan segments as well as relations between individuals. Although a simple memorial death feast may require only one set of mha and one of ashyang-shyangpo in addition to the sponsoring clan, a complex feast can include three sets of ashyang-shyangpo, all from separate clans. Details of the obligations among these groups unfold in the rites around cremation and in the memorial death feast proper (see Figure 11).

[15]The mothers and sisters of unmarried men who have died and mothers, daughters, sisters, and wives of married men receive contributions of grain from their clan sisters or ananenchon. Likewise, the mothers and sisters of unmarried women and the mothers-in-law, daughters, and sisters of married women receive contributions. These groups of women receive two mana of rice and one-quarter or one-half a rupee from each of their clan sisters. The rice contributed to these women (and specifically that of the daughters and sisters) is cooked in a large cauldron at the death feast and after being offered first to an effigy of the deceased is usually combined with the other feasting food for general consumption. The remainder of the rice contributions is combined with that of the sponsors—that is, the husbands, brothers, father, or sons of the women. The money is used to buy butter, which fuels lamps lit by daughters, sisters, and male sponsors in honor of the deceased.

The Structure and Process of Mortuary Rituals

There are three distinct periods in mortuary rites from the moment of death to the final severance of the shadow-soul from relations with the living. Rites conducted at the time of death are followed by an intermediate period of several months and a concluding memorial death feast.[16]

Ritual procedures may vary slightly according to the school of lamas that presides over a particular gral; however, with slight variations, they have a basic structure. The most common divergences revolve around the dances the lamas perform at the climax of the festivities. Villagers assert that the proper number of lamas is nine; however, most mortuary feasts have either slightly more or slightly less than this number. A household invites lamas with gifts of grain and honorific flasks. In Tamdungsa, most village lamas as well as lamas from neighboring villages come to all mortuary events (for details see Holmberg 1980:204–24).

Rites at the time of death and cremation prefigure the memorial death feasts proper and reveal their basic structure. The whole village community and significant categories of kin begin to perform specified tasks announcing distinctions that will continue throughout the mortuary sequences and culminate in the memorial death feasts. Significant kin include close male agnates, the principal mha, an ashyang or shyangpo, and a daughter. Lamas also arrive for the initial rituals. After death, daughters or sisters cleanse the face of the deceased, and lamas separate the nine shadow-souls from the body, conjoining them into a single entity. A procession including the representatives of all the households in the village and key kin outside the village climbs up to the cremation grounds on a promontory above the village. There, villagers make offerings to the deceased, lamas apply blessings, and sons light the funeral pyre. Those who carry grief begin showing signs of mourning.

According to Tibetan formulations, an intermediate period of forty-nine days succeeds death. During this period rebirth occurs, depending on the karma of the deceased. Tamang do not subscribe to the orthodox declaration of a forty-nine-day intermediate period; their intervening period can vary considerably in length, depending on the season of

[16]Although Tamang cremate corpses and the decaying body does not carry the symbolic focality integral to Hertz's (1960) consideration of death rites, the sequence of events and overall process of these rites replicates patterns isolated by Hertz and van Gennep (1960) whereby the social body reconstitutes itself as the physical body disintegrates and the soul achieves a new state (Huntington and Metcalf 1979:66–67).

death. Sponsors must complete a memorial death feast within the calendar year of death, and gral are usually performed within the period between November-December and April-May; memorial death feasts are not conducted in the period from May-June through October-November. Thus, feasts memorializing all those who have died over the monsoon season (May-June—September-October) are delayed until November-December or December-January. Stores of grain for fermenting into whiskey and for feasting are high, and, as importantly, the dry fields where hundreds of people gather are cleared of crops. The actual days of performance are decided by sponsors and other key participants in consultation with lamas. (Some rationalizing lamas now claim that the reason for high infant mortality among Tamang is that when lamas call a shadow-soul after the forty-nine-day period, the shadow-souls are already reborn and thus lamas kill the life-forms that shadow-souls have assumed.)

During the intermediate period, the shadow-soul remains attached to the living and is not yet aware of its new state. Villagers treat the shadow-soul as though it were a member of the society of the living until the completion of the memorial death feast. If the death feast cannot be completed before the inception of the monsoon, lamas and householders feed the shadow-soul and complete *mhane kulpa* or the application of blessings on the sacrificial feast days in July-August and September-October. The final feast for the deceased occurs during the memorial death feasts, when relations with the living are theoretically terminated.

Memorial death feasts take place over three or four days. Events move from the residence of the deceased to an altar constructed nearby in empty, dry fields. The raised altar is adorned with beautiful paintings, dough images of the Buddhas, and offerings of cloth donated by clan sisters of the deceased. Memorial death feasts have many discrete ritual sections, but the main events are as follows.

Day 1

1. Events begin with the recognition of key kin and functionaries. Beer mash is examined for traces of the nature of the rebirth of the deceased.

Day 2

2. The altar is consecrated.
3. In the evening, the formal greeting and seating of the party of the ashyang-shyangpo with whiskey and food is made. A lambu invokes protection for the time of feasting.

4. An effigy (*gur*) of the deceased is constructed in the residence. Lamas bind an oath to the shadow-soul to inhabit the effigy.
5. Ashyang-shyangpo are presented with a tray that holds samples of the food restricted to the mourners. They communicate these kinds of food along with cloth to the mourners on the final day.
6. Lamas apply blessings to the deceased, and householders feed their coresident for the final time.

Day 3

7. Lamas invoke power (wang) from the Buddhas.
8. In the afternoon, the effigy is removed from the house and transported to the altar, led by lamas and sponsors, carried by the mha, and followed by grieving women.
9. The circle of kin makes final offerings, and the lamas apply blessings. Celebratory feasting, drinking, and dancing ensue.
10. The *nebar* text is recited and the shadow-soul is shown the trail to rebirth. The effigy is cremated.

Day 4

11. The ashyang-shyangpo expel grief. They convey the restricted foods and gifts of cloth to the mourners.
12. Lamas distribute power blessings to all and they invoke good fortune for the households of the sponsors.

The social and ritual intensity of the death feast reaches its height on the third day when a large throng gathers for a final feast for the dead. This is followed by more celebratory feasting and dancing and ultimately the cremation of the effigy of the deceased. These events particularly reveal the social and Buddhist registers of mortuary rites.

Death Feasting and Social Order

Throughout the mortuary sequence, the shadow-soul of the deceased is called and fed, and lamas apply blessings to erase demerit. These offerings and blessings (mhane kulpa) are the elementary act of all the rites of the mortuary sequence; and they reach a culmination in a huge feast (*ghewa get juba*) and application of blessings in the memorial death feast proper. Activity at this feast focuses on a bamboo-and-cloth effigy of the deceased, which is transported from the house of residence to the altar. Lamas call the shadow-soul and bind an oath for it to reside in this effigy. They devote their ritual energies to transporting the shadow-soul into rebirth and use the effigy for didactic purposes. For villagers, the effigy takes on a social meaning; it provides the focal point for a drama of exchange through which villagers not only symbolically isolate and separate the deceased but recreate form among the living.

On the third and climactic day, the effigy sits between a line of lamas and a raised altar and is attended by a grasping mha; the circle of kin conveys gifts. Every household in the village and every household outside the village that can trace a trail of relation must attend and give. When they arrive they first contribute raw grain and money to the sponsors to defray the expense of the feasts. They then proceed to the effigy, where they give trays arrayed with pleasing gifts. All households bring leaf plates full of treats for the deceased, including an assortment of cooked and uncooked foods, cigarettes, whiskey, beer, and other pleasing things. As women place these offerings near the effigy, the grasping mha, who attends the effigy throughout the mortuary feast, places token amounts in a receptacle in the effigy and stacks the rest around it. Clan sisters add flowers to the effigy and cook a special pot of rice for the deceased.

Lamas then gather pieces of edible offerings from each of the stacks. They offer these portions twice over to the Buddhas, consume some themselves, and then toss the remainder to the outskirts of the ritual space for lurking evils. Finally they place a selection of food in a broken clay vessel for the deceased. Mha accumulate the remainder of the offerings in a large basket and distribute them to everyone who attends, all of whom must consume some. The grasping mha takes the uncooked offerings of grain, cigarettes, peppers, and the like for his personal consumption. Each offering to the deceased has included liquor, which is also now distributed along with that distilled by the sponsors, and the gral takes on a distinctively more festive air. Singers (shyepompo) dance around the altar singing songs glorifying the Buddhas and to the ultimate good fortune of the deceased. Young men and women, girls and boys sing playful songs of courtship and dance back and forth. Lamas also dance. Interposed in this celebration, the sponsors provide a huge feast of rice, meat, and whiskey.

Villagers give their gifts to the deceased so that the shadow-soul will not feel left out; they treat it like a traveler about to set out on a long or permanent journey. They do not want the shadow-soul to harbor ill feelings or resentment. They also want to set the record of exchange straight, to sate the shadow-soul thoroughly so that it will not be attached to the world and desire repayment of unpaid debts. Although villagers explain their giving as an effort to keep the shadow-soul from feeling alienated and excluded, the symbology of the giving in fact singles out the deceased. From the moment of death, the shadow-soul receives a portion in a fragment of a broken vessel, which villagers present to it separately from the portions distributed among the living. The message of this exclusionary feeding, one villager explained, is to inform the shadow-soul that "you are not one of us." This tense exchange, like those of exorcism of shades, is meant to urge the shadow-soul on its way without feelings of craving or anger. Villagers do not anticipate a direct return, and Tamang say that lamas "expel" the dead, using the same words they do for exorcism.

Thus, the society of the living declares itself as a totality through both the obligatory contributions of grain and money to sponsors and the food offerings to the effigy, offerings that the society of the living communally consume in a commensal solidarity in opposition to the dead. These contributions in their totality do not represent a system of gains and losses; they affirm a community of exchange. The contributors not only get back the grain they contribute when they sponsor gral, they are reciprocated almost immediately in the feasting foods and liquor they consume.

This total society, though, always takes form as opposed patriclans, and the memorial death feast, more than any other ritual, articulates an order generated through principles of exchange embedded in the structure of bilateral cross-cousin marriage. The memorial death feast is about marriage and social groups. It is performed only for mature adults and usually only those with a full social identity—that is, those who are married. Beyond wrenching grief, death implies the dissolution of a marriage (or a potential marriage) and threatens social order. Marriage is the convergence and alliance of exogamous groups through exchange. In the memorial death feast, the relations among patriclans as well as the ethos of opposition and reciprocity are reasserted in a recreation of the elementary form of society. Thus, as Oppitz (1982) stresses in a comparative consideration of Magar death rites and kinship, it is as much the reaffirmation of social form as the alleviation of grief that inspires mortuary rituals.[17]

A tripartite structure of ashyang-shyangpo/sponsors/mha typifies all mortuary rites. These relations double the relation of ashyang-shyangpo or wife-givers and mha or wife-receivers: sponsors stand as mha to their ashyang-shyangpo and as ashyang-shyangpo to their mha.[18] In death feasts, ashyang-shyangpo give goods and receive

[17]The alleviation of grief among Tamang is directly attuned to this recreation of social order.

[18]This is marked terminologically by the practice of a man's calling a daughter's husband "mha" or "mha-kola" and a man's calling a sister's husband "mha."

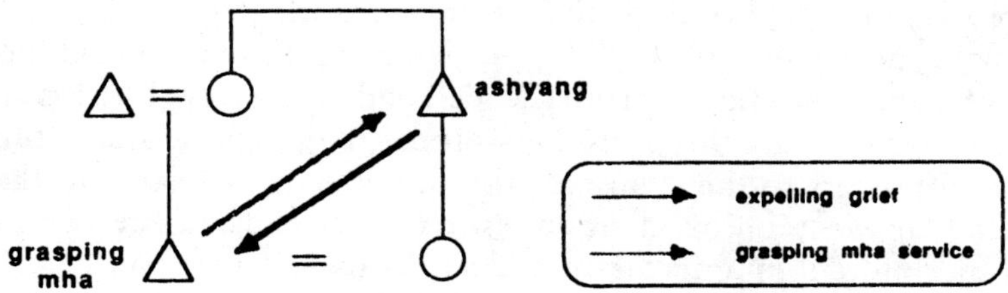

Figure 12. Principal ashyang and the grasping mha in a matrilateral cross-cousin marriage

honor, and mha are obliged to serve, a pattern repeated in everyday life. This elementary structure is condensed in the obligations of ashyang to give their sister's sons cloth to terminate their period of mourning. This cloth moves from the patriclan segment of the ashyang-shyangpo to that of the sponsors. In turn, when an ashyang dies, it is his daughter's husband (either a real or a classificatory sister's son) who acts as his grasping mha or serves him (see Figure 12).[19]

All exchanges conform to this elementary pattern and affirm an order between sponsors and patriclan segments that stand as mha or ashyang-shyangpo in relation to them. Mha provide service both to the deceased and to the sponsors, service that may be, like death itself, polluting. They maintain all direct contact with the corpse and the effigy; they shroud, carry, feed, transfer offerings to, and cremate both the corpse and the effigy; they burn the clothes of the deceased and replaster the house; they dig and clear the cremation site, construct the pyre, and pick through the cremation ashes. In the memorial feasts proper, they construct the altar, distribute the offerings made to the effigy, and cook and serve the feast. They provide these services to the sponsors who are their shyangpo (wife's brothers).

Ashyang-shyangpo come in a complementary role. The sponsors who stand as wife-receivers treat them with special respect and honor, serving them as mha must serve shyangpo. A clan sister (busing) of the sponsors greets them with a special service of whiskey and food, and the sponsors bow formally, touching their heads to the feet of the ashyang-shyangpo. Ashyang-shyangpo also come symbolically as givers, presenting a white cloth for the altar in honor of the dead.

[19]An exact reciprocity between individuals is the case only in actual matrilateral cross-cousin marriages. This occurs only some 13 percent of the time. Figure 12 elucidates this structural relation between clans in a bilateral system rather than in one between individuals acting independently.

Moreover, they give cloth to their sister's children, sister's husband, and sister, depending on who has died. Women receive a colorful sheet of cloth, which they tie on their backsides, and men receive turbans and caps. Ashyang or mother's brothers proper, although in a structural sense wife-givers to the sponsors, also are affectively related to their *kon* and *konme* (terms used for both sister's sons and daughters as well as grandchildren) in a nurturant and supportive position.

These exchanges of goods and services between a particular configuration of patriclan segments are further supplemented by those of women to their parents, children, brothers, and to each other. Although women mourn the deaths of parents, siblings, children, and spouses, crying out laments, and daughters (or sisters) have the special obligation of washing the faces of dead parents and siblings, they also are involved in specific exchanges of goods and services that on the one hand announce their relations to their natal and marital groups and on the other a solidarity among female siblings. These gifts declare a unity among clan sisters and particular bonds between men and women of a common clan.

Memorial death feasts thus recreate a social world based on the restricted and reciprocal exchanges of spouses, service, cloth, food, drink, and other valuables between opposed patriclans. Although a specific event yields a structure composed of three patriclan segments—ashyang-shyangpo/sponsors/mha—temporarily deployed in a hierarchy, this arrangement does not become generalized beyond the egocentric perspectives of the principals and their close kin. Over the years, a patriclan segment may take the role of ashyang-shyangpo in one death feast; in another it may be in the contingent of mha; in yet another it may be associated with the sponsors. In the calculation of all the exchanges among clans and their direction over several years, an overarching dual organization based on principles of equality and restricted exchange (most clearly marked in the de facto division of the village along the lines of the dominant two clans) crystallizes. One side of this duality serves the other by carrying their dead, bearing pollution, and performing menial tasks only to have their roles reversed at the occasion of another death.

Death Feasts as Paratexts

Death feasts are Buddhist rituals. Not only do lamaic dances during the gral associate Tamang with the historical defense of Buddhist dominion in the Himalayas, the symbology fits firmly within a greater Buddhist universe and conforms specifically with Tibetan cultural patterns.[20] Elementary notions of karma, suffering, desire, and disjunctions between this and otherworlds all unfold in a ritual rather than a textual idiom. As Tambiah concludes, "Village religion is expressed in rituals and these rituals in turn clothe abstract philosophical ideals. The underlying rationale of ritual is that ideas so represented and made concrete can be manipulated realistically in an instrumental mode. In this perhaps lies the difference between ritual and philosophy" (1970:377).

Tamang mortuary rituals, although entwined in a nonliterate society of cross-cousin marriage, are paratexts of elementary tenets of Buddhist doctrine. If Tamang appropriations are heterodox, their heterodoxy is one of a field of heterodoxies. Rather than approaching the Tamang practices as a "subversion" (Tucci 1980:194) of doctrine, I attempt to point out here homologies among Tamang, Tibetan, and pan-Buddhist variants, following the insights of Obeyesekere (1963), Kirsch (1972), Tambiah (1970), and Dumont and Pocock (1959a), all of whom have questioned the disjunction between "great" and "little" or "textual" and "folk" in favor of exploring continuities or gradations of common orientations and structures. Although from the vantage of the full field, there is a disjunction between Tamang formulations and the rationalized Buddhist systems of state societies, on the level of the memorial death feasts, paratextual equivalents abound.

Tamang practices are directly linked to those of Tibet, particularly those of the *byang ter* tradition (Skorupski 1982). Tamang attention to the shadow-soul (bla)—which is linked by analogy to consciousness or *sem*—conforms with the general focus on the sem or on consciousness throughout Tibet (Tucci 1980:193–94; Snellgrove 1967:27). Local lamas know of the *bar do thös grol* or *Tibetan Book of the Dead* (Evans-Wentz 1960), but they claim that a recitation of this text is only required when the deceased has accumulated an inordinate amount of demerit or when someone is having a difficult and painful death, in

[20]Different schools of lamas dance different dances, and lay sponsors or ashyang often demand that certain dances be performed even if the lamas are reticent about dancing, as some are. In Tamdungsa one popular set recounts the assassination of Gyalbo Lungdar. Lamas mould a dough image of this king and symbolically execute it with a ritual dagger. Prior to this execution, however, a series of humorous and sometimes ribaldly sexual dances are performed—dances that the ancestors of Tamang reputedly performed to coax the king from his palace. Once the king emerged, the dancer (Dong Chhempo) shot him with arrows and his accomplices rushed in to rub medicine/poison into his wounds, after which they all fled to Nepal.

which case it is recited to hasten death. Although Tamang do not recite the bar do thos grol during the forty-nine-day intermediate period succeeding death, the memorial death feast paratextually accomplishes the same effect: it brings the shadow-soul to an awareness of its new condition and guides it on the way to an improved rebirth. Whereas a recitation of the bar do thos grol should move the "principal of consciousness"—"unaware, as a rule, that it has been separated from a human-plane body"—to a recognition of its new state (Evans-Wentz 1960:29), Tamang lamas accomplish a similar realization through ritual manipulations. Lamas call the shadow-soul and bind it to a new body, the effigy, and display this new body to the shadow-soul through a mirror. The logic behind this display, one lama explained, is to make the shadow-soul realize its new state, a state it had not fully comprehended.

The recitation of the bar do thos grol in Tibet is also supposed to describe the path to rebirth. Lamas accomplish a similar end through the display of iconographic cards. After the feasting, and at the cremation of the effigy, lamas display the cards to the deceased and chant the nebar text (cf. Skorupski 1982:361–62). This display, intended to guide the shadow-soul of the deceased to rebirth, is the paratextual equivalent of the recitation of the bar do thos grol. As one lama explained: "[The cards] are instructions for the shadow-soul. They inform the shadow-soul of the different lives it can take. They tell the shadow-soul which are good lives to take and which are bad: 'You should be like this.' It is training after death. Lamas cannot take people to the heavens; they can only tell the way: 'You are on your own. Don't linger on the way; don't stop halfway. Don't stay with the shades and harmful agents.'"

Mortuary rites are the primary context for expression of karma: the accumulated effect of good and bad deeds during the life of an individual. On the one hand, Tamang accept the general law of karma as an explanation of the process of rebirth and the presence of suffering. Overall, they resign themselves to the turn of rebirths and worldly suffering, both of which are the focal subjects of songs of lament. Tamang agree that there is nothing to be done for those who accumulate vast stores of demerit, and more than anything they view their acts as a send off rather than a final determination. On the other hand, each application of blessings performed from the time of cremation to the conclusion of the mortuary sequence conjoins the presentation of food and other gifts to the erasure of demerit or transference of merit. Lamas, grievers, and the circle of kin all work to erase the demerit of the deceased through the blessings of Chenreshih, the illumination of butter lamps, chants of "Ong song mhane peme hung ri," and songs glorifying the Buddhas.[21] The kin of powerful villagers and prominent lamas also erect mhane (small stupa), a work that benefits both the deceased and the living.

Although Tamang subscribe in general to the operation of the law of karma, they also attempt to modify this theoretically unalterable force. Tamang death rites again follow the bar do thos grol, which Tucci notes is intended "to afford relief from the appointed processes of karma" (1980:194). Theravada Buddhists in Thailand (Tambiah 1970; Keyes 1983) and in Sri Lanka (Gombrich 1971a, 1971b) likewise work to alter the karmic condition of the deceased by making and transferring merit both in rites directly tied to death and in those that become related to death. This adherence to the ideology of karma coupled with an attempt to modify it appear contradictory; however, they may simply be complementary. As Gombrich has suggested, evil and suffering have intellectual and emotional dimensions. Sinhalese adherence to "karma solved the intellectual problem of evil, but the solution was too perfect for emotional comfort," for which pre-Buddhist gift giving transformed into a symbology of a transfer of merit to the deceased (1971a:219). The climactic offerings of the final feast directly juxtapose these two movements. Villages pile their offerings around the effigy at the exact moment that lamas apply blessings to erase demerit. Women with unbraided hair wail stylized chants to their deceased kin:

> Mother, mother, why have you left me? When you were alive,
> You lived by your son's word and affection.
> Now after death, accept our affectionate offerings.
>
> Don't continue to be attached to your sons and daughters,
> Or to your grandsons and daughters,
> Or to your various livestock and things!
>
> Don't take rebirth as a mule, or as a dog or as a pig!
> Come back again in human life-form![22]

Mortuary rites, then, can simultaneously communicate the essential principles of the mechanics of karma to rationalize death and suffering

[21] The chant is the Tamang variant of "Om mane padme hum."
[22] This chant was recorded by Kathryn S. March.

in the cosmos and provide an opportunity to modify it. These apparently contradictory ritual statements are invoked for different reasons and in different contexts. The declaration of the law of karma provides an abstract theory for making death, suffering, and rebirth meaningful. At the same time, it provides a pragmatic course for modifying the condition of the deceased. Rebirth allows a consolation to mortality in the form of an immortality.

In conjunction with this commentary on karma, lamaic practice orders suffering and worldly existence according to an overarching separation between the world of the living and the world of the dead. The movement of the shadow-soul is from the confines of the domestic and worldly space of its former home, where the effigy is constructed, to the open ritual ground. When lamas lead the effigy from the house of residence to the altar, they are transferring it from this to the otherworld. This movement of the effigy parallels the movement of the shadow-soul from the world of the living to the authority of the Buddhas. One lama explained that the altar is brilliantly decorated in order to attract the shadow-soul away from its home in the world to a new home with the Buddhas. Moreover, at the climactic moment of feasting, lamas and villagers chant the blessings of Chenreshih in direct counterpoint to the wrenching wailing of women who, with their hair mournfully unbraided, stand over the effigy. These measured lamaic cadences superimposed over the expressions of worldly suffering mark out an opposition between the world of the Buddhas as a perpetual presence and the human world as transitory and full of suffering. This contrast is amplified by the focality of the effigy—a symbol of the transitory and false nature of existence—over which women weep.

This reconstruction of Tamang lamaic practice raises several comparative issues. I introduce them here but take them up more directly in the next chapter. Two contradictory reconstructions of Tamang practices are possible. On the one hand, they appear to violate essential criteria of Buddhist societies and to be non-Buddhist; on the other they show a continuity with greater Buddhist ideology. The following are some examples of these contradictions. Lamas marry and remain part of the world, but they attend disciplined retreats where values of celibacy and social removal are expressed. Lamas do not beg (true of greater Tibet as well), but they make annual rounds through the village to collect grain. They do not moralize, but they articulate a karmic ideology in death rites. Lamas employ lambus for sacrifice even though sacrifice violates expressed values of nonviolence. Lamas have no permanent habit but don red for rituals. Lamas do not debate doctrine, but they have sects. They say bombos lie, but lamas employ bombos for ritual service.

These contradictions result from a shift in vantage point. If one looks at the totality of practice, lamas and Tamang villagers are heterodox. If one looks from the perspective of specific rituals, they appear more orthodox. Tamang, then, are truly unreformed. The ritual logic that governs the memorial death feast remains contained within ritual boundaries; Buddhist ideology has not reorganized or rationalized the symbolic field. Outside these confines, the lamaic manifests itself as one dimension of a system of complementarities. (To apprehend the system requires that we shift from a ritual vantage to a mythic vantage, which we shall do in the concluding chapter.) In the complementarities the shamanic appears on the edge of the lamaic domain.

An Asocial Feast at the Margins of Order

While humans feast the dead and themselves in gral, lamas convey offerings to Buddhas, divinities, and harmful agents and lambus, prior to human feasting, pass their offerings to the divinities and harmful agents. Measured feasting and the exchanges of the gral belie a precarious potentiality confirmed cosmographically by the reality of harmful agents. A counter society lurks on the outskirts of ritual space. Swarms of blood-eating fiends and cannibalistic ogres, local shades, regional spirits, and rarified cosmic evils throng on the margins ready to disrupt. They represent the potential of an asocial feast and an insufficiency in the order of reciprocity. The lama's principal chore is to assure that the deceased does not become a member of this contrary world of shades who, wrenched inauspiciously from life, are unbound to the order of human life and unrestrained by the ethos of balanced reciprocity. They grasp human flesh and feed on it. Humans try to appease them but get nothing for their efforts but more hardship. In gral, feasting among humans, the deceased, divinities, and harmful agents, coupled with lamaic ritual, works to control this counter world and to impose a determinate order in the cosmos and society. The shadow-soul of the deceased is always on the verge of becoming a shade and joining the hosts of harmful agents in their hellish, permanently intermediate places. Lamas attempt to keep the shadow-soul from the society of fiends by drawing it away.

This ritual logic is revealed in the process lamas use to call the shadow-soul throughout the mortuary rites. Shadow-souls have a tendency to stray and become enticed or entrapped by a world of ravenous, unsated, and tortured harmful agents, those excluded from the closure of exchange. Lamas extricate the shadow-soul from this possibility through the power of the letter or, as one lama put it, "by the book." They close their eyes, chant special mantras, place their hands in special binding gestures, and call the shadow-souls, who come as pure emanation, "white like milk, clear like water," in contrast to shades, who come with wild hair, bloody faces, and fierce expressions. When asked about lamaic techniques of shadow-soul calling, one lama responded with a graphic demonstration. He drew the first letter of the Tibetan syllabary in the dust of his yard and added a hook to the top:

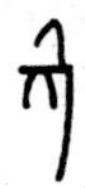

He explained that the letters of their books and the words of their chants hook the shadow-soul into the sway of Buddhist oaths and the authority of the Buddhas. On the one hand the letter separates the shadow-soul from teeming evil and on the other consigns it to the measured and determinate order of oaths.

Moreover, when lamas construct the effigy of the deceased, they attach a wood-block print to the head. This print has a blank spot where lamas write the name of the deceased in red ink (see Figure 13). When mha burn the effigy, destroying the social body of the deceased, lamas burn the wood-block print. They say the shadow-soul resides in the print. When lamas burn it in their butter lamps, the shadow-soul passes into the hands of the Buddhas for rebirth. The shadow-soul is saved from the group of evils.

The efforts of lamas in death feasts, supplemented by the parallel propitiatory efforts of lambus, combine to construct an encompassing order. During the gral, the lamaic altar becomes the abode of the Buddhas (whose presence Tamang detect in faint westerly breezes or in shimmers of light flashing off tormo), merging the heavens of the Buddhas with the world of humans. By their presence the Buddhas determine this order, and by repeating oaths, reciting texts, and applying the power of letters lamas embody the Buddhas' authority in the world. The throng of harmful agents latently attending memorial death feasts are a constant reminder of the potential dissolution of order and reciprocity with which death as social breach confronts Tamang villagers. This potentiality, though, is written into the cosmos with the announcement of reciprocity itself, an announcement that implies its

Figure 13. Death print. Name is inserted in upper right.

antithesis. The possibility of unrestrained collapse erupts at moments during all feasts, usually in the heat of intoxication when ashyang-shyangpo often make demands on their mha and voice complaints to their hosts about the quality of food, service, or lamaic dancing. These eruptions expose the inherent contradictions in the Tamang ethos of balanced reciprocity. Tamang base unity on social difference. The order of the feast is tenuous and incomplete and opens the way for bombos to sound. Bombos, rather than hook shadow-souls out of intermediate voids, delve into these voids.

8 Ritual Polarities, Mythic Imagination, and History

> Moreover, there is no special rite that is not complex in itself, for either it pursues several ends at the same time, or, to attain one end, it sets in motion several forces.
>
> Henri Hubert and Marcel Mauss, *Sacrifice*

The rituals of lambus, bombos, and lamas generate in containment select communications within a field of possibility. A specific ritual symbology momentarily silences others, and the system of relations that forms the full field is announced on the level of specific rituals through absences. These absences become highly charged in reference to death and death rites, where restrictions apply to bombos, revealing a structural incompatibility in Tamang imagination between shamanic soundings and the lamaic cum sacrificial declarations in memorial death feasts: "lamas deliver the dead; bombos cure the living." The cultural construction of the shamanic vocation condenses incongruities between the lamaic and the shamanic. Lente or ancestral spirits of dead bombos—who invigorate bombos, charging them to practice, and who are thereby the inspiration of soundings—exist because death feasts fail to sever the relations of dead bombos to the living and to assure their rebirth in new life-forms. Lente, like shades, who occupy the margins of the death feast, return to haunt, immune to the determinations of exclusively sacrificial exchange or the lamaic letter. It is, however, around tsen or midspace sprites that the countervailing tendencies of the shamanic are extensively figured. Tsen direct us to general ethnological conclusions concerning the dynamics of ritual fields. Villagers explain that contact with death or consumption of the offerings to the deceased would sully tsen with whom bombos are associated. Bombos therefore cannot touch corpses or act like mha and carry corpses to the cremation grounds; they cannot enter the houses of the recently deceased. Most important, they cannot consume the food offered to the effigy, which villagers communally consume during rites of cremation, the feasts of the intermediate period, and the concluding death feasts. Participation in these feasts marks membership in the circle of kin. For bombos to maintain the marginality necessary for mediation, they must remain on the outskirts of memorial death feasts.

Tsen and the origination account of tsen, moreover, point to a fundamental paradox in Tamang culture, a paradox obscured in the symbology of memorial death feasts, which regenerate orders based on opposition of patriclans, reciprocity, and a dynamic balance of dualities. Memorial death feasts and the origination account of tsen proceed from the same social order but in quite different directions, and this disjunction allows us to apprehend in elementary form the relations between an encompassing sociocultural order and ritual divergences. To arrive at this general conclusion, however, we must first reconsider the origination account of tsen, which as we have seen is central to shamanic practice, and relate it to memorial death feasts. The structural dynamics exaggerated in this contrast allow us to compare the Tamang ritual field with other Himalayan religious systems having a Buddhist or lamaic component and to locate this field within the general theoretical problem of ritual polarities with which we began this reconstruction.

Enigmas of Cousin Marriage

The account of tsen and the rituals of death revolve around a common breach, a breach celebrated in the origination account of tsen. This account focuses on the relations of a father tsen, a daughter tsen, and a brother tsen to a human (chapter 6). The daughter tsen is married to the human, making tsen the ashyang-shyangpo of humans, who in turn become mha to tsen. The human husband and his wife's brother go hunting, and the husband captures a tiny bird, large in the eyes of the tsen but miniscule to the human. A quarter of the butchered bird is sent home with the husband to his wife as a gift from her natal kin. The husband, who thinks of the quarter as insignificant, breaks his wife's leg when he tosses it to her. The angered tsen divide from humans, ceasing the possibility of marriage exchange.

The social structure of this account is the elementary order of Tamang social life, an order celebrated in memorial death feasts. The focal characters—a woman, her father, her brother, and her husband—become exchanging halves, and it is around the exchanges of opposites encoded in relations of mha and shyangpo that Tamang imagine ideal order. Yet a paradox is implicit in this system of difference and reciprocity. Tamang attempt to establish unity or social whole through exchanges; yet to activate exchanges they separate themselves into irreconcilable opposites—exogamous patriclans formed into de facto moieties. In other words, they construct order from inherent rift. This rift implies an immediate violence, for within the social collectivity it is women in their passages from natal to marital affiliations (and back again) who directly bear the contradictions of marriage exchanges. From a woman's perspective, marriage represents a rupture from her natal kin and the never-complete incorporation in her husband's patriline; like the tsen wife, Tingtsa Rani, she bears the pain of a broken body. Her movement to a new marital home is the very image of suffering and desire in the laments of Tamang poetic songs. A contradiction between ideals of symmetrical reciprocity and the facts of asymmetrical hierarchy between actual ashyang-shyangpo and mha are also an object of reflection in this account. Divine tsen are ascendant ashyang-shyangpo and in their superior difference from human mha separate, again a socially impossible course of events; inequalities in actual exchange must be sustained in the encompassing ideology of equality.

The harm to Tingtsa Rani vividly condenses the contradictions of cross-cousin marriage, and the movement of Tamang imagination in the tsen account can be understood as a radical solution to these contradictions: tsen retreat from sight, effecting a permanent cessation of social relations between the wife and her natal kin and humanity. In practice, this solution to the contradictions of exchange is an impossibility, for social reproduction demands the retention of communication and sight between groups, communications in which women are essential. In reference to a Tsimshian myth in which residence rules are violated, Lévi-Strauss concludes that Tsimshian myths "do not seek to depict what is real, but to justify the shortcomings of reality, since the extreme positions are only *imagined* in order to show they are *untenable*. This step, which is fitting for mythical thought, implies an admission (but in the veiled language of the myth) that the social facts when thus examined are marred by an insurmountable contradiction" (1968:30). It is in the insurmountable contradictions implicit in cross-cousin marriage that bombos sound. Bombos contrapuntally play off the dominant rhythms of Tamang life that reproduce patriclan continuity and opposition; bombos celebrate a matrilineally figured spirit associated with mediation. Shamanic soundings are thus linked to the intermediacy of women, and the shamanic takes definition by association with paradoxes that erupt through the lives of women.[1]

Death feasts respond to a situation that is identical to the solutions posed by the origination account of tsen and the ultimate separation of human and divine; thus we can make a direct contrast between the lamaic and sacrificial death feasts and shamanic soundings. Villagers perform death feasts for married adults, and death implies the dissolution of a marriage and of relations between ashyang-shyangpo and mha. One partner (like tsen) goes the way of divinities and out of sight. Where the shamanic dwells in that breach, revelling and revealing enigmas of experience and order, the memorial death feasts attempt to overwhelm these possibilities in a surfeit of exchange and sociality, overdetermining patriclan opposition and the orders of reciprocity. Where the sufferings, marginality, and intermediacy of women become material for shamanic meanings, the dual affiliations of women go unelaborated in death rites as they act either as siblings tied to natal patriclans or as wives to marital patriclans; the enigmas sounded in shamanic rituals are damped.

The field thus allows two responses to the enigmas of necessary breach, one embedded in the account of tsen and the other in memorial death feasts. These responses are supplemented by a third response to the predicament, one we encountered at the outset: the formative incestuous marriage of Ingkyal and Tikiri (see chapter 3), which not only generates the focal clans of Tamdungsa duality but also overcomes the inherent ruptures of marriage union by linking husband-brother to wife-sister. These two extremes—to marry a sibling or not to marry at all—cannot become praxis for villagers, who are bound to reproduce restricted exchanges and hence their paradoxes. This dilemma becomes the axis of ritual divergence within the total field, where the lamaic and the sacrificial recreate determinate orders and the shamanic resounds through their arbitrariness. The field is not reducible, though, to this axis alone, and the enigmas of cousins are subsumed within a more generalizing field of contrasts, which are condensed in an account of a competition of a lama and a bombo known in several variants throughout the Buddhist Himalayas.

[1]In this sense the shamanic is female in Tamang symbology and the lamaic and sacrificial male. I should caution that this does not mean the shamanic is of women or the lamaic and sacrificial of men in the ways construed by functionally oriented theorists of the sociology and psychology of possession and shamanisms (see Holmberg 1983). On the intermediacy of women see March (1979, 1984, 1987).

Rational Irresolvability of the Ritual Field: From Ritual to Myth

More often than not if one asks Tamang villagers directly, "What is the difference between a lama and a bombo?" they will respond with the origination account of *kalten sangkye* and *dungsro bon*, primeval brothers, the former a lama, the latter a bombo. A coda to the main events of the account also introduces the lambu and situates sacrificial practice in the field. If societies "contain their own interpretations" (Geertz 1973:453) narrated in ritual performances, then mythic accounts like that of Kalten Sangkye and Dungsro Bon are interpretations but, in contrast to rituals, on a more totalizing level. Contemporary lamas and bombos trace descent directly to Kalten Sangkye and Dungsro Bon, the latter transformed into *nharu bon*. This account of ritual divergence and ritual authority is about the total field and provides an overview unattainable on the level of ritual. Lévi-Strauss, in characterizing the relations of ritual and myth, emphasizes that myths operate as metatexts that refuse to resolve into the images demanded in ritual narrations: "Myth and ritual do not always correspond to each other. Nevertheless, they complete each other in domains already presenting a complementary character. The value of the ritual as meaning resides in instruments and gestures: It is a *para-language*. The myth, on the other hand, manifests itself as *meta-language*; it makes full use of discourse, but does so by situating its own significant oppositions at a higher level of complexity than that required by language operating for profane ends" (1976:66). With less abstraction, the accounts of Dungsro Bon and Kalten Sangkye are an indigenous commentary on the same problem that has dominated anthropological and comparativist concern with what is often conceptualized as "syncretism." Through the account, Tamang attain a vantage outside the constructions of particular ritual symbologies; this exegesis can be brought into direct dialogue with anthropological reconstructions of complex ritual systems.

As we shall see, the account, like the tsen account discussed above, portrays irresolvable tension; however, tensions are more generalized in this account and allow us to make more extensive comparisons on ritual polarities across the Himalayas. The account appears to be widely known in Nepal and Tibet, and versions have been recorded among Tamang from several areas and among Gurung (Höfer 1975; Peters 1981; Pignède 1966:387–88); western Tamang not only regularly recount colloquial versions but bombos must formally recite (or at least cryptically refer to) them at the time of the erection of the *so dungma* or life-force tree in soundings. Reformist versions are part of Sherpa lore (Ortner 1978b) and of Tibetan literature (Dás 1881; Mi-la-ras-pa 1962).

The Account of Kalten Sangkye and Dungsro Bon

I shall begin with a variant told by a prominent lama in Tamdungsa and consider other variants subsequently: "In a time of only earth and stones, there were two brothers. The older brother was a lama, Kalten Sangkye, and the younger brother was a bombo, Dungsro Bon. At that time, Dungsro Bon did all things. He cured people; he expelled the dead, and he performed the memorial death feasts. The lama did nothing.

"One day, the lama's wife chided her husband, asking him what good he was; why he did nothing and why he had nothing. She told him that Dungsro Bon, the bombo, called the dead, that the dead appeared to the community and ate their food offerings. Kalten Sangkye told his wife that it was all a trick and that those who actually came to eat the offerings were evil spirits and shades.

"He told his wife to take his *dorje* [symbol of truth and power] and when Dungsro Bon called the shadow-soul of the deceased to display it. If it was an evil spirit that came, it would be destroyed, and if it was the shadow-soul, it would come under the care and protection of the Buddhas.

"The wife went and at the appropriate time displayed the dorje. It was revealed to be evil spirits that came to eat the offerings of food. Dungsro Bon was humiliated. He was made speechless.

"The bombo said to his brother, 'You have made me out like a senseless, drunken fool. You have made me your rival and now we must have a competition. Let's go on a pilgrimage to Chhomamo Ngyingtso [a high mountain lake]. You have never been on pilgrimage before.'

"The bombo set off on the three-day trail to the high mountain lake. His people went with him, carrying his drum, his altar, and some snacks for the way.

"The lama sat at home alone. His daughter became worried and said, 'Father, the other has left on the competition. Why are you staying here? They left three days ago and they have probably already arrived.' The lama asked his daughter to cook him some soup. Then he transformed himself into a bird and flew up to Chhomamo Ngyingtso. There he planted his staff.

"The lama perched in the center of the lake. The bombo arrived and looked into the lake. He saw nothing there but a vulture. Then, wondering what the vulture would do, he threw things at it trying to drive it away. The lama thought to himself, 'Ahaa, he would do a thing like that to me. He must not recognize me.' The bombo was thinking to himself, 'My older brother is below and has not yet arrived.' The bombo threw more things at the vulture.

"This time Kalten Sangkye became angry at his younger brother. He took his spoon, dipped it in the water, and flipped the lake over, driving Dungsro Bon down and into the midst of the lake. The lama thought he had finished off Dungsro Bon and returned to his home.

"Kalten Sangkye's daughter, out of affection for her father, had gone to the lake, but when she arrived he had left, descending by a different trail from hers. All she heard was the sound of a drum beating. She looked over and down into the lake and saw Dungsro Bon dancing and beating his drum. She wondered what had happened. Three days went by while she looked. Up from the midst of the lake, Dungsro Bon sent the curse of the porcupine quill and ruined the eyes of Kalten Sangkye's daughter.

"Kalten Sangkye came and tried to cure his daughter. He consulted his books and blew his mantras onto her, but could not find the cure. Finally, he called out to his brother, who was still dancing and beating his drum while lodged in the midst of the earth. The lama said, 'Look here, big man. Don't call yourself Dungsro Bon anymore; call yourself Nharu Bon. Chant only for the living; I will give you five rupees and nine level measures of grain if you cure my daughter's eyes.' He then extracted the bombo from the midst of the lake.

"The lama then bound the following oath: 'Look, I will take care of the dead and you will take care of the living.' The bombos now go crazy if they eat the food of the communal death feast. The bombos cannot touch the dead either. The portions were divided between lamas and bombos."

On one level, this exegetic account confirms ritual reality. In fact, lamas recount it to legitimate their authority over death rites and their superiority over bombos. Other versions assert an alternate authority, and bombos add new dimensions to the competition, announcing the limits of lamaic power. For instance, one respected bombo opened the account with an inversion of the relation of the brothers: "In ancient times, Dungsro Bon and Kalten Sangkye did battle for three years. The lama said to his brother, 'You will take care of the living and I will take care of the dead.' The bombo responded, 'I will not stay under my younger brother's order.' The bombo did not obey the lama so the lama said, 'We two must go to Palkutang. We will meet there.' The bombo went ahead. Along the way he expelled the dead, he called the shadow-soul, and he performed the death feast."

Bombos also add greater detail to the events surrounding the bombo's emergence from the lake: "Trouble and confusion overcame Kalten Sangkye. He sat with his eyes closed and meditated to reveal the cause of his daughter's affliction. He knew if Dungsro Bon did not emerge, his daughter's eyes would crack and break. So Kalten Sangkye placed a tall palm tree and a cedar tree as *so dungma* or life-force trees. He [erected the wrong species of tree] as a joke and to trick Dungsro Bon. Then he placed the sapling of the chestnut tree, and Dungsro Bon emerged from the center of the earth beating his drum."

Ritual Contradiction and the Structure of the Myth

These versions, whether in lamaic or shamanic rendition, stand in contrast to reformist variants, which I consider below, largely because they authorize all forms of practice, not simply the Buddhist or lamaic. The problem of ritual divergence is not resolved by a final privileged position. In all versions, the bombo is not absolutely defeated and silenced, erased from practice, as in literate renditions, but drums and dances incessantly eventually to rise up and sound. Although the lama declares the bombo a bumbling charlatan in the performance of death feasts, one who fools through sleight of hand, in another passage in the account the lama attempts to deceive the bombo by implanting false life-force trees. The lama reveals truth, but it is the bombo who gives sight to the daughter. The myth concludes with an oathbound division of ritual labors, but the submission of the bombo is never fully accomplished: after driving the bombo into the bowels of the earth, the lama accedes to his demands. These versions, whether taken singly or in combination, can be conceived not only as a complex confirmation of ritual reality but as expressions that reveal the dynamics of Tamang religion.

Events in the account, in fact, do not conform to the actual division of labor between lamas and bombos, and our interpretation must take this into consideration. Like the account of tsen, it poses direct contradictions and inversions of actual conventions; its power for Tamang derives again from presenting impossibilities: the bombo becomes a lama and the lama a bombo. In all Tamang versions, the bombo performs death rites; he expels the dead and feeds the dead. Likewise, the bombo's name is Dungsro Bon, who Tamang say sounded in the daylight like lamas in contrast to present-day bombos who, except during pilgrimages, only sound at night. On the other hand, Kalten Sangkye becomes a bombo when he transforms into a bird and flies to the high mountain lake; it is bombos not lamas who wear the feathers of the impeyan pheasant or peacock when they travel on pilgrimage and who adorn their altars with images of flight. Moreover, the lama, again like a bombo, tries to cure his daughter and places the life-force tree to remove his brother from the earth and lake.

These inversions no doubt work to define proper ritual roles through exaggeration, but the contrary reality created in the account also directs us to consider the account as more than a mechanism for rephrasing a logically prior ritual necessity. The mythic disruption of ritual reality discloses but does not resolve the opposition between lama and bombo; the variants are speculative and reveal dynamic tensions in Tamang consciousness, just as the variants of Shivaic myths expose an elementary paradox in Hindu worldview (O'Flaherty 1973; cf. Lévi-Strauss 1967a:229–30, 1968:30, 1976:65–67). The Tamang account poses a death-oriented lama to a life-reviving bombo, a binder of oaths to an irrepressible sounder, the power of Buddhist oaths to uncontrollable forces, order to counter order, determinacy to indeterminacy. The account rescues the bombo, a deconstructor of lamaic declarations, at the same moment that it asserts oathbound lamaic order and, as we shall see, the exorcistic powers of lambus.

Tamang exegesis of ritual divergences condenses another dimension of cultural contradiction, one that operates at an encompassing remove from the particular paradox of cousins and reciprocity around which the tsen account revolves. The account of Kalten Sangkye and Dungsro Bon recognizes a necessity for all forms of ritual practice. The prevailing strategies for explaining such "syncretism," "complexity," or multiplicity found throughout the greater Himalayas, South Asia, and Southeast Asia, as I noted at the outset, work from theories of extrinsic motivation, whether historical, sociological, or psychological. The accounts of Kalten Sangkye and Dungsro Bon transcribed here suggest that an arbitrary dynamic is at play in the formation of the field; ritual polyphony becomes more than the cacophony of an irretrievable history or of fragmented functions; complementarity and opposition are cultural processes erupting out of necessary contradictions that operate like orthodoxies and heterodoxies historically. Attention to this dynamic does not demand a denial of history nor of psychosocial dimensions of symbolic life but rather a reorientation toward what has been formulated as an "interface" of Hindu/Buddhist/"indigenous" elements in the Himalayas: at the same time that rituals of the word (and of sacrifice) declare determinate orders in the cosmos, displacing the forces of indeterminacy and the counter world of shamanic soundings, they implicitly announce their reality.

Anthropological writing on cultures tends toward closure— in functional studies by discovering extracultural motivation and in semiological studies in the systemic laws of signification. I have represented the dynamics of Tamang ritual polarities here in synchronic terms, yet this narrative systemization must remain heuristic, for the ritual field defies a final, unitary synthesis. As Boon remarks: "The dangerous tendency in studies of significant forms and in seeing 'culture' as holistic significant form is to 'over-literalize' the facts at hand. The investigator attracted by bound, multivocal, sensory rich productions only derives full satisfaction if he can finally abstract and completely interrelate the total range of components" (1973:16). In an essay on festivals in Andhra, Herrenschmidt (1982b) makes a related point when he demonstrates that a unitary reconstruction of a village festival cycle may be impossible and that we are confronted with multiple points of view.

A similar orientation has organized this reconstruction of the Tamang field, and our attention has focused as much on the relations among differences as on discovering final, grammatical structures of Tamang religion. The field is not closed into a coherent and tensionless order. What emerges through an overview of Tamang symbology is not consistent order but the juxtaposition of contrary orders. The ritual triad that has formed the subject of this book, for instance, takes shape in several different ways. Lamas oppose themselves to both lambus and bombos as the ones who have unique access to final truth and authority; they often say lambus and bombos "lie." In another context, lamas and bombos ally themselves in opposition to the lambu, who by his own hand kills. In yet another configuration, as we have seen, the lama and the lambu conjoin in the determination of social and cosmic order. A final, totalizing picture of Tamang religion never takes form; the field can be conceived only through the apperception of several ritual, mythic, and anthropological vantages. From this point of view (see Tambiah 1970), the field, like a kaleidoscope, never resolves into a totalizing image of all its variants. Nevertheless, by examining relations among the symbolic constructions of different ritual components, a logic of differences that form a total field can be abstracted.

Tamang exegesis, like anthropological exegesis, also demands narrative closure, and as we have seen, Tamang revert to glosses. They bring an overarching closure to their ritual polarities by according the lamaic an encompassing position. The account reiterated above ends in an oathbound order with the bombos confined paradoxically to lamaic authority. Likewise the bombo ritually claims authority from primordial lamas for many ritual activities as does the lambu, whose ritual powers to exorcise Nakhle Mhang emanate from ancient lamas. The system remains irresolute, however. Although the lama binds the bombo to an oath, it is an oath to sound, which as we have seen implies that the bombo celebrates indeterminacy and inherent contradiction. Tamang are fond of pointing out that Guru Rhimborocche was both a bombo and a lama; his matted hair (*rhalbo*) can be detected in iconographic renditions. The overstructuring that remains a risk in our interpretation is ultimately tempered not only by the deconstructive voice of the bombo but by the operation of historical forces as well.

A Sacrificial Coda: From Structure to Event

To this point, I have conflated the sacrificial and lamaic in an opposition to the shamanic. This has been justified in part by the convergence of the practice of lama and lambu in the memorial death feast and elsewhere toward the generation of elementary orders, even though they diverge in their bases of authority and orientation: lamas work from repeated Buddhist oaths and frame death rites in otherworldly schemes, and lambus proceed from acts in exclusive attention to worldly well-being. An association of lamaic and sacrificial in death feasts is further reflected in several other linkages between them.

The lamaic, although deriving justification in oaths, does not erase sacrificial acts. Lamaic practice in Tibet makes no pretense of disguising essentially sacrificial practices. Buddhist practitioners mold substitute offerings in place of living victims: "The animals and their body parts, which were used in the earlier sacrifices, were not completely displaced but were represented by replicas and by symbolic figures made of wood, dough, and butter. . . . In form, they may be representations of gods, men, beasts of prey, domesticated or game animals, birds, or reptiles" (Ekvall 1964:164). Tamang lamas do likewise, creating all sorts of effigies, including human ones, some of which they hack to pieces with ritual daggers or curved knives. Lamaic practice among Tamang, however, does not end with substitute offerings, and actual sacrifices accompany many contemporary lamaic rites and were an integral part until recently of the all-important death rituals. In the village festival Chhechu, lamas regularly exorcise Nakhle Mhang. Although the intense chants of the lamas are theoretically effective in sending this evil upon its way, lambus sacrifice a small chick for the evil on the lamaic ritual grounds with the tacit approval of lamas. Likewise, before the celebration of the festival of Chhechu, lambus must conduct sacrifices to all the neighborhood divinities in the vicinity of the performance and to Shyihbda and Shyingmardung. These sacrifices supplement the lamaic offerings of incense and beer at the site of the Buddhist altar.

Sacrifices that reveal the most to us, however, occur during memorial death feasts. In the not-too-distant past, death feasts included the sacrifice of a goat known as *gyam rhit* or trail begging. The head and tail of the sacrificial goat were placed under the Buddhist altar on an earthen mound, much as lambus place the heads and tails of animals on the sacrificial altar. Villagers and lamas explained that the goat was a "friend" of the deceased, who by grasping the tail could cross into rebirth (cf. Oppitz 1982:390–94). Quarters of the sacrificial animal were also given to significant categories of kin—apparently the sets of ashyang-shyangpo and mha—thus declaring the social order of the death feasts in sacrificial and Buddhist terms simultaneously. It would not be farfetched to surmise that in prelamaic times death rites, which are now the absolute prerogative of lamas, were sacrificial events not unlike those of ancient Tibet (see Tucci 1980:231).

The linkage of sacrificial and lamaic ritual functions from the perspective of the total field is also contained in a coda to the account of Kalten Sangkye and Dungsro Bon. According to one lambu, the bombo refused to abide by the lama's oath, and they fell into dispute once again: "[After the bombo emerged from the water] they argued again. Kalten Sangkye put Dungsro Bon back into the earth. Traveling within the earth, Dungsro Bon went to Gang Gangde and came out again. With his dorje, Kalten Sangkye made him dissolve into the earth again. Then Dungsro Bon went to Parping Godavari and stayed there, becoming the [evil spirit] Aktang Mhang." In this rendition of the origins of Aktang Mhang—which is one of several—Dungsro Bon is transformed not into the oathbound Nharu Bon from whom contemporary bombo trace affiliation but into an evil spirit subject to the repetitive exorcisms of lambus. The irrepressibility of the bombo becomes transfigured to necessary evil. The bombo becomes thus an ambiguous character, oscillating from containment in oathbound legitimacy to a reflection of the irrepressible evils that humanity battles.

With the convergence of lamaic and sacrificial ritual orientations, the question of their simultaneous perpetuation arises. The lamaic, through oaths and substitute victims, properly should subsume the practice of lambus. This incorporation has occurred among the Sherpa where Buddhist ritual and village lamas have displaced sacrificial practices that had continued in at least some Sherpa villages until this generation.[2] As Paul (1979) has argued, Sherpa religion presents itself as a unitary construction in which sacrificial and shamanic practices have been subsumed in a totalizing lamaism.

The perpetuation of the sacrificial in tandem with the lamaic reflects the general worldly orientation of Tamang: "The real world and man's this worldliness are taken for granted. Benefit, instead of moral merit, and tabu, instead of sin, are the notions governing man's attitude towards the superhuman. Far from being an illusion to be transcended, man must accommodate himself with the world in which both the 'good' and the 'bad' are imminently present" (Höfer 1981:37). On the one hand, the lamaic repertoire, although including propitiatory and exorcistic techniques, abstracts the forces of evil into generalized images. Lamaic ritual does not encounter in particularized symbolic constructions what for villagers is the quite real presence of shades, evils, and temperamental divinities. The erection of a *mhane* or an earthen work in an image of the ascendancy of the Buddhas over the earth, for instance, does not celebrate the autonomous powers of the divinities but the power of the Buddhas and the Word over all divinities and evils. For Tamang the earth divinities remain irrepressible by oaths. The sacrificial, in its direct encounter and engagement with these beings in their own terms, remains necessary.

An active sacrificial component has also been fostered in the historical circumstances of Tamang in Nepal. Buddhism and lamas were and are associated not only with a ritual orientation and authority but with sociopolitical formations. The lamaic announcement of the values of *ahiṃsā* or nonviolence, for instance, does not simply have ethical implications. Opposition to bloody sacrifice was and is a direct challenge to a ritual polity symbolically effected in sacrificial performances.[3] Buddhist institutions, however, never came to dominate and encompass local Tamang polities. The marginality of the Tamang to Tibetan theocratic polities and the rise of the Hindu state insulated the lamaic and tribalized lamaic practice outside the monastic and state evolve-

[2]Personal communication from Kathryn March.

[3]The early Buddhist assertion of nonviolence and a universalizing ethic were also framed in complement to the ossified orders of Vedic sacrifice.

ments that unfolded in Tibet. Labor, land, and surpluses that could have supported a lamaic monasticism were siphoned into the feudallike Rana polity. Some lands in the Tamdungsa region still support Hindu institutions in the Kathmandu Valley, and Tamdungsa and neighboring villages are officially recognized as the begging preserve of a sect of mendicant Hindus. Not only was lamaic monasticism infrastructurally precluded, the universalizing ethics of Buddhism were never fully incorporated in Tamang culture.

As Buddhism became contained in the Tamdungsa region, intensified relations with greater Nepalese polity encouraged a continuance of sacrificial forms. The pan-Nepal sacrificial celebration of Dasain became the context for legitimating local polities during the formative decades of the Nepalese state. According to local historical tradition, Tamang *pompo* or headmen would travel north during Dasain to receive blessings (*ṭikā*) and a turban from princely overlords of the early state. Dasain continues to play a legitimating role. Non-Tamang regularly ask whether Tamang celebrate Dasain, with the direct implication that if they do not, they are outsiders to greater Nepalese society. Contemporary Tamang celebrate Dasain; lamaic involvement, however, is indicative of the ambiguity of lamas and Buddhism in political terms. Tamdungsa villagers slaughter several buffalo on the occasion of Dasain, and village lambus perform propitiation to the nine Durgas, offering blood and meat in patterns convergent with those of greater Nepal. Moreover, on Dasain proper, the lambu consecrates the blessings that the village headmen distribute to all villagers. In the past lamas and the lama associated with the village gombo played a central role in the consecration of the blessings, but this is no longer the case. Blessings were kept in the gombo and then distributed to villagers. Although villagers gather on the nine nights before Dasain to sing songs glorifying the Buddhas and for the well-being of the headmen, the events of Dasain are now distinctively sacrificial in tone. The reinforcement of sacrifice as the idiom for the declaration of local polity reflects as well the localization of Tamang sociopolity in the rise of the state. Lambus practice exclusively in specific villages. Thus, at the same time that local lamas and society turned in upon themselves in the rise of the state, sacrificial forms received an encouragement. Moreover, the intensifying relations with greater Nepal introduced an array of new divinities and harmful agents into the Tamang ritual field, and relations with them, as in greater Nepal, were in large measure sacrificial. The lambu continues, then, in an essential position in Tamang practice.

The retention of the sacrificial in tandem with the lamaic thus has historical correlates, and the multiplicities of the field reflect both the systemic correlates of Tamang religiosity and these events. The retention of the sacrificial along with the lamaic and the shamanic can also be considered from another vantage not dissociated from the systemic and the historical. Tamang religious imagination allows the suspensions of contradictory forms and does not demand the consistency characteristic of rationalized renditions of Buddhism associated with monasticism and state societies. The words of lamas, the acts of lambus, and the soundings of bombos, though contradictory, can co-exist.

Between Mythic and Reformed

The ritual field responds not only to cultural contradictions and sociopolitical circumstances but to the powers of Tamang symbology. Tamang culture does not yield to the demands for the rational synthesis characteristic of reformist renditions of Buddhism. Tamang symbology in Weber's (1963) broad comparative and evolutionary scheme is traditional as opposed to rationalized; in structuralist metaphors Tamang are more like tribal *bricoleurs* than engineers (Lévi-Strauss 1966:16–22). Tamang incorporate ethicalized notions of karma in their practice and celebrate renunciation but keep them circumscribed to bounded ritual events.

Outsiders, whether other Buddhists of a Tibetan persuasion or Buddhologists, tend to relegate the Tamang to a position of degradation and heterodoxy. Tamang become figures of inconsistency, contradiction, and violation against the norms of reformed Buddhist ideology and practice. In the reformist Buddhisms of greater Tibet, Dungsro Bon and Kalten Sangkye appear in new guise as a practitioner of the Bon religion, Naro-Bon-chhun, and a Buddhist adept, Milarepa. These versions, in contrast to Tamang renditions recounted above, introduce the moralizing tones of world rejection and the play of karma. The account in the translation of Dás (1881:206–11)—which has more contemporary correlates—begins with a dialogue between Milarepa and Naro-Bon-chhun that is as much a disputation of doctrine as a competition. Milarepa in fact encounters Naro-Bon-chhun on his way to meditate at Mount Tesi (Kailash) and accuses him of being a "juggler." Naro-Bon-chhun responds with a challenge to race to the top of Mount Kailash. Milarepa accepts and tells Naro-Bon-chhun that it is a pity that "you mistake the light of Bon-bum for the chief perfection. He who possesses it should be able to see his own face. In order to be able to do so, one must embrace the system of meditation prescribed in our religion" (Dás 1881:210).

In an opposition of propitiation to meditation, Naro-Bon-chhun prays to a tutelary and Milarepa pursues ascetic practices. The race then begins:

> At the dawn of the 15th [day], Naro-Bon-chhuñ, being dressed in a blue fur-dress, playing the cymbal, called "*shang*," and mounting a tambourine, went towards the sky. The pupils of Je-tsun [Milarepa], seeing this, went to him and found him fast asleep. One of the pupils named Re-chhuñ addressed him:—"Venerable Sir! Naro-Bon-chhuñ, early in the morning, riding his own tambourine, flew towards the sky. By this time he has reached the waist of Tesi." Je-tsun being still in bed, his pupil thought that the Bonpo had gained the day and carried off the possession of the place. Earnestly he pressed Je-tsun to get up, and the same was done by all the pupils. Je-tsun now looked with fixed eyes toward Tesi and said—"Behold! the Bonpo, being unable to climb the precipice, has gone round it." Then in a finger's snapping he mounted the sun-beam and, by spreading his raiment as outspread wings, flew towards the top of Tesi, which he reached in a moment along with the glowing sun. At this time the Lamas belonging to Je-tsun's order and the god Chakra Sambara witnessed the spectacle, and were delighted with the triumph of Je-tsuñ. When Naro-Bon-chhuñ was attempting to rise above the neck of Tesi, he fell down, and his tambourine rolled down towards the southern valley of Tesi. (Dás 1881:211)

In this account, Milarepa, the advocate of ascetic renunciation and of the dharma of the Buddhas, and Naro, the adept of Bon, cannot accommodate each other except in mutual exclusivity. The account enshrined in the Tibetan canon and retold by reformist Tibetan Buddhists reaches a final conclusion in which the juggler Naro is deposed and his tambourine rolls down the valley. In other translations of this song of the Buddhist adept Milarepa, this finale is supplemented with pedagogical verse:

> I bow down to my Guru, the gracious Marpa!
>
> Through His mercy and the compassion of all Buddhas
> I heard the wondrous Lord Buddha Śākyamuni,
> He who subdued the heretics and followers of the Six Schools
> With the rightful teaching of Dharma.
> The doctrine of Buddhism has thus been spread over the world.

On the Mountain, the Snow Di Se,
I, the Yogi of Tibet, with the Dharma conquer Bon,
And make the Buddha's Practice Lineage
Illuminate Tibet. (Mi-la-ras-pa 1962:221–22).

This doctrinal account stands in relief to Tamang versions, which conclude with inclusive complementarity.

In both word and practice Tamang accommodate multiplicity without final privilege. Lamas at one moment will assert the strictures of karma and declare that sacrificial slaughter is the worst form of demerit and the next moment carry a rooster to the site of a village divinity to be killed by a lambu. They allow lambus to sacrifice chicks within the confines of their ritual domain. They likewise will say bombos lie, yet assist bombos in soundings, on pilgrimages, and in the banishment of evil. They erect prayer flags to protect bombos from onslaughts and equip them with talismans. They do not now compete with bombos on pilgrimages toward a mutual exclusivity but practice in tandem. Tamang houses are often festooned with both lamaic prayer flags (*lungdar*) and shamanic life-force poles (so dungma), and villages partake of the blessings of each.

Although multiple practice remains a reality in other Buddhist societies like the Thai and the Sherpa, sacrifice and the shamanic are marginalized and subsumed to an orientation that privileges karma and world renunciation as ultimate values. The Tamang appear as unreformed, even tribal, in their symbology. On the one hand this is announced in the absence of monasticism and on the other in the inclusivity of their symbology, which does not move toward synthesis according to karma and world renunciation. The history of Buddhism in Tibet in large measure is one of the genesis of large monastic communities and the general transformation of religious culture toward salvation through ethical action. Beginning in the fourteenth century, celibate monasticism became a predominant ideal of religious action and the dichotomies between lay and monastic a basic feature of Tibetan society.

The recent history of the Sherpa reflects a similar progression. Over the last century Sherpa monasticism has been on the rise in a general climate of reformism. Monasteries of married monks are on the wane, and large communities of monks and nuns thrive (Ortner 1978a). Accompanying these developments have been the diminishment and marginalization of other ritual practices. Shamanism is in sharp decline

(Ortner 1978b; Paul 1976). Even the thought of sacrifice, the smell of blood, or proximity to butchers can bring Sherpa to a quite physical revulsion.[4] Sherpas as well as many people in the greater Tibetan-culture area appear orthodox, even by Theravada standards (Ortner 1978a:157–68). Monastic Tibetan forms then appear as a reformed tantrism from the perspective of Tamang, who were contained historically as "tribals."

The division of lay and monastic, with all its philosophical justifications, does not overcome the division of clans among Tamang. According to Tamang lamas, the truths of Buddhism can be achieved in heterodoxy. Some lamas find a greater truth in heterodox practices than in orthodox ones. One lama accounted for sacrifices that used to occur in conjunction with memorial death feasts by alluding—in good tantric fashion—to the possibility of several paths to salvation:

> A long time ago, we used to do these things [sacrifice in death rites]. Now they ask, "Why did you do them?" Well, you need meat for a death feast. They ask, "Why kill?" They say, "Demerit will come." But a death feast is no good unless you have meat. The dead animal is the friend of the deceased. If you go by the book, you cannot sacrifice because demerit will come; you cannot fornicate because demerit will come. If you do not fornicate, how can there be children? So, too, how can you not have meat in a death feast? Supposedly, if you spin a prayer wheel [full of Buddhist mantras] demerit goes away, is erased; they just put it aside. It is only one trail—not the real trail. This trail is just for learning. This only shows one way to the heavens. They say you cannot light lamps because the bugs die. But how can you sit at night? They say you have to light butter lamps [in order to honor the Buddhas], but how can you do that without killing bugs? In ancient times, they used to do it like that but not now.

This lama has not only converted celibacy into naïveté, he has conjoined the philosophical and mystical ends of Buddhism with the strictures of life in general and of the exchanges of clan society in particular. This conjunction reveals the mythic logic of Tamang culture as the suspension, articulation, and integration of what are incompatibilities from the rationalized perspectives of orthodox systems. Their system is both "tribal" and tantric.

[4]This revulsion may well be a function of the fact that blood indicates a pollution (*grib*) as much as a demeritorious act.

This pursuit of life escapes the tensions that inhere implicitly in the elevation of renunciatory celibacy. In a broad comparison of types of religiosity, considering both ideological and institutional implications, Boon has contrasted tribal and tantric logics to reformist monasticism in the following terms:

> Nonmonastic traditional systems, including, I would argue, both tribes and Tantrisms, are *generalized*. (Again, Tantrism can contain monastic and ethical elements, but they do not symbolize the whole.) In a generalized order, each smaller division—two exogamous clans, say, or some other type of alliance partners—replicates the full degree of differentiation recognized; small-scale wholes engage in rituals of the total whole. Compared to such systems monasticism appears revolutionary, or at least antithetical: Celibacy, which must remain ambivalent or even deviant in tribal (or tantric?) systems, becomes institutionalized in monasticism. "Asociality" is legitimated as an alternative to "society." From the vantage of society and its perpetuation, the monastery epitomizes incompleteness: not self-regenerating, often not self-sustaining. Yet although the monastery can survive only through recruitment, it presumes to represent the entire cosmos, society included. Hence from the vantage of "life" there is a fundamental discrepancy: The cosmic whole is lodged in social part (*ceremonies* of monks), not in social whole (*rituals* of clans or ancestor groups). (1982:202)

Among Tamang, Buddhist ideals of salvation through renunciation and meritorious acts are certainly condensed in the memorial death feasts but subsumed to the "generalized" order of patriclan exchange.

The "asociality" of reformist ethos introduces a superstructuring tension in Sherpa religion but remains unelaborated institutionally or ethically in Tamang society. The ethnology of Sherpa takes this tension as a primary problem in a comparison with other types of religion. Among Sherpa, the ascetic rites of Nyungne are characterized by fasting and other asocial declarations, leading Ortner to conclude her study of Sherpa ritual with the following words:

> There is, then, an a priori logic to the argument that Buddhism, given its premises, will be antagonistic to social life and will thus be problematic for lay people operating in religion's shadow. The Sherpa case seems to manifest this logic. Sherpa Buddhism, which in many respects can hardly be called orthodox, nonetheless retains the central Buddhist tendency to isolate and atomize the individual, and devalue social bondings and social reciprocity. Indeed it is hard to imagine how Buddhism could be

> Buddhism without retaining this bias. A Buddhism of social bonding and communal solidarity seems a contradiction in terms. (1978a:157)

Paul, likewise, portrays Sherpa as caught in existential paradox affirming both world denial and affirmation: "A salvation religion in a routinized social context must at the same time affirm and deny the value of life in the social world. It must, therefore, contain some practices designed to 'save' the individual from an intolerable life in this world and others designed to lengthen, enhance, and bestow riches and health on the same existence in this world" (1979:274). Tamang lamaic ritual, particularly death feasts, generate "social bonding" and "communal solidarity." The disjunction between monastic and lay does not structure the Tamang religious field.[5] One pole of this meta-opposition that infuses Sherpa religious consciousness is virtually absent except as a distant unattainable and impractical end.[6] Renouncers enter the Tamang social field only as true outsiders—ascetic Hindu beggars, monastics encountered at urban centers—not the inside outsiders of societies that institutionalize monasticism. Buddhist values are articulated and subsumed within the regenerative reciprocities of clan-based society and the confined alliances of a dual organization condensed in preferential cross-cousin marriage, not vice versa. The purpose here is not to quibble about whether or not the essentially life-affirmative character of Tamang lamaic ritual makes them aBuddhist, for definitions of what is and what is not Buddhism can only be taken by privileging some forms over others, but to suggest that Tamang ritual practice counters reformist and ethically rationalized patterns.

Tambiah, in his comprehensive overview of Thai ritual and myth, likewise finds that lay religion directly incorporates the ideals of world denial. He has demonstrated how historical transformations have generated continuities and homologies between lay and monastic, village and literary renditions. Primary examples of this convergence are "the union of monkship (renunciation) with the concept of filial obligation and merit transfer, the union of lay sponsorship of religion for support of sons in robes, and the union of temporary monkhood with the exigencies of a life-cycle rooted in this world." The latter example refers to the common practice of a Thai man who "shifts from ascetic

[5]Paul (1979) elaborates a distinction of the same order between celibate and removed monastic renouncers and village lamas who marry and perform life-affirming rites.

[6]Lichter and Epstein (1983) have stressed a distinction between lay and clergy among Tibetans. In particular, they suggest that karma (for both laity and monastics) is linked to conceptions of happiness.

monkhood to marriage and family life and then becomes an increasingly pious layman who in old age begins to approach monkhood again" (1970:376). Like the life stages of Hindu ideology, which ideally move individuals from positions of chaste student, through householdership, to forest dweller, and eventually to complete renouncer, renunciation and engagement are artfully made possible for all. The intensified religiosity of older Sherpas is analogous. The reciting of mantras and texts, the turning of prayer wheels, and attendance at ascetic rituals all mark a life-cyclical incorporation of Buddhist ideals.

This lay Buddhism with its diachronic adaptation to prestructuring values of the Hindu-Buddhist world, though, can be contrasted to that of the Tamang precisely because the orientation of even the laity is framed in the values of the monastic. Among Tamang, the tensions introduced in consciousness by an asocial world denial and in social organization by monasticism are undeveloped. Thai, like Sherpa villagers, support monasticism and remain in close communication with renouncers. Tamang, in Tambiah's terms, have an exclusively lay elaboration. They are like Sherpa village lamas without renunciatory counterparts. The historical containment of the Tamang and the involution of their ritual field, however, contain the seeds for reformism, the expressions of which are evident in contemporary Nepal as their social and experiential reality transforms.

One could make the historical conjecture that if Tamang had continued intensive contact with monasticized Tibet, reformist processes would have been encouraged. The rise of the state of Nepal truncated an economic and religious potentiality for gradual transformation toward monasticism, transformation that would have de-emphasized the local alliances that formed the basis of a confined sociopolity and that would have marginalized shamanic and sacrificial practices in patterns analogous to those of the Sherpa. Contemporary social transformations are unsettling the basis of these historical orders and are opening Tamang to the outside in new ways; a reformist voice has entered into village life.

These trends prompt disputes among lamaic schools over ritual practice. The Dukpa school of lamas has become prominent in the greater western Tamang region through the activities of their millenial guru. He was a respected teacher until his departure at age ninety-six for more important Buddhist sites; during his residence—with two "nuns"—he held numerous retreats and initiated some fifteen Tamang lamas. He also embellished the lore of local geography by linking it to Buddhist prophesies and legend. Although villagers recount that Tibetan lamas regularly visited the region prior to Chinese administration in order to locate significant points in Guru Rhimborochhe's journey to Tibet, the Bhutanese teacher was able to identify footprints and prophesied the discovery of texts hidden by the guru on his journey. His students reported, for instance, that on a peak sacred to a mountain divinity—whom, according to local legend, Guru Rhimborochhe could not subdue—there was a book with golden and diamond letters lodged in the midst of a block of granite. After the teacher left the region, his students went to the peak with sledgehammers but could not crack open the block; this failure confirmed in their minds the real presence of the texts. When a tree fell over at the site of a regional goddess and several ancient Buddhist figurines were discovered, these lamas asserted that the figurines had been hidden by Guru Rhimborochhe and that their discovery confirmed the predictions of their teacher. Two disciples of the Bhutanese lama also pointed out that golden and diamond relics (a dorje and a bell) were embedded in rocks in a site sacred to local divinities in their village.

Although the Bhutanese teacher articulated Guru Rhimborochhe's exploits to local geography, these evolvements were less new than more forcefully and millenially emphasized. As we have explained, Buddhist monuments are often found in juxtaposition with sites of chthonic divinities. What is new with the school of Dukpa lamas is their refusal to accommodate heterodox practice—not only that of lambus and bombos but of unreformed lamas. They claim that sacrificial and shamanic rituals are evil and accumulate demerit, and they recount yet another version of the Kalten Sangkye and Dungsro Bon competition to make their point. In this version, bombos sacrifice, accumulating huge amounts of sin. They prophesy a future in which proper Buddhist action will overtake all other ritual forms. Moreover, unlike most Tamang, the Dukpa lamas regularly invoke terms such as dharma, karma, and demerit (pap/dikpa), which are rarely heard in local discourse. They avoid the excessive alcoholic consumption common at most rituals and wear more correct habits. Several have become teachers in their own right and are exercising influence well beyond the locale. Two with skill in Buddhist arts are not only acting as teachers in distant regions but have been commissioned to construct gombos in distant Tamang villages as well. Another resides periodically in a monastery in the Kathmandu Valley. Their reformism has overtones of the civic; in one village a "committee" of lamas has been involved in several local projects, most notably the construction of a gombo. They are in contact with reformed Newar Buddhists who have encouraged Theravada practices in Nepal and monastic institutions in the Kathmandu Valley.

This reforming orientation is most evident in the performance of memorial death feasts. Disciples of the Bhutanese teacher uncompromisingly insist on reformed practice in opposition to sponsors and powerful headmen, who demand traditional performances. The changes demanded by Dukpa lamas go beyond the usual procedural strife over tormo, texts, and the like that mark school differentiation. They assert that death feasts should dispense with merriment and all other heterodox activities not focused on the progression of the soul to rebirth or not framed in an otherworldly mentality. In particular, they refuse to dance and condemn excessive drinking, feasting, and celebratory dancing and singing on the part of villagers. They refuse to recite their texts or conduct their rites at the raised altars around which village clans exchange among themselves and with the deceased; instead they erect sheds where they serenely chant toward the improvement of the karmic condition of the deceased. Not all reformism comes from the Dukpa, and other schools of lamas have adopted reformist practices. In particular, all schools, including the Nakpadoser or the most "unreformed," have dropped the former practice of gyam rhit or trail begging in which a goat was sacrificed.

These reformist expressions may well define patterns of religious change among western Tamang. Dukpa lamas, as I noted, have acted as masters for lamas throughout the western Tamang territory, and they have constructed the finest gombo in the region. They proselytize for a more reformed lamahood and view dharma as serious. Like some Karmapa lamas, they introduce a new tenor in religious motivation, one based on individually constructed goals oriented to an otherworld. With these changes come corresponding devaluations of sacrificial and shamanic practice. These changes may also be a response to broader transformations in western Tamang society, where there are many more lamas being trained than bombos or lambus and where one hears tales of bombos converting to lamas. The reformism is complemented and further supported by Tamang villagers who communicate regularly with other Nepalese in the more cosmopolitan regions of Nepal and who break out from the isolation of the local socioeconomy embedded in the alliances and hierarchies of reciprocity into an expanded social experience. A true transformation to monastic patterns probably requires the formation of an elite sector of Tamang—perhaps, as we have seen, a contradiction in terms. Tamang are emerging in modern Nepal as a laboring class.

These developments, though, remain in process and contained in an antecedent cultural logic. Dukpa lamas remain Tamang lamas, and unless they renounce to monastic institutions of greater Nepal, they must be responsive to local demands and social structure. Reformist ideals are now articulated in the field, but to this point they have yet to overtake the field. They introduce yet another voice. The multiplicities contained in the ritual field through Tamang symbology reflect a tantric-tribal resistance to reformist trends. Tamang suggest inclusion of another term in the comparative studies of Buddhist societies beyond the philologically established Mahayana, Vajrayana, and Theravada.

Not coincidentally, Dukpa lamas did not preside over death feasts in Tamdungsa. When they came to a neighboring village they made demands in reference to the performance of the death feasts that provoked a sharp dispute with both the sponsors and the headmen, which led to a near collapse of the proceedings. Villagers and headmen have firm ideas about the proper course of the death feasts and insist on the continuation of celebratory practices. Memorial death feasts are not only rites motivated and marked by Buddhist precepts, an otherworldly orientation, and textual recitation, they are celebrations in which systematic exchanges and revelry abound. Moreover, they usually include several types of dancing and singing. Lamas dance the postures of sangkye as painted in their thangku; they represent in dance incidents in Buddhist legend; they perform ribald skits. Villagers sing songs in glorification of Buddhas, and young people revel through the night, singing playful songs that sometimes lead to elopement. Whiskey flows freely. The death feast is far from a sober reflection on the implications of death and rebirth; grief is cured in social regeneration and reciprocity. As a Tamang song goes, "Why oh why do the lamas dance? To fill their bellies full, full!"

Glossary

Words are Tamang unless otherwise noted.

acho-ale — One's clan brothers or those men who share the same patriclan on the local level. See also *busing; ananenchon.*

ahiṃsā (Sanskrit) — Hindu-Buddhist stricture of nonviolence or noninjury to living beings. The killing of living beings is associated with demerit/sin (*pāp*).

ananenchon — A woman's clan sisters or those women who share the same clan on the local level. See also *acho-ale; busing.*

ashyang — Mother's brother or anyone who stands in this relation in a classificatory sense. Also, father's sister's husband or spouse's father (*ken*).

ashyang-shyangpo — Mother's brothers and wife's husbands; translated as "wife-givers." Used to refer to those who come to expel the grief of mourners in a memorial death feast. See also *ashyang.*

bāhun (Nepali) — Nepali term for Brahman, the highest caste grouping in the Nepalese hierarchy. Significant subgroups in Tamang areas are *upādhyaya bāhun* and *jaisi bāhun.*

bar do thos grol (Tibetan) — Text recited at the time of death by Tibetan Buddhists to guide the consciousness of the deceased to a fortunate rebirth.

beyhul — Secret heavens of the bombos to which they travel at times of revelation. Their spiritual ancestors are thought to reside there.

bhoṭe (Nepali) — Used by Nepali speakers to refer to many hill-dwelling, Tibeto-Burman-speaking groups, in particular, those along the northern border of Nepal with Tibet who are ethnically associated with Tibetan peoples. Used to refer pejoratively to Tamang populations. See also *lama; murmi.*

bir — Animallike familiar thought to be kept by wealthy people to steal the well-being and prosperity of others. Bombos and lambus expel *bir* along with its master, *baramāsu* or wealthy ones.

birtā (Nepali) — Income-producing estates granted to military, administrative, and noble functionaries during the nineteenth century and the first half of the twentieth century; no longer recognized.

bla — Tamang term for souls; shadow; translated as "shadow-souls." Humans have nine *bla. Bla* dream, persist beyond death, and can become lost.

bokshyi Nepali word used by Tamang for people who ruin things out of jealousy; translated as "witch."

bombo One of the major ritual practitioners in Tamang life. Bombos have unique powers of sight and capture lost shadow-souls (*bla*), revive life-force (*so*), and reveal the sources of distress.

brāhmaṇ (Sanskrit) Highest caste group in the Hindu varna system; in Sanskritic ideology, priests.

brangke Raised altar constructed for all major rituals.

brui hong Prosperous essence of grain.

busing A man's clan sisters or those women who share patriclan membership on the local level. See also *ananenchon*.

chhangma Mistress of feasting at the festival of *chhechu*. Responsible for the organization and distribution of food and whiskey; usually assisted by other men and women.

chhechu Village festival of dances and Buddhist rites. *Chhechu* is in many respects a village version of the monastic pageants of Tibet.

chhetri (Nepali) Term for Kshatriya or the warrior or ruling castes.

chhoppa Sequences of rituals in which offerings are conveyed to divine or demonic powers.

damla Oath. Tamang lore recounts that in primordial times Buddhas bound oaths to create order in the world.

dasaĩ (Nepali) Festival held in September-October in honor of the goddess Durga. *Dasaĩ* is an important national festival with symbolic functions in Nepalese sociopolity.

dharma (Sanskrit) Religious obligation or duty; proper and virtuous behavior including the social.

dikpa Sin or demerit in the Buddhist sense.

ḍimḍung One of the leading clans of Tamdungsa. Descendants of *dong chhempo*.

dong chhempo Assassin of an anti-Buddhist king of Tibet who fled to Nepal. Ancestral hero of Tamdungsa Tamang.

dorje Powerbolt; a Tibetan Buddhist ritual implement that symbolizes absolute truth and power.

du Formal grief carried by the children, parents, spouse(s), and inheritors of the property of the deceased.

gle A subsector of the larger Tamang population. Princely clans prior to the conquest of Nepal. In Nepali, *ghale*.

gombo Tamang term for a small temple located in a village and housing images of the Buddhas. In Tibetan *gombo* means monastery or hermitage.

gral Memorial death feasts or large Buddhist rites held after a death. Largest of Tamang social rites.

gurpa Buddhist specialist who invokes *wang* or magical power.

guru (Nepali) Teacher or preceptor; religious master. See also *lopan*.

guru rhimbo-rochhe	Buddhist hero or saint who in large measure represents the Buddhas in western Tamang imagination.
guṭhi (Nepali)	Land endowed in support of institutions, particularly religious and charitable institutions.
gyut	Patriline. See also *santān.*
himḍung	One of the major clans of Tamdungsa.
jāgir	Income-producing estate used to support a functionary of the state.
jaisi bāhun (Nepali)	Type of Brahman in the hills of Nepal. Lower in status than other types of Bahun; often referred to as widow-remarrying Bahun.
jarti	Tamang term for Chetri and Bahun peoples. Any high-caste Nepali speaker.
jāt (Nepali)	Ethnic group, tribe, caste, or clan. Among themselves Tamdungsa Tamang use *jāt* for patriclan. See also *khor.*
jhā̃khri (Nepali)	Nepali term for specialists in the mediation between humans and spirits or divinities.
jimiwāl (Nepali)	Local official during the Rana era. *Jimiwāl* technically were responsible for collecting taxes on irrigated fields but were also the final authority in village matters.
kāmi (Nepali)	Caste Blacksmiths (Tamang *kami*). Found throughout the hills of Nepal and in most Tamang villages, *kāmi* work iron and provide field and other wage labor. They are an untouchable caste (*pāni nachalne jāt*) and are generally impoverished.
karche	One of two types of offerings conveyed to divinities: white or non-blood offerings. See also *marche.*
karma (Sanskrit)	Effects of action in this world on rebirth.
kerap	Account of rebirths or origination.
khanḍangmo	Female furies who accompany Tamdungsa bombos on their forays into divine realms.
kharṭa	Divinity in Tamdungsa situated between two other village divinities, *shyihbda* and *shyingmardung.*
khor	A term sometimes used for clan.
khurpa	To carry on the shoulders. Used to describe the bombos shouldering of divinities during soundings.
khyung	Primordial bird associated with bombos in Tamang mythology. Symbolized by the beak of the great hornbill.
kipaṭ (Nepali)	Form of land tenure whereby land is held inalienably by ethnic or clan groups.
kṣatriya (Sanskrit)	Warrior varna of ancient Indian society. Chetris and Thakuris of Nepal were classed in legal codes as Kshatriya.
la	General term for divinity.
lai ne	Place of the divinities; a heaven of the deities.
lama	Buddhist specialist in Tamang society. Also used to refer to Tamang peoples.

lambu — Sacrificial specialist who is responsible for most propitiations and exorcisms in everyday life.

lasol — Ritual bombos perform every year or every three years to honor their *lenṭe* and their *tsen*. Similar to *mālo lhoba*.

lenṭe — Spirits of deceased bombos.

lhai mhang — Evil spirit of the high country.

lopan — Preceptor or teacher of lamas or bombos; guru or religious teacher.

lu — Type of spirit that inhabits the earth and waters; associated by Tamang with pollution and polluting places.

lungdar — Prayer flag or luck flag erected by lamas for the general well-being of people.

mālo lhoba — Shamanic ritual performed in lay houses, usually those with attached *tsen*. Includes a full complement of shamanic displays. See also *lasol*.

māna (Nepali) — Nepalese measure equivalent to roughly a cup and a half.

mantra (Nepali) — Magically powerful set of syllables that can be activated in writing or incantations.

marche — One of two types of offerings conveyed to divinities: bloody or red offerings. See *Karche*.

mengko — Poisoner.

mhā — Sister's husband; translated as "wife-takers." *Mhā* must provide services to wife's brothers (*shyangpo*). Also, daughter's husband (*mhā kola*).

mhane — Buddhist earthen work; a small stupa.

mhang-mhung — General term for evil spirit.

mharsung — One of two ritually significant halves of the Tamang year: the period between the full moon of February–March (*phālgun*) and the full moon of August-September (*bhadāu*). See *yharsung*.

mukhiyā (Nepali) — Influential political-judicial authorities on the village level. Villagers recognize many more people as headmen or women than does the government.

murmi (Nepali) — Nineteenth-century term for peoples now called Tamang.

nakhle mhang — Winnowing-tray-evil spirit also known as the four orphans. *Nakhle Mhang* attacks the well-being and prosperity of Tamang houses and fields. Lambus exorcise it on a regular basis.

ne — Place associated with divine or demonic beings; a heavenly or hellish place. Also used to describe the groves sacred to divinities.

nhorgi yang — Essence of wealth.

panchāyat (Nepali) — Contemporary administrative system of elected councils on village, town, and district levels; an administrative "village" composed of nine wards.

pāni nachalne jāt (Nepali) — Castes from whom water is not accepted; untouchables.

pāp (Nepali) — Sin or demerit in the Hindu-Buddhist sense.

pāthi (Nepali) — Nepalese measure of volume equivalent to about one gallon.

phamo — Guardian, mother; the divine and spirit guardians of bombos.

pujāri (Nepali) — Term for a ritualist; someone who performs a ritual.

raikaṛ (Nepali) — Common system of land tenure in contemporary Nepal where individuals retain usufruct of land in return for the payment of taxes to the state.

rakam (Nepali) — Form of land tenure important during the Rana era; as in feudal corvée, land rights were maintained only if labor was supplied to overlords.

rhalbo — Matted locks of bombos who never cut the hair on the back of their heads.

rhikap — Recitation of places; an integral element of sacrificial and shamanic rituals.

sangkye — Tamang term for Buddhas.

sangrap — Part of rituals in which incense is offered.

sangtung — Type of ritual specialist like a bombo but uninitiated. *Sangtung* beat on bronze plates instead of drums and perform minor cures.

santān (Nepali) — Patrilineage. The effective patriclan segment in a village; usually those patrilineally related men who can trace a common ancestor six or so generations back. See also *gyut*.

sehgi chut — Essence of strength in things.

sem — Heart-mind and seat of emotions.

śūdra (Sanskrit) — Lowest of the four varna of ancient Indian society. Shudras do not wear sacred threads; they perform services for the three higher varna.

shyepompo — Experts in the performance of songs, particularly songs in recognition of, and in honor to, the Buddhas and songs that record the history of things.

shyerap — Internal strength or power.

shyihbda — Master-mistress of the earth and the most important of village divinities.

shyingmar-dung — Primary site of divinities in Tamdungsa; includes a male and a female deity.

shyingo — Ghost or shade; the spirits of the deceased.

so — Life-force; grows up through the body like a tree.

so dungma — Sapling erected by bombos outside houses as a symbol of life-force (*so*).

sounding — Ritual performed by bombos.

tālukdār (Nepali) — Local official during the Rana era. *Tālukdār* were technically responsible for collecting taxes on dry fields in the Tamdungsa area and were seen as less important than the *jimiwāl*.

tembe la — Supporting divinity or clan divinity.

tengba — Tamang verb for tossing something about in the air with the hands as one tosses a small child. Used by bombos to describe how they deal with divine and demonic beings during soundings.

ṭhakuri (Nepali) One of the ruling Kshatriya or warrior castes of Nepal.

ṭhungrap-kerap Origination or rebirth account; myths that relate the origin and coming into being of things or beings.

tihār (Nepali) Ritual event celebrated throughout Nepal. Among Tamang *tihār* is the occasion on which brothers and sisters show solidarity.

ṭikā (Nepali) Mark placed on the forehead as a kind of blessing.

tormo Images of divinities and Buddhas molded from dough. Among Tamang *tormo* are made from rice.

tsen Spirit who mediates between humans and divinities and earth and sky. Tsen reside in high passes and cliff faces and have special associations with women and bombos.

tshe Long life or immortality; an important blessing of ritual.

ui same Site of the first Buddhist *gombo* in Tibet; the site for Tamang of many primordial events and the place of their own origins. In Tibetan, *bSam yas*.

upādhyaya bāhun (Nepali) Relatively high sector of the Brahmans in Nepal.

vaiśya (Sanskrit) The third of four varna in Hindu social theory; classically, merchants or herders.

varṇa (Sanskrit) System of distinguishing and interrelating the four main caste groupings in Indic social theory: Brahman, Kshatriya, Vaishya, Shudra.

wang Magical power or potency.

yambu Tamang term for the Kathmandu Valley.

yambui mhang Evil spirit of Kathmandu.

yharsung One of two ritually significant halves of the Tamang year: the period from the full moon of August–September (*bhadāu*) until the full moon of February–March (*phālgun*). See also *mharsung*.

Bibliography

Allen, Michael. 1973. Buddhism without Monks: The Vajrayana Religion of the Newars of Kathmandu Valley. *South Asia* 3:1–14.

Allen, Nicholas J. 1976. Shamanism among the Thulung Rai. In John T. Hitchcock and Rex L. Jones, eds., *Spirit Possession in the Nepal Himalayas*, pp. 124–40. New Delhi: Vikas.

——. 1981. The Thulung Myth of the Bhume Sites and Some Indo-Tibetan Comparisons. In Christoph von Fürer-Haimendorf, ed., *Asian Highland Societies in Anthropological Perspective*, pp. 168–82. New Delhi: Sterling.

Ames, Michael M. 1964. Magical-Animism and Buddhism: A Structural Analysis of the Sinhalese Religious System. In Edward B. Harper, ed., *Religion in South Asia*, pp. 21–52. Seattle: University of Washington Press.

Aziz, Barbara. 1976. Reincarnation Reconsidered; or, The Reincarnate Lama as Shaman. In John T. Hitchcock and Rex L. Jones, eds., *Spirit Possession in the Nepal Himalayas*, pp. 343–60. New Delhi: Vikas.

Babb, Lawrence A. 1975. *The Divine Hierarchy: Popular Hinduism in Central India*. New York: Columbia University Press.

Bachofen, Johann J. 1967. *Myth, Religion and Mother Right: Selected Writings of J. J. Bachofen*. Ralph Manheim, trans. Princeton: Princeton University Press.

Barth, Fredrik. 1965. *Political Leadership among Swat Pathan*. London: University of London, Athlone Press.

Bateson, Gregory. 1958. *Naven: A Survey of the Problems Suggested by a Composite Picture of the Culture of a New Guinea Tribe Drawn from Three Points of View*, 2d ed. Stanford: Stanford University Press.

——. 1972. Culture Contact and Schismogenesis. In *Steps to an Ecology of Mind*, pp. 61–72. New York: Ballantine Books.

Bennett, Lynn. 1983. *Dangerous Wives and Sacred Sisters: Social and Symbolic Roles of High-Caste Women in Nepal*. New York: Columbia University Press.

Berglie, Per-Arne. 1976. Preliminary Remarks on Some Tibetan "Spirit-Mediums" in Nepal. *Kailash* 4.1:85–108.

Berreman, Gerald D. 1960. Cultural Variability and Drift in the Himalayan Hills. *American Anthropologist* 62.5:774–94.

——. 1964. Brahmins and Shamans in Pahari Religion. In Edward B. Harper, ed., *Religion in South Asia*, pp. 53–69. Seattle: University of Washington Press.

Beyer, Stephan, V. *The Cult of Tara: Magic and Ritual in Tibet*. Berkeley: University of California Press.

Bharati, Agehananda, ed. 1976. *The Realm of the Extra-Human: Agents and Audiences*. The Hague: Mouton.

Bista, Dor Bahadur. 1971. Political Innovators of Upper Kali-Gandaki. *Man* (N.S.) 6:52–60.

——. 1972. *People of Nepal,* 2d ed. Kathmandu: Ratna Pustak Bhandar.

——. 1982. The Process of Nepalization. In *Anthropological and Linguistic Studies of the Gandaki Area of Nepal. Monumenta Serindica* no. 10, pp. 1–20. Tokyo: Institute for the Study of Languages and Cultures of Asia and Africa.

Bloch, Maurice, and Jonathan Parry, eds. 1982. *Death and the Regeneration of Life.* Cambridge: Cambridge University Press.

Boon, James A. 1973. Further Operations of Culture in Anthropology: A Synthesis of and for Debate. In Louis Schneider and Charles M. Bonejean, eds., *The Idea of Culture in the Social Sciences,* pp. 1–32. Cambridge: Cambridge University Press.

——. 1982. *Other Tribes, Other Scribes: Symbolic Anthropology in the Comparative Study of Cultures, Histories, Religions, and Texts.* Cambridge: Cambridge University Press.

Bourguignon, Erika. 1967. World Distribution and Patterns of Possession States. In R. Prince, ed., *Trance and Possession States,* pp. 3–34. Montreal: Bucke Memorial Society.

——. ed. 1973. *Religion, Altered States of Consciousness, and Social Change.* Columbus: Ohio State University Press.

Brown, W. Norman. 1957. The Sanctity of the Cow in Hinduism. *Journal of the Madras University* 28.2:29–49.

Burghart, Richard. 1984. The Formation of the Concept of Nation-State in Nepal. *Journal of Asian Studies* 44.1:101–26.

Burke, Kenneth. 1961. *The Rhetoric of Religion: Studies in Logology.* Boston: Beacon Press.

Caplan, Lionel. 1970. *Land and Social Change in East Nepal: A Study of Hindu-Tribal Relations.* Berkeley: University of California Press.

Carrithers, Michael, Steven Collins, and Steven Lukes, eds. 1985. *The Category of the Person: Anthropology, Philosophy, History.* Cambridge: Cambridge University Press.

Clarke, Graham. 1980. Lama and Tamang in Yolmo. In Michael Aris and Aung San Suu Kyi, eds., *Tibetan Studies in Honour of Hugh Richardson,* pp. 79–86. Warminster: Aris and Phillips.

Claus, Peter. 1979. Spirit Possession and Spirit Mediumship from the Perspective of Tulu Oral Traditions. *Culture, Medicine and Psychiatry* 3:29–52.

Cohn, Bernard S. 1968. Notes on the History of the Study of Indian Society and Culture. In Milton Singer and Bernard Cohn, eds., *Structure and Change in Indian Society,* pp. 3–28. Chicago: Aldine.

Crapanzano, Vincent. 1980. *Tuhami: Portrait of a Moroccan.* Chicago: University of Chicago Press.

Crapanzano, Vincent, and Vivian Garrison, eds. 1977. *Case Studies in Spirit Possession.* New York: John Wiley and Sons.

Csordas, J. Thomas. 1985. Medical and Sacred Realities: Between Comparative Religion and Transcultural Psychiatry. *Culture, Medicine and Psychiatry* 9:103–16.

Dahal, Dilli R. 1985. *An Ethnographic Study of Social Change Among the Athpahariya Rais of Dhankuta*. Kirtipur: Centre for Nepal and Asian Studies, Tribhuvan University.

Daniel, E. Valentine. 1984. *Fluid Signs: Being a Person the Tamil Way*. Berkeley: University of California Press.

Dás, Sarat C. 1881. Dispute between a Buddhist and a Bonpo Priest for the Possession of Mount Kailasá and the Lake of Mánasa. *Journal of the Asiatic Society of Bengal* 1:206–11.

Derrida, Jacques. 1976. *Of Grammatology,* 1st American ed. Gayatri Chakravorty Spivak, trans. Baltimore: Johns Hopkins University Press.

Detienne, Marcel. 1986. *The Creation of Mythology*. Margaret Cook, trans. Chicago: University of Chicago Press.

Dobremez, Jean F., ed. 1986. *Les collines du Népal central* 2 vols. Paris: Institut National de la Recherche Agronomique.

Doherty, Victor S. 1978. Notes on the Origins of the Newars of the Kathmandu Valley of Nepal. In James F. Fisher, ed., *Himalayan Anthropology: The Indo-Tibetan Interface,* pp. 433–45. The Hague: Mouton.

Dumont, Louis. 1970a. *Religion, Politics, and History in India: Collected Papers in Indian Sociology*. The Hague: Mouton.

——. 1970b. *Homo Hierarchicus: An Essay on the Caste System*. Mark Sainsbury, trans. Chicago: University of Chicago Press.

Dumont, Louis, and David Pocock. 1959a. On the Different Aspects or Levels of Hinduism. *Contributions to Indian Sociology* 3:40–54.

——. 1959b. Possession and Priesthood. *Contributions to Indian Sociology* 3:55–74.

Durkheim, Emile. 1965. *The Elementary Forms of the Religious Life*. Joseph W. Swain, trans. New York: Free Press.

Ekvall, Robert B. 1964. *Religious Observances in Tibet: Patterns and Function*. Chicago: University of Chicago Press.

Eliade, Mircea. 1972. *Shamanism: Archaic Technique of Ecstasy*. William R. Trask, trans. Bollingen Series 76. Princeton: Princeton University Press.

English, Richard. 1985. Himalayan State Formation and the Impact of British Rule in the Nineteenth Century. *Mountain Research and Development* 5.1:61–78.

Euler, Claus. 1984. Changing Patterns of a Subsistent Economy. *Contributions to Nepalese Studies* 11.3:63–98.

Evans-Pritchard, E. E. 1956. *Nuer Religion*. Oxford: Oxford University Press.

Evans-Wentz, W. Y., ed. 1960. *The Tibetan Book of the Dead; or The After Death Experiences of the Bardo Plane, According to Lama Kazi Dawa-Samdup's English Rendering*. London: Oxford University Press.

Fisher, James F. 1985. The Historical Development of Himalayan Anthropology. *Mountain Research and Development* 5.1:99–111.

——. 1986. *Trans-Himalayan Traders: Economy, Society and Culture in Northwest Nepal*. Berkeley: University of California Press.

Fournier, Alain. 1976. A Preliminary Report on the Puimbo and the Ngiami: The Sunuwar Shamans of Sabra. In John T. Hitchcock and Rex L. Jones, eds., *Spirit Possession in the Nepal Himalayas*, pp. 100–123. New Delhi: Vikas.

——. 1978. The Role of the Priest in Sunuwar Society. In James F. Fisher, ed., *Himalayan Anthropology: The Indo-Tibetan Interface*, pp. 167–78. The Hague: Mouton.

Frank, Walter A. 1973. *Ethnische Grundlagen der Siedlungsstrucktur in Mittelnepal, Unter Besonderer Berücksichtigung aer Tamang*. Innsbruck and Müchen: Universitätsverlag Wagner.

——. 1974. Attempt at an Ethno-Demography of Middle Nepal. In Christoph von Fürer-Haimendorf, ed., *Contributions to the Anthropology of Nepal*, pp. 85–97. Warminster: Aris and Phillips.

Frazer, James George. 1963. *The Golden Bough: A Study in Magic and Religion*, abridged ed. New York: Macmillan.

Freed, Stanley A., and Ruth S. Freed. 1967. Spirit Possession as Illness in a North Indian Village. In John Middleton, ed., *Magic, Witchcraft, and Curing*, pp. 295–320. Garden City, N.J.: Natural History Press.

Fricke, Thomas E. 1986a. *Himalayan Households: Tamang Demography and Domestic Processes*. Ann Arbor, Mich.: UMI Research Press.

——. 1986b. Marriage, Household Cycles, and the Maintenance of Equality among the Tamang of North Central Nepal. Paper presented at the annual meeting of the American Anthropological Association, Philadelphia, December 3–7.

Fürer-Haimendorf, Christoph von. 1955. Pre-Buddhist Elements in Sherpa Belief and Ritual. *Man* 55.61:49–52.

——. 1956. Ethnographic Notes on the Tamangs of Nepal. *Eastern Anthropologist* 9.3–4:166–77.

——. 1964. *The Sherpas of Nepal: Buddhist Highlanders*. London: John Murray.

——. 1966. Caste Concepts and Status Distinction in Buddhist Communities of Western Nepal. In Christoph von Fürer-Haimendorf, ed., *Caste and Kin in Nepal, India, and Ceylon*, pp. 140–60. Bombay: Asia Publishing House.

——. 1975. *Himalayan Traders: Life in Highland Nepal*. London: John Murray.

Gaborieau, Marc. 1982. Les fêtes, le temps et l'espace: structure du calendrier hindou dans sa version indo-népalaise. *L'Homme* 22.3:11–30.

Geertz, Clifford. 1973. *The Interpretation of Cultures*. New York: Basic Books.

Gellner, David. 1986. Language, Caste, Religion, and Territory: Newar Identity Ancient and Modern. *European Journal of Sociology* 27:102–48.

Girard, René. 1972. *La violence et le sacré*. Paris: Bernard Grasset.

Glover, Warren W. 1974. *Semantic and Grammatical Structures in Gurung (Nepal)*. Norman: Summer Institute of Linguistics, University of Oklahoma.

Gombrich, Richard F. 1971a. *Precept and Practice: Traditional Buddhism in the Rural Highlands of Ceylon*. Oxford: Oxford University Press.

——. 1971b. "Merit Transference" in Sinhalese Buddhism: A Case Study of the Interaction between Doctrine and Practice. *History of Religions* 11.2:203–19.

Goody, John R., ed. 1968. *Literacy in Traditional Societies*. Cambridge: Cambridge University Press.

Gordon, Antoinette K. 1959. *The Iconography of Tibetan Lamaism*, Rev. ed. Tokyo, Rutland, Vt.: C. E. Tuttle.

Gorer, Geoffrey. 1967. *Himalayan Village: An Account of the Lepchas of Sikkim*, 2d ed. New York: Basic Books.

Great Britain, Ministry of Defense. 1965. *Nepal and the Gurkhas*. London: H.M. Stationery Office.

Greenwold, Stephen Michael. 1978. The Role of the Priest in Newar Society. In James F. Fisher, ed., *Himalayan Anthropology: The Indo-Tibetan Interface*, pp. 461–82. The Hague: Mouton.

Greve, Reinhard. 1981–82. A Shaman's Concept of Illness and Healing Ritual in the Mustang District, Nepal. *Journal of the Nepal Research Centre* 5–6:99–124.

Hagen, Toni. 1971. *Nepal: The Kingdom in the Himalayas*. Chicago: Rand McNally.

Hall, Andrew R. 1978. Preliminary Report on the Langtang Region. *Contributions to Nepalese Studies* 5.2:51–68.

Hamayon, Roberte. 1982. Des chamanes au chamanisme. *L'Ethnographie* 78.87–88:13–48.

Hamilton, Francis B. [1819] 1971. *An Account of the Kingdom of Nepal: And of the Territories Annexed to This Dominion by the House of Gorkha*, reprint ed. New Delhi: Mañjuśrī.

Harper, Edward B. 1957. Shamanism in South India. *Southwestern Journal of Anthropology* 13.3:267–87.

——. 1963. Spirit Possession and Social Structure. In L.K. Bala Ratnam, ed., *Anthropology on the March: Recent Studies of Indian Beliefs, Attitudes, and Social Institutions*, pp. 165–97. Madras: The Book Centre.

——. 1964. Ritual Pollution as an Integrator of Caste and Religion. In Edward B. Harper, ed., *Religion in South Asia*, pp. 151–96. Seattle: University of Washington Press.

Herrenschmidt, Olivier. 1982a. Sacrifice: Symbolic or Effective? In Michel Izard and Pierre Smith, eds., John Leavitt, trans., *Between Belief and Transgression: Structuralist Essays in Religion, History and Myth*, pp. 24–42. Chicago: University of Chicago Press.

——. 1982b. Quelles fêtes pour quelles castes? *L'Homme* 22.3:31–55.

Hertz, Robert. 1960. *Death and the Right Hand*. Rodney and Claudia Needham, trans. Glencoe, Ill.: Free Press.

Hitchcock, John T. 1966. *The Magars of Banyan Hill*. New York: Holt, Rinehart and Winston.

——. 1967. Nepalese Shamanism and the Classic Inner Asian Tradition. *History of Religions* 7.2:149–58.

——. 1974. A Shaman's Song and Some Implications for Himalayan Research. In Christoph von Fürer-Haimendorf, ed., *Contributions to the Anthropology of Nepal*, pp. 150–58. Warminster: Aris and Phillips.

——. 1976. Introduction. In John T. Hitchcock and Rex L. Jones, eds., *Spirit Possession in the Nepal Himalayas*, pp. xii–xxviii. Delhi: Vikas.

——. 1978. An Additional Perspective on the Nepali Caste System. In James F. Fisher, ed., *Himalayan Anthropology: The Indo-Tibetan Interface*, pp. 111–20. The Hague: Mouton.

Hitchcock, John T., and Rex L. Jones, eds. 1976. *Spirit Possession in the Nepal Himalayas*. New Delhi: Vikas.

HMG (His Majesty's Government of Nepal). 1966. *Shri panch surendra vikram shahadevakā shasan kālmā baneko muluki ain* (The law of the land of the reign of His Majesty Surendra Vikram Shah Deva). Kaṭhmandaun: Shri Panch Ko Sarkār, Kānūn Tathā Nyay Mantralāya.

——. 1975. *1971 Population Census of Nepal.* Kathmandu: Central Bureau of Statistics.

——. 1984. *Population Census—1981,* Volume I, Part III: *Social Characteristics Tables.* Kathmandu: Central Bureau of Statistics.

Hocart, Arthur M. 1950. *Caste: A Comparative Study.* London: Methuen.

Höfer, András. 1969. Preliminary Report on a Field Research in a Western Tamang Group, Nepal. *Bulletin of the International Committee for Urgent Anthropological and Ethnological Research,* Vienna, 11:17–31.

——. 1971a. Notes sur le culte du terroir chez les Tamang du Népal. In L. Bernot and J.M.C. Thomas, eds., *Langues et techniques, nature et société* (Essays in honour of André Haudricourt), Vol. 2, pp. 147–56. Paris: Klincksieck.

——. 1971b. Some Non-Buddhist Elements in Tamang Religion. *Vasudha* 14.3: 17–23.

——. 1974. Is the "Bombo" an Ecstatic? Some Ritual Techniques of Tamang Shamanism. In Christoph von Fürer-Haimendorf, ed., *Contributions to the Anthropology of Nepal,* pp. 168–82. Warminster: Aris and Phillips.

——. 1975. Urgyen Pema und Tüsur Bon: Eine Padmasambhava-Legende der Tamang, Nepal. In Hermann Berger, ed., *Mündliche Überlieferunger in Südasien,* pp. 1–70. Wiesbaden: Franz Steiner.

——. 1979. *The Caste Hierarchy and the State in Nepal: A Study of the Muluki Ain of 1854.* Innsbruck: Universitätsverlag Wagner.

——. 1981. *Tamang Ritual Texts,* I: *Preliminary Studies in the Folk-Religion of an Ethnic Minority in Nepal.* Wiesbaden: Franz Steiner.

Höfer, András, and Bishnu P. Shrestha. 1973. Ghost Exorcism among the Brahmans of Central Nepal. *Central Asiatic Journal* 17:51–77.

Holmberg, David. 1980. Lama, Shaman, and Lambu in Tamang Religious Practice. Ph.D. diss., Cornell University.

——. 1983. Shamanic Soundings: Femaleness in the Tamang Ritual Structure. *Signs* 9.1:40–58.

——. 1984. Ritual Paradoxes in Nepal: Comparative Perspectives on Tamang Religion. *Journal of Asian Studies* 43.4:697–722.

Hubert, Henri, and Marcel Mauss. 1964. *Sacrifice: Its Nature and Function.* W. D. Halls, trans. Chicago: University of Chicago Press.

Hultkrantz, Å. 1978. Ecological and Phenomenological Aspects of Shamanism. In V. Dioszegi and M. Hoppál, eds., *Shamanism in Siberia,* pp. 27–58. Budapest: Akadémiai Kiadó.

Huntington, Richard, and Peter Metcalfe. 1979. *Celebrations of Death: The Anthropology of Mortuary Ritual.* Cambridge: Cambridge University Press.

Hyde, Lewis. 1979. *The Gift: Imagination and the Erotic Life of Property.* New York: Vintage Books.

Iijima, Shigeru. 1982. The Thakalis: Traditional and Modern. In *Anthropological and Linguistic Studies of the Gandaki Area in Nepal. Monumenta Serindica,* no. 10, pp. 21–39. Tokyo: Institute for the Study of Languages and Cultures of Asia and Africa.

Jäschke, H. A. [1881] 1972. *A Tibetan-English Dictionary*. London: Routledge and Kegan Paul.

Jerstad, Luther G. 1969. *Mani-Rimdu: Sherpa Dance-Drama*. Seattle: University of Washington Press.

Jest, Corneille. 1976. Encounters with Intercessors in Nepal. In John T. Hitchcock and Rex L. Jones, eds., *Spirit Possession in the Nepal Himalayas*, pp. 294–308. New Delhi: Vikas.

Jones, Rex L. 1968. Shamanism in South Asia: A Preliminary Survey. *History of Religions* 7.4:330–47.

——. 1976a. Spirit Possession and Society in Nepal. In John T. Hitchcock and Rex L. Jones, eds., *Spirit Possession in the Nepal Himalayas*, pp. 1–11. New Delhi: Vikas.

——. 1976b. Limbu Spirit Possession and Shamanism. In John T. Hitchcock and Rex L. Jones, eds., *Spirit Possession in the Nepal Himalayas*, pp. 29–55. New Delhi: Vikas.

Jones, Shirley Kurz. 1976. Limbu Possession: A Case Study. In John T. Hitchcock and Rex L. Jones, eds., *Spirit Possession in the Nepal Himalayas*, pp. 22–28. New Delhi: Vikas.

Kakar, Sudhir. 1982. *Shamans, Mystics, and Doctors: A Psychological Inquiry into India and Its Healing Traditions*. New York: Alfred A. Knopf.

Kapferer, Bruce. 1983. *A Celebration of Demons: Exorcism and the Aesthetics of Healing in Sri Lanka*. Bloomington: University of Indiana Press.

Karan, Pradyumna P. 1960. *Nepal: A Cultural and Physical Geography*. Lexington: University of Kentucky Press.

Keyes, Charles F. 1983. Merit Transference in the Karmic Theory of Popular Theravada Buddhism. In Charles F. Keyes and E. Valentine Daniel, eds., *Karma: An Anthropological Inquiry*, pp. 261–86. Berkeley: University of California Press.

Keyes, Charles F., and E. Valentine Daniel, eds. 1983. *Karma: An Anthropological Inquiry*. Berkeley: University of California Press.

Kirkpatrick, William. 1811. *An Account of the Kingdom of Nepaul, Being the Substance of Observations Made during a Mission to That Country, in the Year 1793*. London: W. Miller.

Kirsch, A. Thomas. 1967. Phu Thai Religious Syncretism: A Case Study of Thai Religion and Society. Ph.D. diss., Harvard University.

——. 1972. The Thai Buddhist Quest for Merit. In John T. McAlister, Jr., ed., *Southeast Asia: The Politics of National Integration*, pp. 188–201. New York: Random House.

——. 1977. Complexity in the Thai Religious System: An Interpretation. *Journal of Asian Studies* 36.2:241–66.

Kumar, Satish. 1967. *Rana Polity in Nepal: Origin and Growth*. Bombay: Asia Publishing House.

Lall, Kesar. 1969. The Tamangs. *Nepal Review* 1.3:39–41.

Lama, Santabir. 1959. *Tambā Kaiten Hvāi Rimṭhim*. Darjeeling.

Lambek, Michael. 1981. *Human Spirits: A Cultural Account of Trance in Mayotte*. Cambridge: Cambridge University Press.

Landon, Perceval. [1928] 1987. *Nepal* (2 vols.), reprint ed. Kathmandu: Ratna Pustak Bhandar.

Leach, Edmund. 1970. *Political Systems of Highland Burma: A Study of Kachin Social Structure*. London: Athlone Press.

Lévi-Strauss, Claude. 1963a. *Totemism*. Rodney Needham, trans. Boston: Beacon Press.

——. 1963b. The Bear and the Barber. *Journal of the Royal Anthropological Institute of Great Britain and Ireland* 93.1:1–11.

——. 1966. *The Savage Mind*. Chicago: University of Chicago Press.

——. 1967a. Structure and Dialectics. In Claire Jacobson and Brooke Grundfest Schoepf, trans., *Structural Anthropology*, pp. 229–38. New York: Anchor.

——. 1967b. The Effectiveness of Symbols. In Claire Jacobson and Brooke Grundfest Schoepf, trans., *Structural Anthropology*, pp. 181–201. New York: Anchor.

——. 1968. The Story of Asdiwal. In Edmund Leach, ed., *The Structural Study of Myth and Totemism*, pp. 1–47. London: Tavistock.

——. 1969. *The Elementary Structures of Kinship*, rev. ed. James Harle Bell, trans., John Richard von Sturmer and Rodney Needham, eds. Boston: Beacon Press.

——. 1976. Comparative Religions of Nonliterate Peoples. In *Structural Anthropology, Volume II*. Monique Layton, trans., pp. 60–67. New York: Basic Books.

——. 1981. *The Naked Man*, 1st U.S. ed. John and Doreen Weightman, trans. New York: Harper and Row.

Levine, Nancy E. 1987. Caste, State, and Ethnic Boundaries in Nepal. *Journal of Asian Studies* 46.1:71–88.

Levy, Robert I. 1973. *Tahitians: Mind and Experience in the Society Islands*. Chicago: University of Chicago Press.

Lewis, I. M. 1966. Spirit Possession and Deprivation Cults. *Man* (N.S.) 1.3:307–29.

——. 1967. Spirits and the Sex War. *Man* (N.S.) 2.4:626–28.

——. 1971. *Ecstatic Religion: An Anthropological Study of Spirit Possession and Shamanism*. Baltimore: Penguin Books.

Lewis-Williams, J. D. 1986. Cognitive and Optical Illusions in San Rock Art Research. *Current Anthropology* 27.2:171–78.

Lichter, David, and Lawrence Epstein. 1983. Irony in Tibetan Notions of the Good Life. In Charles F. Keyes and E. Valentine Daniel, eds., *Karma: An Anthropological Inquiry*, pp. 223–60. Berkeley: University of California Press.

Lienhardt, Godfrey. 1961. *Divinity and Experience: The Religion of the Dinka*. Oxford: Oxford University Press.

Macdonald, Alexander W. 1973. A Nepalese Copper-Plate from the Time of Prithvinarayan's Father. *Kailash* 1.1:6–7.

——. 1975. *Essays on the Ethnology of Nepal and South Asia*. Kathmandu: Ratna Pustak Bhandar.

——. 1980. Creative Dismemberment among the Tamang and Sherpas of Nepal. In Michael Aris and Aung San Suu Kyi, eds., *Tibetan Studies in Honour of Hugh Richardson*, pp. 199–208. Warminster: Aris and Phillips.

Manandhar, Thakur Lal. 1986. *Newari-English Dictionary: Modern Language of Kathmandu Valley*. Delhi: Agam Kala Prakashan.

Manzardo, Andrew E. 1985. Ritual Practice and Group Maintenance in the Thakali of Central Nepal. *Kailash* 12.1,2:81–114.

March, Kathryn S. 1979. The Intermediacy of Women: Female Gender Symbolism and the Social Position of Women among Tamangs and Sherpas of Highland Nepal. Ph.D. diss., Cornell University.

——. 1984. Weaving, Writing, and Gender. *Man* (N.S.) 18.4:729–44.

——. 1987. Hospitality, Women, and the Efficacy of Beer. *Food and Foodways* 1:351–87.

——. n.d. Words and Worlds of Tamang Women. Department of Anthropology, Cornell University, Ithaca. Photocopy.

Marriot, McKim. 1955. Little Communities in an Indigenous Civilization. In McKim Marriot, ed., *Village India: Studies in the Little Community,* pp. 171–222. The American Anthropological Association Memoir no. 83.

——. 1976. Hindu Transactions: Diversity without Dualism. In Bruce Kapferer, ed., *Transaction and Meaning: Directions in the Anthropology of Exchange and Symbolic Behavior,* pp. 109–42. Philadelphia: Institute for the Study of Human Issues.

Marriot, McKim, and Ronald B. Inden. 1977. Toward an Ethnosociology of South Asian Caste Systems. In Kenneth David, ed., *The New Wind: Changing Identities in South Asia.* The Hague: Mouton.

Marsella, Anthony J., George Devos, and Francis L. K. Hsu, eds. 1985. *Culture and Self: Asian and Western Perspectives.* New York: Tavistock.

Mauss, Marcel. 1967. *Thc Gift: Forms and Functions of Exchange in Archaic Societies.* Ian Cunnison, trans. New York: W.W. Norton.

Mazaudon, Martine. 1973. *Phonologie Tamang.* Paris: Société d'Études Linguistiques et Anthropologiques de France.

——. 1978. Consonantal Mutation and Tonal Split in Tamang Sub-Family of Tibeto-Burman. *Kailash* 6.3:157–79.

McHugh, Ernestine. 1984. Concepts of the Person among the Gurungs of Nepal: The "Heart-Mind." Paper presented at the annual meeting of the American Anthropological Association, Denver, November 14–18.

Meeker, Michael E., Kathleen Barlow, and David M. Lipset. 1986. Culture, Exchange, and Gender: Lessons from the Murik. *Cultural Anthropology* 1.1:6–73.

Messerschmidt, Donald A. 1976a. *The Gurungs of Nepal: Conflict and Change in a Village Society.* Warminster: Aris and Phillips.

——. 1976b. Ethnographic Observations of Gurung Shamanism in Lamjung District. In John T. Hitchcock and Rex L. Jones, eds., *Spirit Possession in the Nepal Himalayas,* pp. 197–216. Delhi: Vikas.

——. 1982. The Thakali of Nepal: Historical Continuity and Socio-cultural Change. *Ethnohistory* 29.4:265–80.

Messerschmidt, Donald A., and Nareshwar Jang Gurung. 1974. Parallel Trade and Innovation in Central Nepal: The Cases of the Gurung and Thakali Subbas Compared. In Christoph von Fürer-Haimendorf, ed., *Contributions to the Anthropology of Nepal,* pp. 197–221. Warminster: Aris and Phillips.

Michl, Wolf D. 1976. Notes on the *Jhā̃kri* of Ath Hajar Parbat/Dhaulagiri Himalaya. In John T. Hitchcock and Rex L. Jones, eds., *Spirit Possession in the Nepal Himalayas,* pp. 153–64. New Delhi: Vikas.

Mi-la-ras-pa. 1962. *The Hundred Thousand Songs of Milarepa* (2 vols.). Garma C C. Chang, trans. New Hyde Park, N.Y.: University Books.

Miller, Caspar J. 1979. *Faith Healers in the Himalayas.* Kirtipur: Centre for Nepal and Asian Studies, Tribhuvan University.

Moerman, Michael. 1965. Ethnic Identification in a Complex Civilization: Who Are the Lue? *American Anthropologist* 67.5:1215–30.

Mumford, Stanley. n.d. Transmutation and Dialogue: Lama-Shaman Interaction in Nepal. Department of Anthropology, Princeton University. Photocopy.

Myerhoff, Barbara G. 1976. Shamanic Equilibrium: Balance and Mediation in Known and Unknown Worlds. In W.D. Hand, ed., *American Folk Medicine: A Symposium,* pp. 99–108. Berkeley: University of California Press.

Nebesky-Wojkowitz, René de. 1975. *Oracles and Demons of Tibet: The Cult and Iconography of the Tibetan Protective Deities.* Graz: Akademische Druck-u. Verlagsanstalt.

——. 1976. *Tibetan Religious Dances: Tibetan Text and Annotated Translation of the 'Chams Yig.* Christoph von Fürer-Haimendorf, ed. The Hague: Mouton.

Noll, Richard. 1988. Shamanism and Schizophrenia: A State-Specific Approach to the "Schizophrenic Metaphor" of Shamanic States. *American Ethnologist* 10.3:443–59.

Northey, William Brook. 1928. *The Gurkhas: Their Manners, Customs and Country.* London: John Lane the Bodley Head.

Obeyesekere, Gananath. 1963. The Great Tradition and the Little in the Perspective of Sinhalese Buddhism. *Journal of Asian Studies* 22.2:139–53.

——. 1966. The Buddhist Pantheon in Ceylon and its Extensions. In Manning Nash, ed., *Anthropological Studies in Theravada Buddhism,* pp. 1–25. Cultural Report Series no. 13. Southeast Asian Studies, Yale University.

——. 1968. Theodicy, Sin, and Salvation in a Sociology of Buddhism. In Edmund R. Leach, ed., *Dialectic in Practical Religion,* pp. 7–40. Cambridge: Cambridge University Press.

——. 1969. The Ritual Drama of the *Sanni* Demons: Collective Representations of Disease in Ceylon. *Comparative Studies in Society and History* 11.2:174–216.

——. 1977. Psychocultural Exegesis of a Case of Spirit Possession in Sri Lanka. In Vincent Crapanzano and Vivian Garrison, eds., *Case Studies in Spirit Possession,* pp. 235–94. New York: John Wiley.

——. 1981. *Medusa's Hair: An Essay on Personal Symbols and Religious Experience.* Chicago: University of Chicago Press.

O'Flaherty, Wendy Doniger. 1973. *Asceticism and Eroticism in the Mythology of Śiva.* London: Oxford University Press.

——. trans. 1975. *Hindu Myths: A Source Book.* Baltimore: Penguin Books.

——. ed. 1980. *Karma and Rebirth in Classical Indian Traditions.* Berkeley: University of California Press.

Okada, Ferdinand E. 1957. Ritual Brotherhood: A Cohesive Factor in Nepalese Society. *Southwestern Journal of Anthropology* 13:212–22.

——. 1976. Notes on Two Shaman-Curers in Kathmandu. *Contributions to Nepalese Studies* 3 (Special Issue June 1976):107–12.

Oppitz, Michael. 1974. Myths and Facts: Reconsidering Some Data Concerning the Clan History of the Sherpa. In Christoph von Fürer-Haimendorf, ed., *Contri-*

butions to the Anthropology of Nepal, pp. 232–43. Warminster: Aris and Phillips.

——. 1982. Death and Kin amongst the Northern Magar. *Kailash* 9.4:377–421.

Ortner, Sherry. 1978a. *Sherpas through Their Rituals.* New York: Cambridge University Press.

——. 1978b. The Decline of Sherpa Shamanism. Department of Anthropology, University of Michigan. Photocopy.

Östör, Ákos. 1980. *The Play of the Gods: Locality, Ideology, Structure, and Time in the Festivals of a Bengali Town.* Chicago: University of Chicago Press.

Pardue, Peter A. 1971. *Buddhism: A Historical Introduction to Buddhist Values and the Social and Political Forms They Have Assumed in Asia.* New York: Macmillan.

Parry, Jonathan. 1982. Sacrificial Death and the Necrophagous Ascetic. In Maurice Bloch and Jonathan Parry, eds., *Death and the Regeneration of Life,* pp. 74–110. Cambridge: Cambridge University Press.

Paul, Robert A. 1976. Some Observations on Sherpa Shamanism. In John T. Hitchcock and Rex L. Jones, eds., *Spirit Possession in the Nepal Himalayas,* pp. 141–51. New Delhi: Vikas.

——. 1979. Dumje: Paradox and Resolution in Sherpa Ritual Symbolism. *American Ethnologist* 6.2:274–304.

——. 1982. *The Tibetan Symbolic World: Psychoanalytic Explorations.* Chicago: University of Chicago Press.

Peters, Larry G. 1981. *Ecstasy and Healing in Nepal.* Malibu, Calif.: Undena Publications.

Peters, Larry G., and Douglass Price-Williams. 1980. Towards an Experiential Analysis of Shamanism. *American Ethnologist* 7.3:397–418.

Pignède, Bernard. 1962. Clan Organization and Hierarchy among the Gurungs. *Contributions to Indian Sociology* 6:102–19.

——. 1966. *Les Gurungs, une population himalayenne du Népal.* The Hague: Mouton.

Rahmann, Rudolf. 1959. Shamanistic and Related Phenomena in Northern and Middle India. *Anthropos* 54:681–760.

Regmi, D. R. 1975. *Modern Nepal.* Calcutta: Firma K. L. Mukhopadhyay.

Regmi, Mahesh C. 1963, 1964, 1965, 1968. *Land Tenure and Taxation in Nepal* (4 vols.). Berkeley, Calif.: Institute of International Studies.

——. 1976. *Landownership in Nepal.* Berkeley: University of California Press.

——. 1979. *Readings in Nepali Economic History.* Varanasi: Kishor Vidya Niketan.

Regmi, Mahesh, C., ed. and trans. 1969. Ban on Cow Slaughter. *Regmi Research Series,* Year 1, no. 1, p. 51.

——. 1972. Imposition of Fines on Gurungs and Lamas, 1810 A.D. *Regmi Research Series,* Year 4, no. 3, pp. 42–43.

——. 1975. Fiscal and Labor Obligations of Inhabitants of Panchsayakhola in Nuwakot. *Regmi Research Series,* Year 7, no. 4, p. 78.

——. 1979a. The Hides and Skins Levy. *Regmi Research Series,* Year 11, no. 2, pp. 21–27.

——. 1979b. Ban on Cow Slaughter, 1809. *Regmi Research Series,* Year 11, no. 8, pp. 126–28.

——. 1979c. Ban on Cow Slaughter in Solukhumbu. *Regmi Research Series,* Year 11, no. 9, pp. 129–30.

——. 1980. Cow Slaughter. *Regmi Research Series,* Year 12, no. 11, pp. 169–70.

——. 1983. Imposition of Fines on Sino-Eating Communities. *Regmi Research Series,* Year 15, no. 11–12, pp. 168–69.

Reinhard, Johan. 1976. Shamanism and Spirit Possession: The Definition Problem. In John T. Hitchcock and Rex L. Jones, eds., *Spirit Possession in the Nepal Himalayas,* pp. 12–21. New Delhi: Vikas.

Rinpoche, Guru (According to Karma Lingpa). 1975. *The Tibetan Book of the Dead: The Great Liberation through Hearing in the Bardo.* Francesca Freemantle and Chögyum Trungpa, trans. Berkeley: Shambala.

Risley, H.H. 1891. *The Tribes and Castes of Bengal.* Calcutta: Bengal Secretariat Press.

Rose, Leo E., and Margaret W. Fisher. 1970. *The Politics of Nepal: Persistence and Change in an Asian Monarchy.* Ithaca: Cornell University Press.

Rosser, Colin. 1966. Social Mobility in the Newar Caste System. In Christoph von Fürer-Haimendorf, ed., *Caste and Kin in Nepal, India, and Ceylon,* pp. 68–139. Bombay: Asia Publishing House.

Rubin, Gayle. 1975. The Traffic in Women: Notes on the "Political Economy" of Sex. In Rayna R. Reiter, ed., *Toward an Anthropology of Women,* pp. 157–210. New York: Monthly Review Press.

Sagant, Philippe. 1973. Prêtres limbu et catègories domestiques. *Kailash* 1.1:51–75.

Sahlins, Marshall. 1972. *Stone Age Economics.* Chicago: Aldine-Atherton.

Samuel, Geoffrey. 1978a. Religion in Tibetan Society: A New Approach. Part One: A Structural Model. *Kailash* 6.1:45–67.

——. 1978b. Religion in Tibetan Society: A New Approach. Part Two: The Sherpas of Nepal: A Case Study. *Kailash* 6.2:99–114.

Schieffelin, Edward L. 1976. *The Sorrow of the Lonely and the Burning of the Dancers.* New York: St. Martin's Press.

Seddon, David, P. Blaikie, and J. Cameron, eds. 1979. *Peasants and Workers in Nepal: The Condition of the Lower Classes.* Warminster: Aris and Phillips.

Sharma, Prayag Raj. 1977. Caste, Social Mobility and Sanskritization: A Study of Nepal's Old Legal Code. *Kailash* 5.4:277–300.

——. 1978. Nepal: Hindu-Tribal Interface. *Contributions to Nepalese Studies* 6.1:1–14.

Shirokogoroff, Sergei M. 1935. *Psychomental Complex of the Tungus.* London: Kegan Paul, Trench, Trubner.

Shweder, Richard A., and Robert A. Levine, eds. 1984. *Culture Theory: Essays on Mind, Self, and Emotion.* Cambridge: Cambridge University Press.

Siegel, James. 1978. Curing Rites, Dreams, and Domestic Politics in a Sumatran Society. *Glyph* 3:18–31.

Skorupski, Tadeusz. 1982. The Cremation Ceremony according to the Byang-Gtar Tradition. *Kailash* 9.4:361–76.

Slusser, Mary Shepherd. 1982. *Nepal Mandala: A Cultural Study of the Kathmandu Valley*. Princeton: Princeton University Press.

Snellgrove, David L. 1957. *Buddhist Himalaya: Travels and Studies in Quest of the Origins and Nature of Tibetan Religion*. New York: Philosophical Library.

——. 1967. *Four Lamas of Dolpo: Tibetan Biographies*. Ed. and trans. David L. Snellgrove. Cambridge, Mass.: Harvard University Press.

Snellgrove, David L., and Hugh Richardson. 1968. *A Cultural History of Tibet*. New York: Frederick A. Praeger.

Snodgrass, Adrian. 1985. *The Symbolism of the Stupa*. Ithaca: Southeast Asia Program, Cornell University.

Spiro, Melford E. 1967. *Burmese Supernaturalism: A Study in the Explanation and Reduction of Suffering*. Englewood Cliffs, N.J.: Prentice-Hall.

——. 1970. *Buddhism and Society: A Great Tradition and its Burmese Vicissitudes*. New York: Harper and Row.

Srinivas, M. N. 1966. *Social Change in Modern India*. Berkeley: University of California Press.

Stanner, W. E. H. 1959–63. On Aboriginal Religion. *The Oceania Monograph* no. 11. Sydney: University of Sydney.

Stein, Rolf A. 1961. *Les tribus anciennes des marches sino-tibétaines: Legendes, classifications et histoire*. Bibliothèque de l'Institut des Hautes Etudes Chinoises, vol. 15. Paris: Presses Universitaires de France.

——. 1972. *Tibetan Civilization*. Stanford, Calif.: Stanford University Press.

Steinmann, Brigitte. 1987. *Les Tamang du Népal, usages et religion, religion de l'usage*. Paris: Éditions Recherche sur les Grandes Civilisations.

Stiller, Ludwig F. 1973. *The Rise of the House of Gorkha: A Study of the Unification of Nepal, 1768–1816*. New Delhi: Mañjuśrī.

Stone, Linda. 1976. Concepts of Illness and Curing in a Central Nepal Village. *Contributions to Nepalese Studies* 6 (Special Issue):55–80.

Tambiah, Stanley J. 1968a. The Magical Power of Words. *Man* (N.S.) 3.2:175–208.

——. 1968b. Literacy in a Buddhist Village in Northeast Thailand. In Jack R. Goody, ed., *Literacy in Traditional Societies*, pp. 86–131. Cambridge: Cambridge University Press.

——. 1970. *Buddhism and the Spirit Cults in North-East Thailand*. Cambridge: Cambridge University Press.

——. 1976. *World Conqueror and World Renouncer: A Study of Buddhism and Polity in Thailand Against a Historical Background*. Cambridge: Cambridge University Press.

——. 1984. *The Buddhist Saints of the Forest and the Cult of Amulets: A Study in Charisma, Hagiography, and Millennial Buddhism*. Cambridge: Cambridge University Press.

Taylor, Doreen. 1969. Tamang Phonemic Summary. Kirtipur: Tribhuvan University, Summer Institute of Linguistics. Mimeo.

Taylor, Doreen, Everitt Fay, and Karma Bahadur Tamang. 1971. A Vocabulary of the Tamang Language. Kirtipur: Tribhuvan University, Summer Institute of Linguistics. Mimeo.

Toffin, Gérard. 1976. The Peoples of the Upper Ankhu Khola Valley. *Contributions to Nepalese Studies* 3.1:34–46.

——. 1978. Les migrations dans une vallée himalayenne du Népal central (District de Dhading). *L'Ethnographie* 120.77,78(n.s.):121–40.

——. 1984. *Société et religion chez les Néwar du Népal*. Paris: Editions du Centre National de la Recherche Scientifique.

——. 1986. Unités de parenté, système d'alliance et de prestations chez les Tamang de l'Ouest (Népal). *Anthropos* 81:21–45.

Tucci, Giuseppe. 1949. *Tibetan Painted Scrolls* (3 vols.). Rome: La Libreia Dello Stato.

——. 1980. *The Religions of Tibet*. Geoffrey Samuel, trans. Berkeley: University of California Press.

Turner, Ralph L. [1931] 1965. *A Comparative and Etymological Dictionary of the Nepali Language*, reprint ed. London: Routledge and Kegan Paul.

Turner, Victor. 1967. *The Forest of Symbols: Aspects of Ndembu Ritual*. Ithaca: Cornell University Press.

Vajracharya, Dhanavajra, and Tek Bahadur Shrestha. 1976. *Nuvākoṭako aitihāsika ruparekhā* (An Outline of the History of Nuwakot). Kirtipur: Institute of Nepal and Asian Studies, Tribhuvan University, v.s. 2029 Shrāvana.

Vajracharya, Gautamvajra. 1964. Nevārī bhāṣāko Tāmānga bhāṣā tathā Limbu bhāṣāsaṅako sādṛshya (The similarity among Newari, Tamang, and Limbu). *Pūrnimā* 2.1,2:43–49, v.s. 2021 Shrāvana.

Valeri, Valerio. 1985. *Kingship and Sacrifice: Ritual and Society in Ancient Hawaii*. Paula Wissing, trans. Chicago: University of Chicago Press.

van Baal, Jan. 1975. *Reciprocity and the Position of Women: Anthropological Papers*. Assen: Koninklijke van Gorcum.

van Gennep, Arnold. 1960. *The Rites of Passage*. Monika B. Vizedom and Gabrielle L. Caffee, trans. London: Routledge and Kegan Paul.

van Kooij, K. R. 1978. *Religion in Nepal*. Leiden: E. J. Brill.

Victor, Jean-Christophe. 1975. Birdim, village Tamang (Népal): Compte rendu de mission. *L'Homme* 15.2:121–26.

Waddell, L. Augustine. [1895] 1972. *Tibetan Buddhism with Its Mystic Cults, Symbolism and Mythology, and Its Relation to Indian Buddhism*, reprint ed. New York: Dover.

Wadley, Susan S. 1976. The Spirit "Rides" or the Spirit "Comes": Possession in a North Indian Village. In Agehananda Bharati, ed., *The Realm of the Extra-Human: Agents and Audience*, pp. 233–52. The Hague: Mouton.

Watters, David E. 1975. Siberian Shamanistic Traditions among the Kham-Magars of Nepal. *Contributions to Nepalese Studies* 2.1:123–68.

Weber, Max. 1947. *Essays in Sociology*. H. H. Gerth and C. Wright Mills, eds. and trans. London: Kegan Paul, Trench, Trubner.

——. 1958. *The Religion of India: The Sociology of Hinduism and Buddhism*. Hans H. Gerth and Don Martindale, eds. and trans. Glencoe, Ill.: Free Press.

——. 1963. *The Sociology of Religion*. Ephraim Fischoff, trans. Boston: Beacon Press.

Winkler, Walter F. 1976. Spirit Possession in Far Western Nepal. In John T. Hitchcock and Rex L. Jones, eds., *Spirit Possession in the Nepal Himalayas*, pp. 244–62. New Delhi: Vikas.

Wylie, T. V. 1959. A Standard System of Tibetan Transcription. *Harvard Journal of Asiatic Studies* 22:261–67.

Index